TRANSLINGUAL IDENTITIES AND TRANSNATIONAL REALITIES IN THE U.S. COLLEGE CLASSROOM

Exploring the roles of students' pluralistic linguistic and transnational identities at the university level, this book offers a novel approach to translanguaging by highlighting students' perspectives, voices, and agency as integral to the subject. Providing an original reconsideration of the impact of translanguaging, this book examines both transnationality and translinguality as ubiquitous phenomena that affect students' lives.

Demonstrating that students are the experts of their own language practices, experiences, and identities, the authors argue that a proactive translingual pedagogy is more than an openness to students' spontaneous language variations. Rather, this proactive approach requires students and instructors to think about students' holistic communicative repertoire, and how it relates to their writing. Robinson, Hall, and Navarro address students' complex negotiations and performative responses to the linguistic identities imposed upon them because of their skin color, educational background, perceived geographical origin, immigration status, and the many other cues used to "minoritize" them. Drawing on multiple disciplinary discourses of language and identity, and considering the translingual practices and transnational experiences of both U.S. resident and international students, this volume provides a nuanced analysis of students' own perspectives and self-examinations of their complex identities. By introducing and addressing the voices and self-reflections of undergraduate and graduate students, the authors shine a light on translingual and transnational identities and positionalities in order to promote and implement inclusive and effective pedagogies.

This book offers a unique yet essential perspective on translinguality and transnationality, and is relevant to instructors in writing and language classrooms; to administrators of writing programs and international student support programs; and to graduate students and scholars in language education, second language writing, applied linguistics, and literacy studies.

Heather Robinson is an associate professor of English at York College, CUNY, USA.

Jonathan Hall is a professor of English at York College, CUNY, USA.

Nela Navarro is the Director of the Graduate English Language Learners and International Teaching Assistants Program at Rutgers English Language Institute (RELI), and an assistant teaching professor and assistant director of the English Writing Program at Rutgers University, USA.

TRANSLINGUAL IDENTITIES AND TRANSNATIONAL REALITIES IN THE U.S. COLLEGE CLASSROOM

Heather Robinson, Jonathan Hall and Nela Navarro

NEW YORK AND LONDON

First published 2020
by Routledge
52 Vanderbilt Avenue, New York, NY 10017

and by Routledge
2 Park Square, Milton Park, Abingdon, Oxon, OX14 4RN

Routledge is an imprint of the Taylor & Francis Group, an informa business

© 2020 Taylor & Francis

The right of Heather Robinson, Jonathan Hall and Nela Navarro to be identified as authors of this work has been asserted by them in accordance with sections 77 and 78 of the Copyright, Designs and Patents Act 1988.

All rights reserved. No part of this book may be reprinted or reproduced or utilised in any form or by any electronic, mechanical, or other means, now known or hereafter invented, including photocopying and recording, or in any information storage or retrieval system, without permission in writing from the publishers.

Trademark notice: Product or corporate names may be trademarks or registered trademarks, and are used only for identification and explanation without intent to infringe.

Library of Congress Cataloging-in-Publication Data
Names: Robinson, Heather M., author. | Hall, Jonathan, (Professor of
    English) author. | Navarro, Nela, author.
Title: Translingual identities and transnational realities in the U.S.
    college classroom / Heather Robinson, Jonathan Hall, Nela
    Navarro.
Description: New York : Routledge, 2020. | Includes bibliographical
    references and index. |
Identifiers: LCCN 2019050840 | ISBN 9780367026363 (hardback) |
    ISBN 9780367026387 (paperback) | ISBN 9780429398605 (ebook)
Subjects: LCSH: Translanguaging (Linguistics) | English language—
    Study and teaching (Higher)—Foreign speakers. | Language and
    culture.
Classification: LCC P115.35 .R63 2020 | DDC 306.44/6—dc23
LC record available at https://lccn.loc.gov/2019050840

ISBN: 978-0-367-02636-3 (hbk)
ISBN: 978-0-367-02638-7 (pbk)
ISBN: 978-0-429-39860-5 (ebk)

Typeset in Bembo
by Apex CoVantage, LLC

HR:
To Caroline and Harriet. You make everything more fun.

JH:
To the memory of my father, Leonard Hall, first in his family to attend college.
And to the memory of my brother Tim, taken from us during the process of writing.

NN:
To my parents, who cultivated a love of language and who taught me the power of writing.
Para mis adorados padres, Manuel S. Navarro y Ana Inés Angulo Navarro "es puerta de luz un libro abierto."

To Thomas E. LaPointe, who shares my passion for the written word and who embraces my wonder and awe at the possibilities that reading and writing offer.

CONTENTS

Acknowledgments   *ix*

1 Making Translinguality and Transnationality Visible   1

PART I
Everyday Translinguality   **19**

2 Everyday Translinguality: We Meet Our Students   21

3 On Racial Privilege and Accent Hierarchies   39
  Heather Robinson

4 Transing Language Identity   44
  Heather Robinson

5 On Becoming and Beyond: My Liminal Identity   59
  Nela Navarro

6 Language Affiliation and Identity Performance Among Transnational Students   71

7 Confessions of a (Recovering) Monolingual: Translingual Moments and Excursions in Language Ideology   87
  Jonathan Hall

8 Transing Pedagogy 97

PART II
Translingual Transnational Literacies 117

9 Translanguaging, Performance, and the Art of Negotiation 119
   Heather Robinson

10 Translingual Economies of Literacy 142
   Jonathan Hall

11 Translinguality, Grammatical Literacy, and a Pedagogy
   of Naming 156
   Heather Robinson

12 Building Community, Building Confidence: Transnational
   Translingual Emerging Scholars 173

13 Cultivating a Culture of Language Rights 191
   Nela Navarro

14 Conclusion: Negotiated Identities 202

Appendices
  A First Day Thinking 217
  B AutoBio and Literacy Narrative Assignment:
    Guidelines Document 218
  C Language Narrative Assignment [Chapter 2]: Introduction
    to Writing, Rhetoric, and Language Course 220
  D Questions for Transnational Graduate Student
    Interviews 221
  E Initial Assignment 223
  F End of Semester Writing Reflection 225
Index 227

ACKNOWLEDGMENTS

First and foremost, we want to thank the students at York College and at Rutgers University whose work has inspired us over the years. Without them, we would never have been compelled to write this book, and to seek innovative ways to do our best as educators of students from diverse linguistic backgrounds. Specific thanks must go to all of the students whose writing and words are included in this book, who participated in interviews, and who completed surveys. We see your labor. We see you.

Our grateful thanks go to our editor at Routledge, Karen Adler, for her patience, guidance, and support.

Heather: I thank my two daughters, Harriet and Caroline, for needing me not to disappear, and instead making sure I found ways to be an author and a parent at the same time over the last eight years. I also thank Michelle Brazier, my wife, for always helping me find courage and remember what's important, and Matt Garley, Lidia Gonzalez, Shereen Inayatulla, Phebe Kirkham, Patricia Milanes, and Melissa Dinsman, my colleagues at York, for listening. I thank Nela for all the texts in the morning and at night, making sure that I knew we were in this together, and Jonathan for agreeing to do this work in the first place. And again, to the students at York College: every day you remind me what higher education can be.

Jonathan: Thanks of course to my two wonderful collaborators and friends, Nela and Heather. Thanks once again to the students, without whom this would not have happened. Thanks to my mother, Veronica Hall (first in her family to attend college), who every time I called kept me on track by asking about "the book." Well, Mom, here it is!

Nela: I would like to extend my deepest gratitude to my colleagues Dr. Heather Robinson and Dr. Jonathan Hall for inviting me to join them on this

this amazing project and for their leadership and thoughtful contributions, I learned so much from you! Thanks to our thoughtful editor Karen Adler for her extraordinary support and encouragement and for offering us the opportunity to make this book a possibility. Thanks to my colleagues in the Rutgers Writing Program for their generosity and deep commitment to our students. My most important thanks are to our students, you are the reason for my professional aspirations, you are my inspiration to make bold moves, you are why my modest contributions to this volume were possible. *¡Gracias de todo corazón, mis queridos estudiantes!*

1
MAKING TRANSLINGUALITY AND TRANSNATIONALITY VISIBLE

Ask the students. That is the simple premise that underlies the several related studies that are discussed in these pages. All of them focus on college students on U.S. campuses who, in a myriad of ways that we explore, differ from the norms of "typical" college students that were prevalent in the days when the disciplines of rhetoric and composition and writing across the curriculum were being originally formulated, and which prevail across the board in our institutions of higher education. For one thing, almost none of them are white, so to some extent this is an exploration of going to college while Brown, Black, or Asian. But our primary focus will be on their language performances and affiliations, the way in which their language identities are negotiated, and the ways in which the students' various language goals and performances may both develop from and help to form transnational experiences.

Students, that is, are the best experts on their language practices, experiences, proficiencies, and identities, but they often need a space in which they can reflect on what are, for them, often routine activities. That such mundane conversations, which cross supposed linguistic and national boundaries, are of interest to researchers comes as a surprise to some of our students, who find that linguistic identity is less a source of either anxiety or pride than monolingual speakers, looking at it from the outside, might expect. The students do not necessarily see their other languages as sources of weakness, but they don't necessarily see them as sources of academic strength, either, unless prompted.

In the pages that follow, we examine how college students on two campuses conceptualize and articulate their own language identities, based on assigned language narratives, on short stories and their associated commentaries, on surveys and in interviews, and in instructor reflections. In their writings, students negotiate between the linguistic identities that are imposed upon them because of their skin color, educational background, perceived geographical origin, immigration status, and the many other cues that are used to "minoritize" them, and the linguistic identities that they actively construct and perform. Our textual analysis draws upon multiple disciplinary discourses of language and identity, including theories of critical pedagogy, of New Literacies, of translingual agency in rhetoric and composition, of code meshing and other translingual practices in applied linguistics, of language identities in second language writing, and on queer and feminist theories. We examine the rhetorical and performative moves through which students structure relationships with particular language identities, attitudes, ambitions, goals, and visions of future use of English and other languages.

We report on three separate but related studies of translingual practices among two groups of students on two different U.S. college campuses in the northeast of the United States. Chapters 2, 4, 9, and 10 explore the linguistic affiliations and practices of students on a public urban university campus, which we will name Urban College, examine translingual practices within a broad umbrella of "Englishes," with emphases on post-colonial native English speakers and on African-American Vernacular Englishes. Chapters 2, 6, and 13 focus on two distinct groups of "international" students on the campus of a public research university, which we will name State University: 1) first-year undergraduates and 2) graduate students. Despite their cultural and experiential differences, all three groups of students may find themselves marked as outsiders within U.S. language practices that stress a limited definition of "standard English." Using similar methodologies, both projects began from a simple premise: ask the students how they negotiate their language identities on a day-to-day basis, and in their academic work, and examine what they *show* us when they do it. We seek to enter into their subjective linguistic world, by trying to create spaces in which students can speak or write, where they can use their languages and/or language varieties as a person who inhabits multiple language communities and where thinking or speaking or writing calls *all the time*—not just when they are consciously playing or performing—for the integrated use of their full linguistic repertoire, even if, as is almost always the case, the final product is recognizable as being "in" a single language. But what, exactly, do we mean by "in"? In the following sections, we explore this question in detail.

I. Translingual/Transnational Spaces

Translingual practices and transnational connections are frequent topics of investigation today in a variety of disciplines and settings. The translingual approach (Horner, Lu, Royster, & Trimbur, 2011) has drawn increasing interest among scholars in writing studies (e.g. Canagarajah, 2013; Horner & Tetreault, 2017; Barwashi, Guerra, Horner, & Lu, 2016; Lee, 2017), connected with parallel developments in TESOL (Jain, 2014) and applied linguistics (Garcia,

2009; Kubota, 2014); and also elicited some controversy, especially in second language writing (Matsuda, 2014; Atkinson et al., 2015). Transnational issues, meanwhile, have illuminated a number of fields, ranging from the origins of the term in anthropology (Duany, 2008) and sociology (Levitt & Jaworsky, 2007) to, more recently, Writing Program Administration (Martins, 2014); TESOL (Solano-Campos, 2014); composition studies (Donahue, 2009); WAC/WID (Zenger, Haviland, & Mullin, 2013), and mobility studies (e.g. Blommaert & Horner, 2017). But these phenomena are often discussed in separation from each other, as though translingual practices and transnational connections were independent entities. Our approach, by contrast, explores the intersections between translingual and transnational practices. We move now to considering in more detail our terms of engagement for exploring these intersections.

From Translingualism to Translinguality

> *Viewing differences not as a problem but as a resource, the translingual approach promises to revitalize the teaching of writing and language. By addressing how language norms are actually heterogeneous, fluid, and negotiable, a translingual approach directly counters demands that writers must conform to fixed, uniform standards.*
>
> *(Horner et al., 2011, p. 306)*

Students and their instructors—who, as a group, may be more monolingual than the students whose linguistic practices we explore here—often approach translingualism from very different starting points. For monolingual instructors, it may well be that a "translingual approach" is a pedagogical aspiration, or a state of consciousness that they may someday be able to acquire by being open to otherness within language.

For our students, though, translinguality is not somewhere that they have to go, but rather somewhere that they already are, a place that they already inhabit every time they speak and each time they engage in reading and writing practices. They already live and embody translinguality, an often-unconscious state that many of them may not think about much, and that they may never have regarded as important until challenged in a course, when the instructor recast language difference, which they had thought of as negative or at best neutral, as, instead, a potential source of positive strength. Whether the students really come to think of it differently or whether they are just trying to please the instructor by saying so is another question, of course.

So we begin in a somewhat opaque and sometimes disputed theoretical territory of a translingual approach to language difference, and then make a turn simultaneously toward the concrete external conditions and toward the subjective reality of each student. Our various surveys, interviews, and analyses of student writing will help us to do so. For our readers, who may range from experienced researchers in translingual theories and approaches, to those who

4 Visible Translinguality and Transnationality

have not previously fully engaged in these scholarly conversations, we aim for rigorous analysis without getting lost in the theoretical weeds. Translingualism has deep roots in post-structuralism, post-colonial theory, multicompetence theory and other aspects of applied linguistics and second language study, which we will explore as needed. But our approach to translinguality—an existing condition rather than an ideology (that would be translingual*ism*)—is better described as:

- a routine practice, implicated in every act of reading, writing, speaking, or listening, even when not consciously visible.
- something that can be played with and/or performed consciously, exploring the echoes when languages bounce off each other, or blend together to create new language practices.
- a way of thinking about language and especially about language difference. It is here that translinguality morphs, perhaps, into an aspirational ideology of translingualism, a pedagogical consciousness mostly not yet achieved and difficult to access.

Translingual approaches toward language difference in writing are an important current topic in the discipline of rhetoric and composition, in second language writing and second language acquisition, in applied linguistics, and in various allied disciplines. Numerous panels at recent conferences in all these fields and in their publications testify to the interest—sometimes a somewhat controversial interest—in the subject. In this volume we will attempt to engage a nexus of theory and practice, asking how a rather theoretically complex concept can be applied in concrete situations—or at least how attempts are made to do so. As a preliminary definition of a translingual approach to language difference, or to an ideology of translingualism, or, (we will argue) best of all, to the existing, routine, and inescapable condition of translinguality, here are three important translingual assumptions about language:

- Languages are not distinct entities, either at the macro-level of societal practices or at the micro-level of the individual user. Rather, they intersect, interact, and interpenetrate.
- Students learn things in different languages, know things in different languages, and remember things in different languages.
- Teaching language or any aspect of it (writing, reading, speaking, listening) to translingual learners will benefit from affirming and encouraging students' continuing productive reliance on *all* their linguistic resources.
- Sometimes these ideas are referred to in rhetoric and composition as "*the* translingual approach" or "the translingual turn," but we are really articulating multiple approaches toward language difference. There seems to be a tension—perhaps a productive one, but one that should be acknowledged—between

- translingualism as a theoretical research framework, which can used to explain the relation of languages to each other, or to undermine traditional beliefs about the bright lines between languages
- translingualism as a pedagogical framework which is essential for writing instructors to incorporate into their models of instruction and especially of assessment
- translingualism as subject matter for students to understand and practice, sometimes in cross-cultural and cross-linguistic interchanges with students of different language backgrounds, sometimes in exploring their own linguistic repertoires in code-meshing experiments, etc.
- translingualism as a goal to be approached through a careful cultivation of an attitude toward language difference
- translingualism as simply a condition that exists, more or less unconsciously but continually exerting influence, every minute of every day when a speaker of more than one language or language variety reads, writes, speaks, or listens.

In this volume, rather than exploring these varying approaches to translingualism as such, we rather write of translingual*ity*. Of course, there is no such thing as a translinguality that is neutral in terms of post-colonial and racial power relations, or that is not situated in relation to existing ideologies of monolingualism, and so even as we assert that translinguality is everywhere, already operating in invisible and unconscious ways, the following chapters still must always inquire: why translinguality? whose translinguality? what kind of translinguality? for what purpose and where?

In this book, we conceive our task as that of making translinguality visible, by focusing on our students' experiences, as manifested in their writing and in their reported language experiences. Many students have got the message that in U.S. culture at large their non-English languages are not valued, and in fact are often regarded as a handicap to the speakers themselves and even as a provocation to the unconscious English-only ideology which pervades many aspects of U.S. society including academia, and which many of our students have therefore come to internalize. Students are not necessarily eager to make use of their non-English languages in academic contexts, because they have always been told that English is the only way. Indeed, students who are immigrants, and/or whose language backgrounds include minoritized varieties of English, are sometimes the most vehement defenders of "Standard English"—or, as we write here, because it foregrounds its implication in structures of power, Standard*ized* English—because they have worked very hard to acquire it and sometimes consider themselves to have arrived in a linguistic space where Standardized English is all that they need to use. It takes a process not only of education but of self-examination and a questioning of cultural boundaries for students to see, first, that they are already living in translingual spaces in both their daily and their academic lives, and second, that this is potentially a good and useful thing for their own self-expression and for a re-valuation of language difference in the culture of academia and beyond. Translingual pedagogies create spaces where students tell their linguistic stories, implicitly or explicitly, rather than teaching them to stuff themselves into ill-fitting boxes. It can teach them about communication, not perfection. They can multiply their linguistic performances, rather than narrowing them down.

Transnationality and Superdiversity

Transnational identities—memberships or affiliations with multiple national communities—are increasingly common across the globe, even "the norm, rather than the exception" (Levitt & Jaworsky, 2007, p. 146). National boundaries, however, continue to play significant administrative roles in our academic institutions, in terms of tuition structures, visa statuses and placement into English Language Learner (ELL)/English as a Second Language (ESL) and composition classes, and yet these bureaucratic categories fail to capture the complex nature of our students' lived identities. Ahmad and Nero (2012) argue that

> Internal migrations and interaction of diverse peoples coupled with the transnational nature of twenty-first-century populations make for multiple homes and identities—real, imagined, claimed, and fluid. By extension, home languages can be real, imagined, claimed (or even rejected), and fluid but never static or monodimensional.
>
> *(p. 73)*

The twentieth and twenty-first centuries have been periods of immense continual movement of people, ideas, currency, items, and practices, back and forth between different nation states, but our academic institutions have been slow to keep up.

College students at both the undergraduate and graduate level are often members of transnational communities, even when what we see mostly is how they are enmeshed in their local ties. No matter what their citizenship status—U.S. citizen by birthright or naturalization; permanent resident, F-1 visa holder—many of our students live in a world in which their behaviors, their stuff, their food, their money, connects them to one or more nations and communities outside the United States. However, these connections often disappear behind the assumptions that instructors make in the college classroom: assumptions of the primacy of American English, and of the inadequacy of other languages and other varieties of English in our students' academic lives—including an assumption that students with other language affiliations will only use English as a "school language."

Yet despite institutional efforts to maintain these categories—standardized English, English as a Second Language, "international student"—as destinations but never as points of embarkation, students and faculty cross and re-cross, transgress, transcribe, translate, and transform these boundaries every day through their language work. Therefore we need to ask the question, "what does transnationality mean for language work in our classrooms and other institutional spaces?"

We have defined our expanded sense of translinguality—distinct from the ideology of translingual*ism*—as both an everyday, pervasive phenomenon, a routine workhorse, and yet also as potentially a sophisticated tool for self-conscious expression of complex language identities. Transnationality is similarly approached both as a conscious claim or performance of identity and as also a largely unconscious immersion in cultural traces, connections, and memories, often mediated by the ongoing use of a minoritized language in a particular displaced setting.

Trans- and Transnationality

As we have shown previously, conversations about translinguality are well established in composition studies, and the field is now turning to considerations of transnationality, and how students' language practices are implicated by students' complex inter- and trans-national affiliations. Blommaert and Horner (2017) characterize, for perhaps one of the first times in composition studies, our students' lives as full of movement without a necessary singular end-point, which is what our narratives of immigration and language acquisition have tended to emphasize: movement towards a goal of linguistic assimilation. Blommaert and Horner argue,

> just as academic literacy researchers' efforts to accommodate students marked by the ideology of monolingualism as linguistically 'different' are now leading to challenges to notions of difference (and sameness) in language, what began with studies of the increasing mobility of students, IHEs, and knowledge as a feature distinguishing contemporary forms of these from the norm is now leading to recognition of the susceptibility of all knowledge to transformation through the process of its mobilization and to an alternative sense of mobility, now seen not as a new phenomenon distinguishing some learners, knowledge, and IHEs from others but as an inevitable feature of all these.
>
> *(2017, p. 5)*

With this idea of total movement in mind, we will move to consider the "trans-" part of transnational and translingual, and see what considerations of "trans" from queer studies afford us.

As a prefix, trans- is in common usage; as a theoretical space, trans- is relatively new in applied linguistics and composition studies. The *Oxford English Dictionary*'s definition of trans-, the prefix, demonstrates the movement that is inherent in its use: "across, through, over, to or on the other side of, beyond, outside of, from one place, person, thing, or state to another" (Trans-, 2019). The aspects of this meaning that we would like to emphasize here are those where trans- refers to a process of becoming and of crossing from one space to another. As a metaphor, trans- is inherently spatial. Trans- also connotes a lack of stability: settling at an end point of the crossing is less important, when we use words beginning with trans-, than the movement between points or spaces or times. As such, it can be thought of connoting disruption: its emphasis on movement is inherently destabilizing.

Perhaps the most culturally salient trans- at this moment in time is transgender: an identity performance in which an individual locates themselves outside and between traditional gender binaries, e.g. woman/man, girl/boy. Because of the frontier work being undertaken in transgender studies, we turn to the work with "trans-" being done in that field in order to expand our understanding of what "trans-" might bring to "translingualism" and "transnationalism" as theoretical constructs and descriptions of lived experience.

Writing about the relationship between "transgender" and queer studies, Stryker (2004) suggests that the field of transgender studies,

> offers to queer theory a critique that is becoming a point of departure for a lively conversation, involving many speakers from many locations, about the mutability and specificity of human lives and loves. There remains in that emerging dialogue a radical queer potential to realize.
>
> (p. 215)

The developing interest in and emphasis on translingualism in composition studies and applied linguistics, and transnationalism in sociology (etcetera) suggest to us that these fields are also seeking a mechanism for such critique: one that recenters the conversation away from traditional ideologies of language and nation, towards the possibility of inhabiting intersecting and mutually constitutive spaces at the same time. Trans- focuses on change and individual experience, rather than asking—or requiring—individuals to conform to linguistic and national categories that may not be relevant to their experiences. Thus, we see trans- as similarly offering a critique to traditional concepts of linguistic and national identity as they are embedded in our terminology, such as multilingual, multinational, plurilingual, ESL/SLW, generation 1.5, immigrant, etc. Trans- theory can help us see that critique and reorient our focus to the spaces between nations and languages as places where many of our students spend most of their time.

To pursue this re-conception of our categories of language identity and national identity via consideration of what trans- means, again, we consider Stryker, Currah, and Moore's (2008) articulation of *"trans-"* as a prefix, and as such its "implicit relationality," and therefore its implications for its possible suffixes. Their focus is on -gender, but their analysis also applies to other suffixes, in which list they include "-national, -racial, -generational, -genic, -species," to which we would, of course, add "-lingual." Stryker et al. (2008) describe what the prefix of trans- does in the two following passages, drawing attention to the connections and the movement implied by trans-,:

- Neither "-gender" or other suffixes of "trans-" can be understood in isolation—the lines implied by the very conception of "trans-" are moving targets, simultaneously composed of multiple determinants. "Transing," in short, is a practice that takes place within, as well as across or between, gendered spaces. It is a practice that assembles gender into contingent structures of association with other attributes of bodily being, and that allows for their reassembly. Transing can function as a disciplinary tool [a tool used to discipline individuals—hmr] when the stigma associated with the lack or loss of gender status threatens social unintelligibility, coercive normalization, or even bodily extermination. It can also function as an escape vector, line of flight, or pathway toward liberation.

    (p. 13)

- "Trans-" thus becomes the capillary space of connection and circulation between the macro- and micro-political registers through which the lives of bodies become enmeshed in the lives of nations, states, and capital-formations.

    (p. 14)

Of the many pieces of the conceptual frame established by Stryker et al. (2008) in these two passages, we focus on their description of "transing" as a practice that takes place within spaces and networks of affiliation, and within which "structures of association" are contingent, and in which transing can also be used "at" individuals to keep them within their assigned identity spaces, or, more importantly for our work in this book, in which transing "function[s] as an escape vector, line of flight, or pathway toward liberation" (p. 13). And finally, we want to emphasize their description of "trans" as "the capillary space of connection and circulation between . . . macro- and micro-political registers" (p. 14). Since languages and nations are ideological constructions—status as a language, rather than a dialect, for instance, is intimately connected with nationhood in the adage, popularized by Max Weinrich: "a language is a dialect with an army and a navy"—we want to emphasize the importance of the political and social implications of transing as it challenges our conceptions of the boundaries of "language" and "nation."

Levitt and Jaworsky (2007) write, in their definition of transnationalism, that

> Basch, Glick Schiller, and Blanc-Szanton (1994, p. 6) initially defined transnationalism as 'the processes by which immigrants forge and sustain multi-stranded social relations that link together their societies of origin and settlement.' More recent scholarship understands transnational migration as taking place within fluid social spaces that are constantly reworked through migrants' simultaneous embeddedness in more than one society (Levitt & Glick Schiller, 2004; Pries, 2005; Smith, 2005). These arenas are multi-layered and multi-sited, including not just the home and host countries but other sites around the world that connect migrants to their conationals and coreligionists.
>
> *(p. 131)*

Again, this definition is conceptually contiguous with the theory of "trans-" outlined previously: transnationalism is relational and enacted in the process of creating and maintaining relations between people; the spaces in which transnational migration occurs are "fluid" and "constantly reworked." To be transnational, as this definition indicates, is to occupy a dynamic space, which is defined by acts of affiliation and performance; identity assignments based on national categories will necessarily be unable to capture the fluidity of the identities formed around processes of transnationals' "simultaneous embeddedness." What this definition also makes clear is that transnationalism is as much a set of connections between people as it is between geographical spaces, which connects to the definition of identity offered by Le Page and Tabouret-Keller (1985) and West (1992): people affiliate themselves with social groups through "acts of identity," driven by desire for these affiliations, these connections. We can see translingual and transnational identities emerge by what people do—how they use language, how they describe and claim their national affiliations.

Of the students participating in the studies presented here, the international students whose stories we narrate in Chapters 2, 6, and 13 of this book may seem, at first glance, to more easily fit the paradigm of transnational students. Indeed, by definition, "international" students are in a liminal situation, where their physical location on U.S. campuses is only part of the story of their language practices and personal/national identities. One variable is student aspirations: some students will complete their degrees (or not) and return to their countries of origin; others will attempt to stay in the United States or move to some other country, and such desires have important relevance both to how students regard the relation between their physical location and their sometimes-shifting notions of "home," and also to how they think about the relation between English as (at minimum) the medium of instruction and their other language(s).

"International" students thus cannot escape situating themselves (and being situated institutionally) on a continuum of transnational and translingual practices: they remain connected, to varying degrees and through different modalities, to their home countries, and yet must also establish a successful relation, of one kind or another, with their U.S. institution, its on-campus community, and the larger host culture. We will consider the status of "international" students as transnational sojourners in more detail in Chapter 6 and 13.

In Chapters 2, 4, and 9, the students are often U.S. citizens and permanent residents, but this does not mean that they are not transnationally connected. On the contrary, Urban College, the site of this study, is a campus with a high percentage of immigrants and children of immigrants, where a plurality, but not majority of students identify as "native English speakers," and where multiple Englishes, especially a continuum of African-American and Caribbean Englishes, further complicate students' language backgrounds and transnational identity commitments. These students are undoubtedly "Americans," yet they maintain strong connections with other nation states; their continuing transnational connections have important implications for our study of their languaging. In our writing samples, students at Urban College explore what Glick Schiller (2003) describes as transnational "ways of being," and "ways of belonging," the social relations and practices that form transnational identities and "a conscious connection to a particular group" (Levitt & Jaworsky, 2007, p. 133). For example, we will meet a man who was born in the United States, but who maintains close familial and loose linguistic ties to Guyana; a woman born in Haiti who describes the ambivalence she feels at having left Haiti for the United States after the earthquake; and a man who emigrated to New York from Ghana with his family, and who resists the linguistic colonization that he experienced in Ghana, and which continues in the United States.

In these students' writing, we see how linguistic stories and (trans)national stories intersect, but do not always overlap. A user of a prestige variety of English may be, technically, "a foreigner." A U.S. citizen by birthright may consider their primary linguistic affiliation to be with a language other than English, or, indeed, with English and another language. We see in our students' language work how the negotiation of linguistic identities intertwines with the negotiation of transnational identities.

The Urban College students depicted in Chapters 2, 4, 9, and 10 differ in another important way from the "international students" at State University depicted in Chapters 2, 6, and 13: the latter students are much more homogenous in terms of their national origin. Yet, as we will see, even though we can say that the students from State University who we discuss mostly "came from China," their language use, future ambitions, level of sophistication in regards to their disciplines, familiarity with U.S. culture all vary widely. At

Urban College, the population is better described as superdiverse, defined as the "dynamic interplay of variables among an increased number of new, small and scattered, multiple-origin, transnationally connected, socio-economically differentiated and legally stratified immigrants" (Vertovec, 2007, p. 1024). Blommaert and Rampton (2012) observe that

> super-diversity is characterized by a tremendous increase in the categories of migrants, not only in terms of nationality, ethnicity, language, and religion, but also in terms of motives, patterns and itineraries of migration, processes of insertion into the labour and housing markets of the host societies, and so on. The predictability of the category of 'migrant' and of his/her sociocultural features has disappeared.
>
> *(p. 7)*

In the absence of such "predictability," our methodology must arrive where we began: our only alternative is to Ask the Students.

II. Translingual Identities, Transnational Realities in the U.S. College Classroom

We have offered, in this introductory chapter, our expanded sense of translinguality (as distinct from the ideology of translingual*ism*) as both an everyday, pervasive phenomenon, a routine workhorse, and also potentially a sophisticated tool for self-conscious expression of complex language identities. We have presented, as well, a view of transnational identity and the ways in which it intersects with students' language backgrounds. And we offer an analytical framework based on the prefix trans-, which brings translinguality and transnationality together, and offers us a way forward in our consideration of how these phenomena are implicated and enacted in our classrooms. In the chapters that follow, we will detail and deepen these preliminary definitions by examining the ways in which our students, in their writings, in response to assignments that invite them to explore, to claim, and to create identities for themselves that may differ from those that have been imposed on them by cultures both in the U.S. and elsewhere. To identify the different voices of the seven chapters, we list the author(s) in each chapter.

We will also explore, more briefly, our own linguistic and national identities, in Chapters 3, 5, and 7, in three reflective essays from our perspectives as educators, language students ourselves, and language users, exploring our linguistic, national, and racial perspectives and privileges. It would be unethical to pretend to stand outside the struggles and triumphs of identity that our students put forward in their writings, as though we are somehow separate from that process, somehow already secure and fixed in our own identities. In Chapter 7, Jonathan, a "native" English speaker abroad, struggles to learn Spanish and finds that it's hard to miss that people have English on their minds, which heightens his sense of his own language identity, sometimes in uncomfortable ways. In Chapter 3, Heather, an immigrant to the United States, but one with white skin and who speaks a high-prestige variety of English, discusses the (in)visibility of difference, and its impact on her teaching practice at a majority-minority institution. In Chapter 5, Nela, a child of immigrants raised in a translingual environment explores a translingual identity as a right, a cosmopolitan sensibility, a means of negotiating difference and creating meaning, as well as a creative force, one that informs her critical pedagogy teaching practices in a graduate program that supports translingual students at a state university.

Chapter 2, **"Everyday Translinguality: We Meet Our Students"** introduces the students from Urban College and State University in the educational contexts where we encounter them. Their language narratives reveal how students conceive their language identities based on their description of multiple contexts, codes, dialects, modes, and purposes. These student texts explore language identity as a dynamic textual negotiation between contextual imposed identities (including that of "international student") and claimed identities mediated through student agency as writers (Varghese, Morgan, Johnston, & Johnson, 2005). The chapter examines the rhetorical moves through which students structure relationships with particular language identities, attitudes, ambitions, goals, and visions of future use of English and other languages. While these identities are somewhat different depending on whether the student is a U.S. resident or citizen or an international student, and depending on undergraduate or graduate status, each student had easily described a unique location in a matrix of interlocking languages. Their translingual identities, their infinite variations on the theme of being inside, out of, between, and around languages, are the subject of the brief sketches that we include, a combination of what they wrote in their papers and the details that they added in interviews and conversations with their instructor. Excerpts from interviews with the graduate students from State University round out the chapter and our brief introductions to the students whose translingual transnational lives we explore here.

Chapters 4 and 8 examine the challenges inherent in the effort to create a college classroom that engages translingual/transnational issues. **"Transing Language Identity"** argues that identity is the issue too often left out of even progressive approaches to writing pedagogy, and explores what a translingual and transnational language identity might look like, as well as pedagogies that center these translingual, transnational identity formations in our classrooms. **"Transing Pedagogy"** focuses on the faculty perspective of transing, considering how can we create assignments and classroom spaces and practices that invite students to explore their translingual and transnational identities, and what a transpedagogical methodology and orientation might look like.

In **Chapter 6 and Chapter 12**, we explore, in depth, ways of being an international student at State University, a large, research-intensive land-grant university in the Northeast. Chapter 6 focuses on how international students perform their linguistic affiliations over the arc of a semester. Five of the students whose identity performance we explore are in their second semester in an English for academic purposes sequence of courses at State University; two of them are graduate students studying in PhD programs at that institution. We discuss these students' biographical essays and literacy narratives, and, for the graduate students, interview responses, to consider the emergent linguistic affiliations that they establish during their degree programs at State University. In Chapter 12, we focus on interview responses from three graduate students, showing how students who are able to establish meaningful intersections between disciplinary discourses and everyday Englishes are able to establish translingual, transnational identities in ways that are not well-known in the international graduate student literature. Further, we contextualize these interview responses in the broader landscape of academic support at State University, using reflections from Nela, the director of the Graduate Academic Support Program (GASP) at that institution.

"**Translanguaging, Performance, and the Art of Negotiation,**" **Chapter 9,** explores translanguaging in student writing, considering what kinds of writing assignments might encourage translingual writing among students, and what kinds of philosophical approaches to these translingual assignments instructors might best adopt. The chapter begins by discussing the kinds of translanguaging that students at Urban College do on a regular basis, and some reasons behind this translanguaging, then moves on to discuss how translingual writing can be incorporated into core pedagogies in the classroom—including formal assignments—considering the kinds of assignments that might give students space to perform translingually without requiring them to "out" themselves as translingual. The last part of the chapter explores the work of specific students, all from different linguistic backgrounds, but who are all adept translingual writers though their adeptness comes from different places.

The translingual turn in composition theory is partly a result of increasing engagement in scholarly alliance with other disciplines such as TESOL, applied linguistics, and second language acquisition. Chapter 10, "**Translingual Economies of Literacy**" continues that dialogue by asking how this translingual turn might affect the way in which we apply our research to questions of reading as well as writing. What might the literature on second language reading have to contribute to our attempts to articulate a translingual approach to reading, one that would account for bi-directional flows of language, for interactional exchanges of meaning, for what is called here translingual economies of literacy? In order to anchor these theoretical discussions in actual examples, two case studies are interspersed, one Urban College student and one instructor, Jonathan, who discusses his own experience of translingual reading.

Chapter 11, "**Translinguality, Grammatical Literacy, and a Pedagogy of Naming**" takes as its starting point the end of Canagarajah's 2006 essay "in which he argues for the incorporation of World Englishes into the discourse of composition, and challenges students to use their 'preferred varieties' of English alongside the dominant ones in 'rhetorically strategic ways" (2006, pp. 598–599). Picking up where Canagarajah left off, this chapter explores a pedagogical approach, which moves the "pluralization of English" into the "deep structure of grammar." Using a grammar course as a case study, this chapter outlines an approach to teaching at the sentence-level that embraces linguistic pluralism and anti-racist attitudes to language.

Chapter 13, **"Cultivating a Culture of Language Rights"** explores how employing a language rights as well as a linguistic human rights framework can provide a critical lens for understanding translingual pedagogical practices and spaces as a rights-based imperative. It also aims to underscore the obligations that educational institutions have to promote and protect the linguistic rights and identities of their students as well as recognize and support the use of their languages in the academy. These frameworks can offer an understanding of the limitations of current language policies and programs in which students in the "global university" are expected to assimilate, "mainstream" and work exclusively in the language and identity of the dominant group. This chapter examines why the implementation of language and linguistic human rights is central to cultivating and protecting translingual practices and spaces, embracing inclusion as well as a cosmopolitan sensibility.

Our concluding chapter, **"Negotiating Identities,"** reminds us that our classrooms and our local administrative programs are not isolated spaces, but rather are zones of contact and sites of struggle, locations where every day, in every interaction, students' language rights either are or are not being respected. Instructors are often torn between their roles as involuntary representatives of institutional power, and thus of demands for enforcing monolingualist language norms, on the one hand, and the language needs and desires of their students on the other. From our exploration of everyday translinguality in Part I, to our focus on transnational translingual literacies in Part II, our emphasis is always on moving a consideration of the ways that students negotiate language identities from the margins to the center of our work in the classroom and in our administrative decision-making. We have much to gain, pedagogically, experientially, and in research, from making translinguality and transnationality visible, from making audible the voices of language-minoritized students, and from listening to their experiences and concerns.

References

Ahmad, D., & Nero, S. J. (2012). Productive paradoxes: Vernacular use in the teaching of composition and literature. *Pedagogy: Critical Approaches to Teaching Literature, Language, Composition, and Culture, 12*(1), 69–95.

Atkinson, D., Crusan, D., Matsuda, P. K., Ortmeier-Hooper, C., Ruecker, T., Simpson, S., & Tardy, C. (2015). Clarifying the relationship between L2 writing and

translingual writing: An open letter to writing studies editors and organization leaders. *College English, 77*(4).
Barwashi, A., Guerra, J., Horner, B., & Lu, M.-Z. (Eds.). (2016). Translingual work in composition (Special Issue). *College English, 78*(3).
Basch, L., Glick Schiller, N., & Blanc-Szanton, C. (Eds.). (1994). *Nations unbound: Transnational projects, postcolonial predicaments, and deterritorialized nation-states.* London: Gordon & Breach.
Blommaert, J., & Horner, B. (2017). Mobility and academic literacies: An epistolary conversation. *London Review of Education, 15*(1), 3–20.
Blommaert, J., & Rampton, B. (2012). *Language and superdiversity.* Göttingen: Max Planck Institute for the Study of Religious and Ethnic Diversity.
Canagarajah, A. S. (2006). The place of world Englishes in composition: Pluralization continued. *College Composition and Communication, 57*(4), 586–619.
Canagarajah, A. S. (2013). *Literacy as translingual practice: Between communities and classrooms.* New York and London: Routledge.
Donahue, C. (2009). "Internationalization" and composition studies: Reorienting the discourse. *College Composition and Communication, 61*(2), 212–243.
Duany, J., & CUNY Dominican Studies Institute. (2008). *Quisqueya on the Hudson: The transnational identity of Dominicans in Washington Heights.* CUNY Academic Works. Retrieved from http://academicworks.cuny.edu/dsi_pubs/1
Garcia, O. (2009). *Bilingual education in the 21st century: A global perspective.* Oxford: Wiley-Blackwell.
Glick Schiller, N. (2003). The centrality of ethnography in the study of transnational migration. In N. Foner (Ed.), *American arrivals: Anthropology engages the new immigration* (pp. 99–128). Santa Fe, NM: The School for Advanced Research.
Horner, B., Lu, M.-Z., Royster, J. J., & Trimbur, J. (2011). Language difference in writing: Toward a translingual approach. *College English, 73*(3), 303–321.
Horner, B., & Tetreault, L. (2017). *Crossing divides: Exploring translingual writing pedagogies and programs.* Logan, UT: Utah State University Press.
Jain, R. (2014). Global Englishes, translinguistic identities, and translingual practices in a Community College ESL classroom: A practitioner researcher reports. *TESOL Journal, 5*(3), 490–522.
Kubota, R. (2014). The multi/plural turn, postcolonial theory, and neoliberal multiculturalism: Complicities and implications for applied linguistics. *Applied Linguistics, 37,* 474–494.
Lee, J. W. (2017). *The politics of translingualism: After Englishes.* New York and London: Routledge.
Le Page, R. B., & Tabouret-Keller, A. (1985). *Acts of identity: Creole-based approaches to language and ethnicity.* Cambridge: Cambridge University Press.
Levitt, P., & Glick Schiller, N. (2004). Transnational perspectives on migration: Conceptualizing simultaneity. *International Migration Review, 38*(3), 1002–1039.
Levitt, P., & Jaworsky, B. N. (2007). Transnational migration studies: Past developments and future trends. *Annual Review of Sociology, 33*(1), 129–156.
Martins, D. S. (2014). *Transnational writing program administration.* Boulder, CO: University Press of Colorado.
Matsuda, P. K. (2014). The lure of translingual writing. *PMLA, 129*(3), 478–483.
Pries, L. (2005). Configurations of geographic and societal spaces: A sociological proposal between "methodological nationalism" and the "spaces of flows". *Global Networks, 5,* 167–190.

Smith, M. P. (2005). Transnational urbanism revisited. *Journal of Ethnic and Migration Studies, 31*, 235–244.

Solano-Campos, A. (2014). The making of an international educator: Transnationalism and nonnativeness in English teaching and learning. *TESOL Journal, 5*(3), 412–443.

Stryker, S. (2004). Transgender studies: Queer theory's evil twin. *GLQ: A Journal of Lesbian and Gay Studies, 10*(2), 212–215.

Stryker, S., Currah, P., & Moore, L. J. (2008). Introduction: Trans-, trans, or transgender? *Women's Studies Quarterly, 36*(3/4), 11–22.

"Trans-". (2019). In *Oxford English Dictionary*. Retrieved from www-oed-com.york.ezproxy.cuny.edu/view/Entry/204575?rskey=ZRD5x3&result=4&isAdvanced=false#contentWrapper

Varghese, M., Morgan, B., Johnston, B., & Johnson, K. A. (2005). Theorizing language teacher identity: Three perspectives and beyond. *Journal of Language, Identity & Education, 4*(1), 21–44.

Vertovec, S. (2007). Super-diversity and its implications. *Ethnic and Racial Studies, 30*(6), 1024–1054.

West, C. (1992). A matter of life and death. *October, 61*, 20–23.

Zenger, A., Haviland, C., & Mullin, J. (2013). Reconstructing teacher roles through a transnational lens: Learning with/in the American University of Beirut. In M. Cox & T. M. Zawacki (Eds.), *WAC and second language writers: Research towards developing linguistically and culturally inclusive programs and practices*. Anderson, SC: Parlor Press.

PART I
Everyday Translinguality

2
EVERYDAY TRANSLINGUALITY
We Meet Our Students

Everyone has a language story to tell. The authors of this book, in the sure knowledge that we do not claim to be considering language identity from some kind of impossibly neutral outside perspective, will in subsequent chapters tell some of our own. But first let us meet some of our students. Their translingual and transnational identities, their infinite variations on the theme of being inside, out of, between, and around languages, are the subject of the discussion that follows, a combination of demographic data gleaned from survey responses, narratives written in papers from various courses and in-depth interviews as well as reflections and framings on these papers and interviews offered by the students' course instructors. Here, we begin to get a preliminary idea of how they perform their language identities, as well as describing our methods of engagement for asking these students about their identities.

Linguistically-minoritized students are often asked to choose between educational success and making overt their plural linguistic identities (Rodriguez, 1983; Young, 2004; Anzaldúa, 1987, among many). In the studies reported here we explore how these plural linguistic identities are always just under the surface, even when they are denied a venue for expression in educational contexts. Nero (2005) explains just how important it is to "meet" our students in our classes, especially those from minoritized "raciolinguistic" backgrounds (Flores & Rosa, 2015). She explains that asking students to self-describe their linguistic identities is an important way to establish "a linguistic 'portrait' of students that serves as a point of departure for how [instructors] might begin to construct and negotiate their identities" (2005, p. 199) in our classrooms. Nero's framing is important: it is not only the responsibility—and the fundamental right—of students to construct and negotiate their linguistic identities; rather, it is both an instructional and institutional responsibility to acknowledge and respond positively to our students as they arrive in our colleges and universities. Furthermore, as we contend throughout this book, it is our students' fundamental right to be able to express themselves in the language(s) of their choosing, while acknowledging that they operate, as we all do, in a system structured by many linguistic, racial, social, and academic hierarchies, all of which may constrain the choices that they feel that they are able to make.

Meeting our students in this chapter shows how post-secondary students in the United States, no matter what their linguistic and national backgrounds, share an experience of "everyday translingualism": translinguality that is an ordinary, unremarkable, *necessary* part of their lives, defined by movement between and beyond various language communities. However, we see this everyday translinguality emerging through students' experiences at these two institutions in distinctly different ways. Whereas translingual approaches to students' identities and linguistic practices often suggest that multi- and plurilingual language practices are "exotic" and "different" (cf. Lee, 2017; Canagarajah, 2013), the students whose narratives we discuss here demonstrate quite the opposite: that translinguality and diversity are quite "ordinary"—if challenging—parts of their lives in this twenty-first century globalized and transnational context (cf. Lee, 2017). As Dovchin (2017) argues,

> In fact, there is nothing unusual about linguistic diversity, as people and cultures have historically always been mixing and mingling. Thus, being bi- or multilingual is neither rare nor exotic. Linguistic diversity is "neither to celebrate nor to deplore, but something to observe and examine with interest like anything else."
>
> *(Sarkar & Low, 2012, p. 12)*

Furthermore, since universities such as State University deliberately recruit international students into both its undergraduate and graduate degree programs, and since cities like the one in which Urban College is located have been landing sites for many generations of immigrants to the United States, we might say that these policies create an ordinary translinguality, where campuses become multilingual spaces no matter what the linguistic demographics of the institution's surrounding community. And yet, in centering everyday translinguality we must also center students' sovereignty (Lee, 2017, following Lyons, 2000) over their own linguistic practices, and the necessity of respecting their choices as to what to show, and what to hide, about their linguistic and cultural resources competencies, especially in contexts such as higher education, which have proven to be hostile to cultural and linguistic difference except to reify and exoticize it.

It is from this positionality that we introduce the students whose translingual and transnational lives we explore in this volume. We suggest that the policies and the environments in which these students live, and which go far beyond "home" and "school," *create* everyday translingualism, in their bringing together people with various language inheritances into these language contact situations. Furthermore, we find the students much more prepared to navigate these spaces than their instructors and institutions. Instructors and institutions tend not to recognize students' wide variety of language goals, and their wide range of facility with writing and language use *in any language*. Therefore, we start from the position that the students are translingual and transnational, either as a central part of their lives, or in a way that is incidental to their citizenship of globalized nation states. We are perhaps used to students' translinguality coming out in hybridized final products, or via so-called interference from languages other than English in their writing; however, we suggest that translinguality is at once more pervasive and more evasive than this. In this chapter, we are less interested in the linguistic outputs of student translinguality, and more interested in the negotiations that students describe as being part of their everyday lives as students and members of transnational and translingual communities.

Going from the general institutional context to the specific context of our participants in the studies presented in this book, the student populations from which we draw our participants are quite different. The students from Urban College are drawn from the general student population, which in turn draws from the linguistically superdiverse communities of a major urban center of the United States. At Urban College, we see the effects of "metrolingualism" (Otsuji & Pennycook, 2013) in action: the linguistic effects of the transnational crossings of people from many different language communities brought together in an urban space; the urban space and the language diversity are co-constitutive. The students who we meet at State University, on the other hand, are at that institution because of a set of policy choices made on the part of the university, and which mirror policy choices at large research universities nationally. Thus, while the general undergraduate student population at State University as a whole shows much of the same linguistic and racial diversity as the student population at Urban College (Enrollment Management, 2018), our focus at State University will be on transnational and translingual diversity among students who the university counts as "international students," who are classified, in terms of their visas, "non-resident aliens." We bring these two groups of students together because they represent sites of profound change in the U.S. higher education landscape, since more and more children of immigrants and members of raciolinguistically marginalized groups of U.S. citizens are attending and graduating from college, and U.S. institutions are recruiting more and more international students. We show how, although all diversity within the category of "international student" is often made invisible by the category itself, nonetheless, "non-resident aliens" come to State University with wide variation in their linguistic affiliations, inheritances, and expertise (Rampton, 1990). That is, although the "international" students who appear in this book may seem from the outside to be more linguistically homogenous than the general State University population, an examination of the State University students' narratives demonstrates that this categorization is a significant oversimplification of their backgrounds, their identities, and their practices, a fact that is being increasingly recognized in the policies and practices of the State University programs which engage international and multilingual students.

One of the things that we hope this volume demonstrates is the urgent need for instructors and institutions to learn more about where *all* students come from at a much more granular level than the national, as language practices are highly variable across regions, and students often identify strongly with the languages and dialects of their cities or their neighborhoods, while often affiliating themselves quite forcefully with the hegemonic English of the United States.

Methodologies: Insider/Outsider Research Perspectives

These chapters constitute an exploration of how the participants in the studies we bring together here construct their identities, focusing on the language that they use to do so. However, and of course, these linguistic identity performances are in no way neutral: because the texts that we examine were produced in classroom contexts, and in interviews with instructors and other interlocutors occupying the position of "professor," they are all influenced and shaped by these contexts. Thus, we recognize that when we analyze and interpret language, we co-construct the meanings that we find, and, to paraphrase Ahearn (2001), that these meanings emerge from particular social interactions (p. 111). Our research method is inductive and qualitative (Guba & Lincoln, 1994; Merriam, 2009): in each of the studies presented here, we started with the student texts (including the interviews) and read to find which themes emerged, then based our analyses on these emergent themes, and broadened and deepened them based on re-engagements with the original texts, and on contextualizing information that we could provide from our knowledge of the students whose responses we explored. Participants in the interviews were compensated for their time. In this section, we foreground our researcher positionalities in this book, each focusing on a particular aspect of these positionalities in a chapter of this volume, and giving an overview here.

As a researcher, Heather is an insider at both institutions. A tenured professor at Urban College, the students whose work is represented in Chapter 4 and 9 were students in her classes at that institution. Analysis of these students' work is thus framed by her knowledge of the students over the course of a semester, and is contextualized by other interactions and assignments created by the students in the course, and, for some, as English majors at Urban College. Furthermore, while no longer teaching or studying at State University,

Heather occupies an insider/outsider positionality with respect to the international students whose work and lives we discuss in this chapter, and Chapter 6 and 13. Heather completed her PhD at State University, as an international student, and amidst many international graduate students. She then moved on to working as an administrator in State University's Writing Program, teaching many courses including the one that directly follows English for Academic Purposes II, the course in which our State University undergraduate students are participating. Thus, she has taught and mentored students very similar to those whose writing we look at here. Her perspective as a researcher therefore is framed by her personal experiences as a student similar to—but not the same as—those whose stories we represent here, and as an instructor of students similar to the undergraduates described here.

Jonathan occupies three different research positionalities with respect to the students who we discuss in this volume. In this chapter, he takes the position of a teacher-researcher, engaging from his vantage point as a tenured professor at Urban College: the students from Urban College whose portraits we offer in this chapter were in Jonathan's class, and they are responding to an assignment in which he asked them to think about their own language background and practices in relation to the concepts that they were studying in class. The papers for that course helped to make visible what he had been increasingly aware of during his time at Urban College: that our students' language backgrounds were far more complex than had really been acknowledged in either popular or scholarly forums. So what began simply as a pedagogical mission evolved into a desire to share some of that complexity with a larger audience.

In working with the students at State University, Jonathan was more of an outsider. Having worked with Nela for several years, he understood something of the complex lives that international students brought into their composition classes. He, like Heather, did not meet or interview any of the undergraduate students represented in this volume, but only reviewed their writings, and responses to a survey which contextualized this writing. In the process, Jonathan discovered that he knew very little about undergraduate Chinese students. He thought that the stories of these students could help with pedagogical awareness in many contexts, not just in courses designated for "international students," but in all college courses.

In the context of working with the international graduate students at State University, again, Jonathan's engagement emerged from his long-term collaboration with Nela who directs the Graduate Academic Success Program at State University. Rather than from professional affiliations with the institution. Jonathan and Nela conducted the interviews represented in this chapter and Chapter 13 together, following a set of questions written by Jonathan. Jonathan compiled the transcripts of the interviews and read through to identify emerging themes; Nela and Heather then reviewed the transcripts in order to narrow down the focus on the discussion of these rich interviews.

In the context of this book, Nela considers herself to occupy both "outsider" and "insider" positionalities as well as a position that extends beyond these established binary categories. She envisions her overall and "third" positionality as that of a "transglobal citizen researcher/teacher," one that inhabits the margins of any given teacher/researcher role and cannot be reduced to either. With this third positionality, she has deliberately chosen a marginal position that is shaped by her own experiences living in transglobal spaces. Her decision to inhabit this liminal space is informed by the ways in which she has been identified, classified, and "written" as both an "insider" and an "outsider" in many personal and professional contexts.

In this chapter, Nela is an "outsider" teacher-researcher who has some familiarity with the students at Urban College, both because of her collaboration with Heather and Jonathan on this project, and because of previous teaching experiences in other universities in the United States and abroad. In those university contexts, she has taught students whose language and cultural identity claims and backgrounds are equally diverse, fluid, and elude simplistic definitions.

Nela occupies the position of an "insider" at State University because of her role as a program director for the Graduate Academic Success Program (GASP) and as a member of the academic advisory group convened by her colleague who directs and coordinates the undergraduate "international students" program. She teaches both the undergraduate and graduate students who have so generously shared their reflections, experiences, and aspirations in the assignments explored in this chapter. She reads, privileges, and understands the multiplicity of student voices at State University through the lens of the "rights based," social justice pedagogy that informs her research interests.

Nela sees her choice to reread and explore the autobiography, literacy narratives, and end of semester writing reflection assignments of students at State University as an opportunity to further connect with them. She also considers it her responsibility to create spaces, assignments and learning opportunities in which we can critically read, listen to, and engage with truly transglobal perspectives, identities, and ideas that emerge from the work of student writers (undergraduates) and emerging scholars and colleagues (graduate students). She does so with the understanding that these ideas and identities must be valued, made legible, and become an integral part of a university's mission to prepare students for the promises and perils of twenty-first-century living.

We Meet Our Students: Urban College

We meet one group of our students at Urban College, a four-year campus of a large urban university. The students that we meet in this chapter are taking an "Introduction to Writing, Rhetoric and Language" course, one of the required courses as they begin the English major; in Chapter 4 and Chapter 9, the students are taking a World Englishes course, a class that fulfills the global writing emphasis of the English major, one of the university's general education requirements, and one of the college's writing intensive course requirements. Sometimes, the latter class is mostly filled with English majors; increasingly, though, it has many non-majors in it.

Urban College's students report plural linguistic affiliations, and plural national affiliations. For our Urban College students, in their big city lives (93% of Urban College students live in the large metropolis where the college is situated (Urban College, 2018)), the boundaries between their languages are porous, flexible; while they have been told to keep them separate in educational contexts, in their lives these languages jostle for space. Almost all of the students, too, are Brown, Black or Asian (93.9% in Fall 2018); all of the students who we will discuss have been and continue to be raciolinguistically minoritized in some way. This minoritization manifests itself linguistically in several ways: they have been refused permission to use languages or varieties other than standardized English in educational contexts; they have been excluded from native-speaker-English status; they have been placed in ESL classes, they are marked as speakers of broken, slang, othered Englishes, and as such declared incapable of using standardized varieties of English except sometimes when they belong to so-called model minorities—South and East Asian—in which case their plurilingualism is rendered invisible.

Urban College reports that its students speak over 100 "native" languages from across the globe. Table 2.1 shows the seven most commonly spoken languages at the college. We note that these top seven languages account for only 41.5 percent of the reported native languages in Fall 2018, indicating a still richer, and increasing, linguistic diversity among students at the college.

While Table 2.1 illustrates an interesting profile of students' linguistic identifications within a fairly constrained set of choices, we note the labels for the

TABLE 2.1 Native Languages at Urban College (Top 7)

Fall 2016	N	%	Fall 2017	N	%	Fall 2018	N	%
English	2879	34.4%	English	2776	32.5%	English	2677	30.8%
Spanish	591	6.4%	Spanish	468	5.5%	Spanish	449	5.2%
Bengali	233	2.8%	Bengali	217	2.5%	Bengali	212	2.4%
Creole	158	1.3%	Creole	94	1.1%	Creole	98	1.1%
Urdu	111	1.3%	Urdu	80	1.1%	Urdu	74	0.9%
French	65	0.8%	Chinese	59	0.7%	Chinese	50	0.6%
Chinese	61	0.7%	French	57	0.7%	French	46	0.5%
	4098	47.70%		3751	44.10%		3606	41.50%

Source: Urban College, 2018

languages represented here tell us little about national origin or language variety within these "master" languages. For instance, as Table 2.3 shows us, the Englishes spoken at Urban College come from across the Anglophone diaspora, French is more likely to be Haitian French than European French, and Spanish and Creole could be connected with any number of nation states or with communities in Urban College's host city. Furthermore, these demographic statistics, while giving something of a blurry snapshot of Urban College's linguistic diversity, obscures the "ordinary translinguality" of our students. Moreover, once native speaker status is conferred in one language, it can exclude native speaker status in any other language (Faez, 2011). In order to bring this into sharper focus, in the World Englishes class, we asked students to answer the open-ended question "What languages do you speak?", in-class survey completed in three sections of World Englishes. These surveys, which students completed on the first day of class, asked open-ended questions about the students' language identities, rather than giving them predefined values from which to choose. The open-ended questions gave students space to self-represent the languages with which they affiliate themselves; their answers are represented in Table 2.2.

The data in this table is notable not because it gives a comprehensive view of language diversity at Urban College—the sample is too small to do that—but because it shows the extent to which students identify as multilingual: almost half of the respondents indicate that they speak two or more languages, and only one of the thirty-two students does not identify as a speaker of English. Notable, too, is the fact that one student recognizes "Broken English" as language independent of English, as does another with respect to Patois, a language which other students might consider to be English (cf. Nero, 1997).

TABLE 2.2 What Languages Do You Speak?

What languages do you speak?	Number	%
English "Only"	17	53.1
English and Spanish	4	12.5
English and Urdu	1	3.1
English and Urdu and Pashto	1	3.1
English and Creole	2	6.3
English and Bengali and Urdu and Hindi	1	3.1
English and Patois	1	3.1
English and Broken English	1	3.1
English and Polish	1	3.1
English and Hindi and Fijian	1	3.1
Spanish	1	3.1
English and Italian	1	3.1
Total	32	

When we break the question down further and ask students what Englishes they speak, their answers become much more complex, as we see in Table 2.3. The questions were once again open ended. There are no percentages because students chose more than one English in many cases.

These responses show a wide variety of Englishes from across the Anglophone diaspora, as well as strong links to specific geographical regions. Three students describe their English as being associated with the large metropolis in which Urban College resides; two get even more specific and describe their English as being from one particular borough within the city. Students also use seemingly pejorative identifiers such as "Broken English" and "Slang." We are not sure what Jargon refers to, but two students claim this affiliation. And, notably, 31 students claim standardized American or Standard/Standardized English as one of their varieties. Urban College students have a clear conception of the social and cultural capital (Bourdieu, 2018) that accrues from an affiliation with dominant varieties of English, and so this figure is unsurprising; however, as we discuss in Chapter 11, students from "raciolinguistically" minoritized backgrounds may not be accorded the status of Standardized English speakers, even if their speech patterns are objectively identical to those of white speakers who use standardized English (Flores & Rosa, 2015). Nonetheless, we see Urban College's students claiming this variety as, we suggest, part of their identities as successful college students.

Our students' responses on these surveys are elaborated by language narratives (an assignment derived from the literacy narrative, one of the most popular student genres in composition as discussed, for example, in Inayatulla, 2013). The following snapshots—which are framed and elaborated by Jonathan's reflections on these narratives and conversations that occurred as part of the coursework of "Introduction to Writing, Rhetoric and Language"—fill in some details of our students' translingual, transnational lives. We do not claim these snapshots as anything other than subjective depictions of students' translingual and transnational performances *for their instructor*; however, we do claim that

TABLE 2.3 Which Englishes Do You Speak?

	N		N
Ebonics/AAVE	9	Caribbean/West Indian	2
"standard" American English	10	Trinidadian	1
Standard/Standardized	21	Metropolis	3
Creolese/Guyanese	6	Borough	2
Patois	4	Spanglish	2
Jamaican	2	Jargon	2
British	1	Slang	4
Broken	8	Dominican	2
Chicano	2		

the identities that students perform in these narratives and conversations provide a strong impetus for centering language diversity in our classrooms in the ways in which we see the linguistic and national identities that students claim for themselves, and how they contend with and negotiate the linguistic identities that have been assigned to them.[1]

Growing up, **José** had an elementary level of heritage Spanish from living in his family, and for the most part that was enough—until his grandmother visited from El Salvador and asked him what he wanted for Christmas and he couldn't really answer her. "Yo quiero socks" was his first attempt at code-switching or translinguality. Gradually he learned more Spanish and began to weave it into his conversations with other bilingual people—but usually only after speaking with them in one language or the other for a while, then he would experimentally add a word here or there, then something longer. He found that he got better service in the same Mexican restaurant if he ordered in Spanish rather than English. He made me laugh when he wrote about a conversation with his mother about a bad grade in math class: "She spoke to me in English about it and reprimanded me in Spanish." He also said that sometimes he "hates" being bilingual, because he observed that languages were often used to exclude people from social groups; sometimes he would refrain from code-switching in a mostly (but not completely) Spanish-speaking group because he didn't want to exclude anybody—he remembered how this felt when he was younger and his Spanish was only passive. Other Spanish speakers, he observed, were not so scrupulous about not excluding English speakers.

Daniel was born in New York of Jamaican immigrant parents. From being around Patois, he understands enough of it to decode it but he doesn't have the pronunciation down and seems especially intimidated by the intonation, so he just doesn't do it. With his mother, they've agreed to speak English, but sometimes she forgets—when she's on the phone with a relative from the island and asks her son to hand her something, she'll sometimes forget and ask him in Patois, after which he will hand her what she wants, but give her a dirty look. Daniel observed that he thinks the key to Patois vocabulary is archaic British slang: "noggin" for head, for example.

Courtney, a student preferred the term "Ebonics" over African-American English, or Black English, although she was unfamiliar with the controversy that arose when the Oakland School Board proposed to teach it in school. Courtney and another student expressed ambivalence about the term "African-American" in general, noting that they had nothing to do with Africa, and that at Urban College, they have met people who actually have immigrated from Africa and thought of those immigrants as African-Americans, rather than those who were born in the United States.

Rodney, on the first page of his language narrative, identified himself as a monolingual English speaker, except for some ineffectual Spanish classes, and went on for a couple of pages about changing registers in different situations, including social media. But then it turns out on page four that his parents are Guyanese—and he finds it difficult to understand them sometimes. "Yet they insist that it's English." (He also uses the term "Broken English.")

Brandon lives in a neighborhood with many Caribbean English speakers from various places, and he finds them difficult to understand as well. He feels somewhat cut off from his heritage culture and his neighborhood culture because he feels limited to standardized English.

Nasrin begins her language narrative by saying that she considers herself a Standard English speaker even though others would call her bilingual—actually trilingual, with Bangla and Urdu. She actually can speak all three fluently, though she strongly prefers English. She focuses on speaking "Banglish": her family mostly communicates in pure Bangla, even her older sister, although they do speak English to various degrees outside the house. Their mother knows very little English, but she still does the shopping, etcetera. She incorporates many Americanisms, and is not confident about her Bengali, she hasn't visited Bangladesh as an adult and says that it would be difficult for her to communicate with people who knew no English at all, and she has an "American accent" in pronouncing Bangla words. Her father said that he hadn't really noticed the pronunciations until she mentioned her "Introduction to Writing, Rhetoric and Language" assignment. She gave an example of a mispronunciation that was apparently hilarious in Bengali, but that I of course didn't understand at all—a translingual moment in the text. But actually the key is: her family has no trouble understanding her, or she them, and nobody seems very worried about it: her family doesn't feel culturally threatened or anything like that. They regard it as just the way she happens to talk.

Rather than claiming that the students whose narratives we describe earlier represent the linguistic diversity of all Urban College students, we rather suggest that this breadth of linguistic diversity is typical of the students in any class at the college but the specifics of students' language affiliations will vary from class to class. The students in "Introduction to Writing, Rhetoric and Language", being English majors, may show more than a typical interest in language use, but from our experiences of teaching majors and non-majors alike, when asked, any Urban College student has a language story to tell that includes a facility and comfort with using many varieties and languages, and a deep and thorough sensitivity to linguistic context, in the very way that authors such as Canagarajah (2006, 2011), for example, describe as being an appropriate goal for classrooms that embrace translingual approaches. In the chapters that follow, we discuss how we might make connections between this kind of everyday translinguality and our classroom practice. In the next section we move to a discussion of students in an apparently much more linguistically homogenous environment within the linguistically diverse State University. Nonetheless, as we will show, these students live translingual and transnational lives, which our institutions and pedagogical practices would do well to recognize and embrace as "ordinary" and central.

We Meet Our Students: International Students at State University

The linguistic diversity of State University mirrors that of its home state, which 82 percent of entering students in Fall 2018 claim as their origin (IPEDS). State University advertises the racial and ethnic diversity of its students as a feature for recruitment (Enrollment Management, 2018), and connections are made between that diversity and the linguistic diversity which its students negotiate every day. Furthermore, in 2017, among the 3289 international undergraduate students at State University, hailing from 87 countries; 2216 were from China, 302 from India and 196 from Korea (Enrollment Management, 2018). This number constitutes 9.1 percent of the total undergraduate student population of 36,039, and students from China among these international undergraduates outnumber those from the other two countries named—India and Korea—by a ratio of almost 10 to 1.

In this volume, we present excerpts from literacy narratives and written biography assignments from students enrolled in a course, which we will call English for Academic Purposes (EAP) II, that precedes "regular" composition at State University and which Nela teaches regularly, as well as interview responses from five graduate students who are affiliated with State University's Graduate Academic Success Program, which Nela directs. We show how students position themselves with respect to the linguistic and cultural transitions that their enrollment at State University requires them to negotiate, and note how these students engage with the support structures that State University offers to international students. Their accounts of their experiences expands our understanding of how students construct their linguistic affiliations, and perform their linguistic identities as they study at U.S. institutions on student visas; looking at their engagement with academic support services—curricular and extra-curricular—deliberately designed to help students negotiate their transnational situations offers suggestions of what kinds of support services international students use and need.

As we explore the State University international students' linguistic identities, we look at academic biographies and literacy narratives composed early in the semester in EAP II, at end of the semester final reflections. This course is part of a four-course sequence of credit-bearing courses for matriculated State University students; students place into any one of these courses via written placement examination and a complex system of scoring using institutional metrics. Unlike some courses in State University's "regular" composition sequence, EAP I and II are not considered "remedial." Both EAP I and EAP II courses assume an already existing ability for students to "read, conceptualize and frame complex arguments" (EAP II), again suggesting that these courses are not viewed as remediation, but rather combine academic support and cohort-building alongside an attempt to translate students' "home" language literacies into an English-medium educational context.

Because Nela teaches EAP I and II regularly, we know that State University's EAP courses emphasize the experiences of "international" students in their design. However, despite the fact that most of the students are international students, according to their visa status, students' narratives show that the experiences of "international" students are quite different. Many of the students have, in fact, been living translingual, transnational lives long before their arrival to the State University—and not only because all of them took required English lessons in school and often private English lessons in addition, as well as speaking a wide variety of Chinese languages beyond the official variety, Mandarin. Therefore, while the group of students whose narratives from EAP II we explore is not as linguistically superdiverse as the students from Urban College in the portraits earlier in this chapter, nonetheless their experiences shows us that "everyday translingualism" is still a relevant framework for guiding our pedagogical approaches to these students' writing. That is, these students are negotiating many languages every day as they navigate their tertiary studies, and centering these negotiations is a productive way to help these students succeed in their pursuit of their undergraduate degrees.

Yang, for instance, identifies himself as a native speaker of Chinese, who "speaks English as well." He is from Shanghai, a cosmopolitan city where "there are tons of languages." Yang notes that "China is a pretty big country [that] consists of tons of small cities or regions." He writes, "I can understand three different languages—Shanghaiese, Nantongese and Wuxiese—but can speak none of them." Alongside these four languages, Yang, also studied "a little German when [he] was in fifth grade," and continues to take German classes at State University. Like many of the students whose narratives we examine, Yang comments on how speaking and writing in English changes the way he thinks, in ways that can be disturbing and uncomfortable to manage.

While several of the students whose narratives we will look at describe their English learning starting in China and continuing as they moved to State University, others have a significantly longer educational history in the United States. One student, **Winnie**, graduated from an all-girls high school in central Pennsylvania, having arrived from China three years before her enrollment at State University. She writes that "My English was not so good when I first came to America, due to the differences between papers in Chinese class and English class," but, in her autobiography for this EAP II class at State University, Winnie performs a linguistic identity that is confidently multilingual. She writes,

> I also found out the importance to using not only one language when I am in the United States. All the people around me are speaking and writing in English. I felt how important to know the language well, cause it really makes your life much convenience when you are in other countries.

Unlike Winnie, though, who seems to be immersed in American educational culture and writes about the enjoyment that she gets from learning her "third language," Spanish, many students from EAP II describe the challenges they face in going beyond translation between their Chinese languages and English, and in understanding the difference in cultural logics between China and the United States. **Amy**, for example, describes the challenges that she faces as she works to meet the discourse expectations for her U.S. composition classes. She writes,

> the hard thing when I write in English is not to translation. You know I try to be like American writer and use their expression and sentence construction. The first reaction when I'm writing and speaking is in Chinese and then I need translate in English in my brain. The easy part is the English alphabet is not hard to write as Chinese. To be honest, the two terrible things in my life are writing and speaking English. Even in Chinese writing, I still not have good grade.

We include this excerpt from Amy's narrative as a reminder that, although, from a faculty perspective, students like Amy are doing U.S. academic discourse, the linguistic challenges that international students perceive themselves facing loom large in students' perceptions of their academic successes (see Andrade, 2002 for discussion).

As we will see when we further explore the narratives of Yang, Winnie, Amy, and other students from EAP II in Chapter 6, these students used their biographies and literacy narratives to describe their linguistic performances in their State University classwork, as well as to establish complex linguistic affiliations which go far beyond the common trajectories of "improvement" that we might expect from international students who identify as native speakers of languages other than English as they move through an undergraduate curriculum. The students from EAP II whose narratives we examine perform a combination of having more to learn about English speaking and writing alongside establishing a place for themselves not only at State University, but in the world.

We move now to introducing five international graduate students who are affiliated with State University's Graduate Academic Success Program (a pseudonym). In later chapters (Chapter 6 and Chapter 13) we will go into detail about how these graduate students negotiate their linguistic, cultural and disciplinary affiliations. These graduate students, like the undergraduates introduced earlier, are predominantly from China and other Asian countries. Their linguistic and educational backgrounds show the same diversity as that of the undergraduate students introduced in the current section, but with a stronger emphasis on translinguality as connected to their disciplinary discourses.

We Meet Our Students: International Graduate Students

Graduate schools in the United States are increasingly dependent on international students for their enrollment. According to State University's chapter of their faculty union, over 50 percent of graduate students are international students (Improving Graduate Employment, 2016, p. 11). This financial and indeed existential dependency has not, however, often resulted in a sensitivity to the language and cultural needs of newly-arrived graduate students, nor necessarily to the development of effective support services. The needs of international graduate students are different from those of undergraduates, even international undergraduates such as those we met in the previous section: they face much more advanced and demanding literacy challenges, like their so-called "domestic" counterparts. As we will see in the following portraits, the graduate students' build networks between English and their other languages, and between their everyday English and their disciplinary discourses. The relationships that they describe with English are more directed towards success in their disciplinary fields than of the undergraduates; however, all of them also narrate the challenges and successes of navigating English as an everyday part of their lives as international students living in the United States. All students were interviewed for one hour, and were compensated for their time; Nela and Jonathan conducted all interviews together either in person on campus at State University or via videoconference, except for Li-kuo, who spoke just with Nela.

Among the graduate students, we first meet **Yi-fen**, a PhD student in Mathematical Finance. Yi-fen's discussion of his linguistic background and his experiences in the PhD program at State University shows a thoroughly translingual, transnational life: a speaker of Shanghainese and Mandarin, and educated in English on a "global" track from an early age, Yi-fen's move to the United States to study is in some ways a step on a trajectory that he started in childhood. Yi-fen's experience shows us how, in the translinguality that pervades his life, different languages serve different purposes, and it is their bringing together which might offer challenges.

Qianqian, similarly, keeps her languages rather separate. A violin performance PhD student originally from Taiwan, Qianqian might be described as a long-term English language learner: while State University is the site of her second U.S. graduate program, she relates a continued struggle to feel the kind of comfort in moving between languages, or, more precisely, of demonstrating agency over her language use in all contexts which she encounters, that Yi-fen describes.

Like Qianqian, **Hanfang** has been in the United States for some time, studying as both an undergraduate and graduate student at a large Midwestern university before following her advisor to State University. Hanfang's narrative in some ways relates what we might think of as a typical trajectory of immersion in the culture of U.S. academic discourse in English. She describes an experience of "coming into language," staying silent in class for most of the first year of her graduate studies at the midwestern university, gradually understanding more and more of what was being said in her classes, and now recounting a real comfort with the requirements of her disciplinary discourse, while expressing that she "hates" general writing. For several of the students whose responses we explore in this volume, disciplinary English was an area in which they felt very confident, but more everyday communication was something that proved challenging. The other two students whose interviews we explore describe their efforts to bring the two together, offering, we suggest, a model for building international students affiliations with everyday English and disciplinary discourses.

Xiaoli, a social work PhD candidate originally from Taiwan, and mother of two children in the U.S. public school system, spoke at length about the challenges of navigating family life from the assigned identity of "international PhD student." However, the aspects of her interview responses on which we focus in Chapter 13 are the ways in which she describes having to interact with clients, as a social work student doing fieldwork placements, and how those everyday interactions influenced her engagement with her disciplinary discourse. Similarly, **Li-kuo**, a music performance PhD candidate and professional cellist describes the ways in which he centers the communication required of his professional practice in his narrative of his developing translinguality. That is, describes the ways in which he has had to learn to use English in order to communicate as a principal cellist, and as a cello teacher in U.S. orchestras and studios, with section musicians and with students. These demands of applying their disciplinary discourses in everyday linguistic contexts, we suggest, are informative as U.S. institutions develop ways in which to help international students professionalize, going beyond so-called mastery of disciplinary discourses into being able to perform the breadth of tasks that academic life requires, especially in transnational contexts like U.S. academia. His involvement in GASP, which Nela narrates in a supplement to the interview responses, shows the tensions that emerge between departmental expectations and assessments of English use, and the realities of everyday life as an emerging scholar and established professional for international students working and studying in the United States.

Conclusion

In this chapter, we have taken a glimpse at the linguistic lives of the students whose translinguality and transnationality we will explore in greater detail in the rest of this chapter. We have introduced the institutions with which we are working, too, as both a backdrop to and major player in the experiences of these students, and thus in their language and identity performances. Importantly, though, we do not claim to have given a comprehensive introduction to, or a "thick" description of our students and their lives; to do so would be to irredeemably other them, to treat their lives and their identity as something that we have no impact on, and no part in negotiating. Rather, we have sought to offer a suggestion of who we might meet in our classes, and how we might meet them such that we recognize and center their translinguality as interesting and unremarkable, and as the "normal" background in front of all our own teaching performances should be created.

Note

1. All names in this chapter are pseudonyms.

References

Ahearn, L. M. (2001). Language and agency. *Annual Review of Anthropology*, *30*(1), 109–137.
Anzaldúa, G. (1987). *Borderlands/La Frontera: The New Mestiza*. San Francisco, CA: Aunt Lute Books.
Bourdieu, P. (2018). The forms of capital. In *The sociology of economic life* (pp. 78–92). Abingdon: Routledge.
Canagarajah, A. S. (2006). The Place of World Englishes in Composition: Pluralization Continued. *College Composition and Communication*, *57*(4), 586–619.
Canagarajah, A. S. (2006). Toward a Writing Pedagogy of Shuttling between Languages: Learning from Multilingual Writers. *College English*, *68*(6), 589–604.
Canagarajah, S. (2011). Codemeshing in academic writing: Identifying teachable strategies of translanguaging. *The Modern Language Journal*, *95*(3), 401–417.
Canagarajah, S. (2013). *Literacy as translingual practice: Between communities and classrooms*. Abingdon: Routledge.
Dovchin, S. (2017). The ordinariness of youth linguascapes in Mongolia. *International Journal of Multilingualism*, *14*(2), 144–159.
Enrollment Management Annual Report. (2018). *State University Division of Enrollment Management*.
Faez, F. (2011). Reconceptualizing the native/nonnative speaker dichotomy. *Journal of Language, Identity & Education*, *10*(4), 231–249. http://doi.org/10.1080/15348458.2011.598127
Flores, N., & Rosa, J. (2015). Undoing appropriateness: Raciolinguistic ideologies and language diversity in education. *Harvard Educational Review*, *85*(2), 149–301.
Guba, E. G., & Lincoln, Y. S. (1994). Competing paradigms in qualitative research. In N. K. Denzin & Y. S. Lincoln (Eds.), *Handbook of qualitative research* (pp. 105–117). Thousand Oaks, CA: Sage.
Improving Graduate Employment. (2016). *State University AAU*. Retrieved from http://equitysecuritydignity.org/wp-content/uploads/sites/2/2018/02/TA_GA-CONTRACT-PROPOSAL.pdf
Inayatulla, S. A. (2013). Beyond the dark closet: Reconsidering literacy narratives as performative artifacts. *Journal of Basic Writing*, *32*(2), 5–27.

Integrated Postsecondary Education Data System (IPEDS). *National Center for Education Statistics (NCES).* Retrieved from https://nces.ed.gov/ipeds/

Lee, J. W. (2017). *The politics of translingualism: After Englishes.* New York and London: Routledge.

Lyons, S. R. (2000). Rhetorical sovereignty: What do American Indians want from writing? *College Composition and Communication,* 447–468.

Merriam, S. B. (2009). *Qualitative research: A guide to design and implementation.* San Francisco, CA: Jossey-Bass.

Nero, S. (1997). English is my native language. . . . or so I believe. *TESOL Quarterly, 31*(3), 585–593.

Nero, S. J. (2005). Language, identities, and ESL pedagogy. *Language and Education, 19*(3), 194–211.

Otsuji, E., & Pennycook, A. D. (2013). Unremarkable hybridities and metrolingual practices. In R. Rubdy & L. Alsagoff (Eds.), *The global_local interface and hybridity* (pp. 83–99). Bristol: Multilingual Matters.

Rampton, M. B. H. (1990). Displacing the. *ELT Journal, 44*(2), 97–101.

Rodriguez, R. (1983). *Hunger of memory: The education of Richard Rodriguez: An autobiography.* New York: Bantam.

Sarkar, M., & Low, B. (2012). Multilingualism and popular culture. In M. Martin-Jones, A. Blackledge, & A. Creese (Eds.), *The Routledge handbook of multilingualism* (pp. 417–432). New York and London: Routledge.

Urban College. (2018). *Urban College fact book.* Retrieved from https://www.york.cuny.edu/president/institutional-effectiveness/institutional-research/factbookfall2018_draft.pdf

Young, V. A. (2004). Your average nigga. *College Composition and Communication, 55*(4), 693–715.

3

ON RACIAL PRIVILEGE AND ACCENT HIERARCHIES

Heather Robinson

When I was in my first semester at graduate school, the faculty member with whom I had moved from Australia to work said to me, "You say 'A is different to B.'" He was intrigued. I wanted to know where I had written this comparison; and whether I was wrong in making it: he was, after all, the big deal linguist who I had crossed the world to work with. But, of course, he was commenting on the linguistic structure of the comparison; I, of course, couldn't even hear what was intriguing. This moment was my first experience of being linguistically othered, but the othering was at least affectionate. It was disorienting, but it was mostly harmless. But what would I have heard if my skin had been brown, if I had written like I wasn't a mother-tongue English speaker? How would my other nationality have been erased, replaced with the status of "not-American"?

I look like a nice white lady. I'm told I don't look particularly American, but boy, do I look white. My brown-red hair is often a bit frizzy. It has some grey bits. My skin is more-or-less freckled, depending on the time of year. I think my eyes are green. I know they're nowhere near brown. I think I'm not memorable in any way, but people do remember me. I think it's the accent.

I open my mouth, and I'm not American. At least, the Americans know that. Europeans tend not to hear my accent at first, though Australians who have been here for a while, or Americans who have been in Australia, usually get it. Oh, I love your accent.

People like my accent. They think it's charming. I think it makes me sound smart, like the English people on TV when I was a little girl. And I'm not even English. I'm from one of the charming countries. People have always wanted to go there, you know.

What does it mean to be white and not American? What does it mean to have one of the cute accents, one of the accents that people want to pet, like a kitten?

It means a whole pile of privilege. It means a smile when I get something wrong. It means accommodation when someone doesn't understand me. When they can see me. The automated voice recognition phone systems don't like me, though. I can't speak right for them. But I've practiced.

But I'm a foreigner, just like her. Just like him. I don't speak standardized American English. Just like her. Just like him. I'm not a citizen. Unlike her. Unlike him.

When I came here, it wasn't to stay. I had my F-1 visa and my I-20, which made it clear to everyone that I was going home. I arrived with two suitcases and deeply insufficient clothing, especially the socks. I lived in student housing. My mother put me on a schedule for calling home, otherwise I would have been doing it every day. As it is, I spend days emailing my sister. Back and forth. Back and forth. But as I continued, after that first dark summer where I almost didn't come back, I started changing things. I came home in winter, and stayed in New Jersey for summer. I felt better. Then I got a job, and another. Then the J-1, with the home stay requirement waived. Then the H1-B. Then the green card. I only recently realized that I'm probably an immigrant.

I married an American and had American babies. And I attached the babies to Australia, because I am still attached. A foot in both worlds, as they say. I have told four people at work that I am not a U.S. citizen. Mine is a passing narrative—they assume that I am a citizen because I can perform American. But I am not. Two of the four people have looked worried and encouraged me to do what I have to do. But I know that applying for citizenship will make me feel trapped; trapped by fear and bureaucracy.

I work in Jamaica, New York, which has a racial mix much like, I imagine, Jamaica in the West Indies. A white man asked me today, as I walked through the bus depot, if I knew where the library was. He was white. I have no idea, and I was confused, because I think he asked me because I was white too. I'm the worst person to ask, I thought. I'm not from here. Can't you *see*? Ask someone who knows something useful.

Not being *from* here is pedagogically useful, but I don't want the not-from-hereness to translate into ostentatious whiteness. I walk down Archer Avenue carrying a parasol. I feel ridiculous. But I'd rather feel ridiculous than feel sunburnt. I have to take it down when I walk through the bus depot, though—too crowded. But even there, I'm moving through, not waiting. It's different.

All this to say, it's not mine, I am not of this place, I have no real claim. I want to tread lightly instead. It takes practice.

So I speak in an ostentatiously not American way to my classes. I say, "Tell me. I don't know." And I have learnt so much. I can now say sentences in

Patois (just a couple). I have judgments in AAVE. I figured out the Ebonics choice today. Because it names a language, not a variety, a dialect, just like Tok Pisin does, like Kamtok does. It makes the language of the black community—of black people—not an acronym, but a real language that belongs to people. And yes, I have read James Baldwin. Several times. But he still uses an adjective, not a name. So Ebonics. OK. I said I wasn't from here, but I pass. Or rather, I am passing. Sometimes I work on it. Sometimes I don't. Sometimes I say "throw a spanner in the works" when I know full well that nobody will know what I'm talking about. Sometimes I say "that's different to what I heard," because I know it will make someone shift the way they look at me, just a little.

In one of my classes, I assign a video blog where students perform texts in English vernaculars. I show them what to do by doing it myself. In my videoblog, my linguistic performance demonstrates my "nation language." It draws attention to my foreignness, even after it has faded away in the classroom. This performance shines a light on what Glick Schiller calls transnational "ways of being," and "ways of belonging": the videoblog creates a space that recontextualizes my transnational linguistic affiliations, and suggests that I can "belong" elsewhere (the first videoblog demo that I did was a performance of a Scottish poem in a Scottish accent. The second, I performed Australian). The accent is on a continuum with the one that my students hear every day—and my father tells me it does not sound weird—but I've exaggerated certain features and, importantly, it is explicitly a performance of difference, connected to the content of the class, rather than something that fades into the background and is something that I designedly make non-intrusive in my performance as "teacher in a New York City college classroom." It is designed to function as a reminder that my transnational affiliations and the languaging that these affiliations entail are always activated, interacting with the language that I use in everyday contexts.

My daughters have a mummy, and wore nappies, and slept in a cot. They walk on the footpath. Actually, they walk on the pathwalk. They're translingual, transnational too. A few weeks ago, my daughters' American mother was reading something to the girls. I forget what the word was—something like spork or sporn or Sean or caught. Our elder daughter could not understand what her mother was saying. I had to translate, to get the vowels right for this little girl. Her mothers were both very proud of her, for asserting the strangeness of American English in America. Of course, she's white too, and she's already buying cultural capital with her little Australian accent. Which she trained herself out of when she was four, practicing her r at the end of her words. Little kids use mostly English-derived words, one or two syllables. Lots of consonants at the end.

Both of the girls ask for war-ta. Without the r, of course. I hope you can read this.

When you're a white person, you have to learn how to say certain things out loud. Like how to talk about how linguistic oppression goes hand in hand with racial oppression. How, when Merriam-Webster writes, under "ain't," the following "Usage Guide," it's not just describing something.

> Although widely disapproved as nonstandard and more common in the habitual speech of the less educated, *ain't* in senses 1 and 2 is flourishing in American English. It is used in both speech and writing to catch attention and to gain emphasis <*the wackiness of movies, once so deliciously amusing, ain't funny anymore—Richard Schickel*> <*I am telling you—there ain't going to be any blackmail—R. M. Nixon*>. It is used especially in journalistic prose as part of a consistently informal style <*the creative process ain't easy—Mike Royko*>. This informal *ain't* is commonly distinguished from habitual *ain't* by its frequent occurrence in fixed constructions and phrases <*well—class it ain't—Cleveland Amory*> <*for money? say it ain't so, Jimmy!—Andy Rooney*> <*you ain't seen nothing yet*> <*that ain't hay*> <*two out of three ain't bad*> <*if it ain't broke, don't fix it*>. In fiction *ain't* is used for purposes of characterization; in familiar correspondence it tends to be the mark of a warm personal friendship. It is also used for metrical reasons in popular songs <*Ain't She Sweet*> <*It Ain't Necessarily So*>. Our evidence shows British use to be much the same as American.
>
> *(Ain't, 2017)*

Excuse me, Merriam-Webster. Ain't is used to express negation, not to catch attention and gain emphasis. It is used by humans, not for purposes of characterization, but for purposes of communication. I suppose this latter might be what this passage describes as "the habitual ain't." It's a bad habit, you know. This passage has no examples from speakers to whom it might belong as part of one of their native languages. A person who also knows how to say "isn't." We white people have done nothing if we have not forced black people and brown people to be adept code-switchers, to be multivarietal and multilingual. If only white people could be so adept.

You have to learn to read differently. And to know that some things just aren't for you, and aren't about you.

It's a bit shocking to discover that you're white, that you get a pass for so many things. I wasn't as white like this in Australia. Or maybe I was, but I didn't know. And maybe that's the point.

I've been trying to give the privilege back, to establish myself as the outsider, the one who has to learn, the one who has to change. The one who says it, when I'm the only white person in the classroom. The fact is, there were two other white people in my classroom last semester. I didn't even see one of them for a couple of weeks. He wasn't particularly interesting. The other was an immigrant with an accent. He fit in better. My students are too polite to point it out when I'm the only white person in the classroom. Or maybe they're used to it. Maybe they don't see how extraordinary it is for this white woman from Sydney to be the only white person in the classroom. They say Caucasian. Again, I think they're being polite. I think the term is weird.

I am a white person. And I have a nice accent. And those get me things. But I'm hoping I can give some things back.

4
TRANSING LANGUAGE IDENTITY

Heather Robinson

Language identity among students has been thoroughly investigated in the applied linguistics and composition studies literature, particularly as it pertains to so-called "second language" students. Notable studies include Chiang and Schmida (1999), Leung, Harris, and Rampton (1997), Ortmeier-Hooper (2008), the essays in Cox, Jordan, Ortmeier-Hooper, and Schwartz (2010), the work of Bonny Norton Pierce, Yasuko Kanno, Jan Blommaert, Adrian Blackledge, Shondel Nero, and so on. But these conceptions of identity mostly exclude students who are not immigrants; Linda Harklau's work on "Generation 1.5" students addressed this somewhat, but the term Generation 1.5 has been noted to be potentially problematic by Roberge (2002), Harklau (2003) and Benesch (2008). Shondel Nero, Keith Gilyard, and Vershawn Ashanti Young have also done extensive work on the identities of students who speak two or more varieties of English, especially those whose varieties are stigmatized in the broader U.S. educational culture. In this framing chapter, we seek to extend these discussions by exploring student identity in terms of what it means to have, perform, or to develop, a translingual or transnational language identity. In doing so, we provide frameworks that resist the conceptions, problematized in Leung et al. (1997, p. 546) that all students assigned the identity of "second-language" or "English language" learners must be "social and linguistic outsider[s]," and that so-called native speakers of English cannot and do not belong to racial or ethnic minorities.

In developing our theory of translingual and transnational language identities, we refer to the authors listed earlier, and we also engage with theories of identity developed in queer and gender studies, as laid out in the introductory chapter, to investigate what it means to "trans-" and to be "trans-," and how theories of transgender identity in particular can help us understand what a translingual and transnational identity might look like. To start, we put forward a theory of identity, before "trans-ing" that identity, arguing that a translingual/transnational identity is inherently and explicitly negotiated and performed, and is put in motion by humans' language acts.

We start from the following premises for our definition of identity:

- Identity is performed.
- Identity is dynamic.
- Identity is complex.
- Identity is constructed.

Then we turn to three representations of students' translanguaging and transnational performances, first noting the ways in which our representations of student work limit and negate students' own "acts of identity" (Le Page & Tabouret-Keller, 1985) when we consider language practices without considering their implications for identity, and then considering identity performances as constructed by students themselves.

Identity Is Performed

Judith Butler writes of the construction of a gender identity as follows:

> When Simone de Beauvoir claims, "one is not born, but, rather, becomes a woman," she is appropriating and reinterpreting this doctrine of constituting acts from the phenomenological tradition. In this sense, gender is in no way a stable identity or locus of agency from which various acts proceed; rather, it is an identity tenuously constituted in time—an identity instituted through a stylized repetition of acts.
>
> *(1988, p. 900)*

Butler goes on to describe gender identity as a "performative accomplishment" that "the mundane social audience, including the actors themselves, come to believe and to perform in the mode of belief" (1988, p. 901). That is, the performance is created to "conform to . . . the rules of a conventional style" (Stylize, 2019), and as such is something built, constructed, created in doing the same things over and over again, such that the performer approximates the thing that they imagine as the target. This conception of identity as something that people *do* for themselves and an audience, rather than being based on inherent characteristics, has also proven to be a useful framework for considering the identities of students with respect to language. Ortmeier-Hooper (2008) applies the "identity as performance" framework to her discussion of the identities of "immigrant ESL" students. Ortmeier-Hooper writes,

> immigrant ESL students . . . are seeking to define and often "perform" themselves within the context of the university and their peers, while at

> the same time negotiating the complex realities of their unique linguistic and cultural experiences. Often, composition instructors only see a single aspect of that performance and are perplexed by the "backstage" realities that often influence these students' decisions in the composition classroom and on the written page.
>
> *(p. 392)*

Ortmeier-Hooper's discussion highlights not only the performative nature of identity construction, but also the role that the audience plays in accepting or rejecting an identity performance: a performance is *for* someone, and so the effectiveness of the performance is always contingent on the audience's reception and understanding of what they are seeing, alongside how well the performer believes that they are representing their imagined target. This combination is important: identity is something that people do as well as something that is assigned to them; identity is the result of human action and interaction. The motivation behind these actions is, as Le Page and Tabouret-Keller's (1985) theory of "Acts of Identity" suggests, based on the desire to affiliate with a social group. In the following passage, LePage and Tabouret-Keller describe what a successful identity performance relies upon:

> We can only behave according to the behavioural patterns of groups we find it desirable to identify with to the extent that: (i) we can identify the groups; (ii) we have both adequate access to the groups and ability to analyse their behavioural patterns; (iii) the motivation to join the groups is sufficiently powerful, and is either reinforced or reversed by feedback from the groups; (iv) we have the ability to modify our behaviour.
>
> *(Le Page & Tabouret-Keller, 1985, p. 182)*

The concept of identity described here aligns with the ways that identity is performed, as described by Butler: identity formation is comprised by "the stylized repetition of acts," and such acts help actors to conform to the conventions of a particular group with which these actors wish to affiliate themselves. As Nero (2005) points, out

> Le Page and Tabouret-Keller are suggesting here that identity formation can be attributed to a high level of individual agency, thus framed as 'acts', and that such acts are motivated by the desire for establishing social/ethnic affiliation with, or distinctiveness from, identifiable groups.
>
> *(p. 195)*

The conception of identity that we are using in this book similarly places the agency for identity construction with the student, while acknowledging the power of assigned identities, including those of "native speaker," "immigrant," "ESL," "foreign," "Black," and "student," all of which have the specific effect of centralizing or marginalizing the interests and the experiences of individuals to whom these identities are assigned in our societies.

Beyond focusing on "acts" of identity, language identity scholars such as Nero (2005) and Norton (1997) have incorporated the conception of identity described in West (1992) into their approaches. West writes,

> For me identity is fundamentally about desire and death. How you construct your identity is predicated on how you construct desire and how you conceive of death: desire for recognition; quest for visibility . . . the sense of being acknowledged; a deep desire for association-what Edward Said would call affiliation. It's the longing to belong, a deep, visceral need that most linguistically conscious animals who transact with an environment (that's us) participate in. And then there is a profound desire for protection, for security, for safety, for surety. And so in talking about identity we have to begin to look at the various ways in which human beings have constructed their desire for recognition, association, and protection over time and in space and always under circumstances not of their own choosing. But identity also has to do with death. We can't talk about identity without talking about death. That's what a brother named Julio Rivera had to come to terms with: the fact that his identity had been constructed in such a way that xenophobes would put him to death. Or brother Youssef Hawkins in Bensonhurst. Or brother Yankel Rosenbaum in Crown Heights. Persons who construct their identities and desires often do it in such a way that they're willing to die for it-soldiers in the Middle East, for example-or, under a national identity, that they're willing to kill others.
>
> (p. 1)

West's definition of identity is important because it shows how central to individuals' lives identity is: it is not some academic formulation, or something that is separate from our day-to-day existence. According to West's formulation, finding, building, and being "permitted" the right identity makes life worth living. And West's formulation around desire and death shows us just how critical the work that we do concerning the identities of students is; it describes the motivation for identity performances, and suggests to us the consequences when we get it wrong. Just how problematic traditional formulations of language identity can be has been discussed in detail elsewhere (e.g. Rampton, 1990; Leung et al., 1997; Faez, 2011), but we mention them to remind the reader how important the development of a complex theory of identity is, and how critical it is to center students' performances, affiliations, desires, and acts of identity within it.

Identity Is Dynamic

Since identity is something that is constructed by being performed and/or assigned, it is also something that changes over time and space. The definition of identity from Blommaert (2013), quoted later, bears strong connections with the theory of gender performance offered by Butler, in that it describes identity as being built out of the assembly of acts that approximate cultural norms, even when these norms are applied in novel contexts, and even when their application is somehow "costly" for the performer.

> Social lives are thus organized not in relation to one single complex of norms but in relation to many competing and/or complementary ones—a feature of sociolinguistic superdiversity we call polycentricity (Blommaert, 2010, p. 39ff); individual repertoires bear the traces of such perpetual reshufflings of norms in a polycentric environment (Blommaert & Backus, 2012), and complex forms of identity work can draw on the resources that orient towards the multiple sets of norms present in someone's 'communicative competence' (cf. Rampton, 2006; Jorgensen et al., 2011).
>
> *(Blommaert, 2013, p. 1)*

What is particularly interesting about Blommaert's definition, for our purposes, is the image created of the movement that identity performance requires. In an elaboration of the ideas in the previous passage, Blommaert describes identity formation as emerging from "the rapid shifts to-and-fro between normative orientations within a polycentric environment" (2013, p. 2). With this image in mind, we can think of identity as being built out of a network that ties together many different social identity "centers," and the dynamism of identity coming from the moments between these centers; indeed, an individual's identity is made up of unique paths of travel between these centers. If we think of these centers as comprising both the identity characteristics "assigned to us [in and] by our environment" and the identities "that we assign ourselves" (Brooke, 1991, p. 17), the paths we choose to travel between them indicate what we accept and what we reject as we build our identities. Paths of connection can be abandoned over the course of a lifetime, and new paths can be taken up as our contexts and circumstances change.

Building on this idea of identity as a collection of "centers" connected by paths between them which are travelled with varying frequency during a lifetime, Polkinghorne (1991) also offers a useful theory of what we do as we construct our identities: we make narratives. He writes,

> in addition to . . . public stories, individuals construct private and personal stories linking diverse events of their lives into unified and understandable wholes. These are stories about the self. They are the basis of

self-identity and personal understanding and they provide the answer to the question "Who am I?".

(p. 136)

We can think of narrative as providing the connective tissue, or the pathways, between the centers of the image of the polycentric network provided by Blommaert (2013). The idea that identity is dynamic is particularly important for members of racial, ethnic, and linguistic "minorities," who tend to be assigned marginalized and marginalizing identities which often conflict with their lived experiences and personal identity assertions and performances. Leung et al. (1997) cite Hall (1988), who "suggests [that] members of minority groups are not simple inheritors of fixed identities, ethnicities, cultures, and languages but are instead engaged in a continual collective and individual process of making, remaking, and negotiating these elements, thereby constantly constructing dynamic new ethnicities" (Leung et al., 1997, p. 547). Conceiving of identity as dynamic, as something that is performed and something that changes over time is particularly important in our work to enfranchise students who are members of racial, ethnic, and/or linguistic minorities, because these elements create space for students to affiliate themselves not only with language communities that best fit their present lives, but also with lives that they imagine living (cf. Kanno & Norton, 2003). But we also need to consider how individuals' affiliations interact with those identities assigned to them by their communities and society, and with what they can do (are able to do and are allowed to do), in order to form complex social identities.

Identity Is Complex

Leung et al. (1997) offer a framework for the consideration of language identity, built upon the terms language affiliation, language inheritance, and language expertise, which we take up in this volume. They describe these terms thus:

> In a slight reworking of Rampton's original formulation, the term *language expertise* refers to how proficient people are in a language; *language affiliation* refers to the attachment or identification they feel for a language whether or not they nominally belong to the social group customarily associated with it; and *language inheritance* refers to the ways in which individuals can be born into a language tradition that is prominent within the family and community setting whether or not they claim expertise in or affiliation to that language.

(p. 555)

This framework is important for the identity framework being developed here because it clearly separates out assigned language identity, linguistic performance and desire for affiliation, all elements introduced earlier. People's assigned language identity is often based on perceptions of their *language inheritance*. This inheritance, as Leung et al. (1997) show, may or may not have very much to do with an individual's *language expertise*: the identity that the individual performs through their language use may not connect them very strongly to the community that speaks a particular language, even though the individual is associated with that community through their family, and their racial and ethnic identity. And finally, *language affiliation* is based on the individual's linguistic actions that demonstrate their desire to be included in a linguistic group: that is, how an individual talks and writes actively connects them with the communities that talk and write in that way. Importantly, affiliation, expertise, and inheritance interact constantly as identity is formed, reformed, and performed. Leung, Harris and Rampton's conception of language identity as being made up of several interacting parts brings to mind Crenshaw's theory of intersectionality (1990). Crenshaw's discussion focuses on the intersections between race and gender in the context of violence against women, but they indicate how the theory of intersectionality can and should be generalized: she writes, "My focus on the intersections of race and gender only highlights the need to account for multiple grounds of identity when considering how the social world is constructed" (1990, p. 1245). Focusing on just one aspect of identity—gender but not race, as Crenshaw (1990) discusses, or, in our case, language inheritance but not "national" affiliation, or "citizenship" but not language affiliation—marginalizes people whose identity is constructed around multiple social categories. For example, considering women as a broad, undifferentiated class ignores the specificity of experiences that belong to women of color, women who are members of the LGBTQ+ community, immigrant women, etc. Similarly, considerations of language identity that do not consider immigration status, national identity, race, and class (for example) will not be able to create a complete picture of our students, and thus we will miss important factors that shape our students' educational experiences. Harklau (2004) makes the importance of intersectional descriptions of identity for so-called Generation 1.5 students clear, writing that "we need to understand how Generation 1.5 students' writing is interwoven with multiple, unstable, and ambivalent identities as immigrants, as young adults, as ethnolinguistic minorities, and often as people of color in the United States" (Harklau, 2004).

As we have developed this notion of identity as being performed, dynamic, and complex, with an individual's identity being made up of assigned identity and enacted identity, we have also suggested that identity formation is made out of the movements that we make between these identity centers, or, as Crenshaw puts it, "grounds for identity": how we connect them through our narratives about ourselves and the identity performances that we create. We now turn to revisiting the definition of "translingual" and "transnational," "translinguality" and "transnationalism" as articulated in the introduction to this volume, paying attention to the performances, the "doing," that our definitions imply.

What Does a Translingual or Transnational Language Identity Look Like?

Canagarajah (2011) describes the way in which speakers do "translanguaging" thus: "the ability of multilingual speakers to shuttle between languages, treating the diverse languages that form their repertoire as an integrated system" (p. 401). This definition provides a good starting point for our conception of "transing" (Chapter 1), but we go further, considering transing as rethinking and structuring our ideas of linguistic and identity spaces. Canagarajah's definition mentioned earlier builds on Garcia's (2009) definition of translanguaging: "Rather than focusing on the language itself and how one or the other might relate to the way in which a monolingual standard is used and has been described, the concept of translanguaging makes obvious that there are no clear-cut borders between the languages of bilinguals. What we have is a languaging continuum that is accessed" (Garcia, 2009, p. 47). Garcia's definition, especially if we expand it to encompass multilingual language users, offers a more expansive conception of the movement between languages that translanguaging entails, suggesting that because the boundaries between a speaker's languages are either porous or blurred or overlapping. Her spatial metaphor is important to us, as is her reference to the role that borders play in defining what translanguaging is. However, rather than thinking of languaging as taking place on a continuum, we consider languaging as a network, a three-dimensional space which multilingual people access and move about in, building on Blommaert's conception of identity formation as described earlier, and also the conceptualization of trans- offered by Stryker, Currah, and Moore (2008). Lines of connection may intersect, creating new language spaces, and the spaces occupied by these ideological constructions, languages, may also come to intersect over time. A translingual identity performance, then, is built by movement between these linguistic spaces, by moving between but also integrating the languages of an individual's affiliation.

Focusing on linguistic performance without considering its identity implications—and how the identities that we assign might go against a student's claimed and performed identity—has serious consequences for the continued marginalization of translingual and transnational students. A translingual identity may not be an immigrant identity, but it might be; a transnational identity may be based on places where people have actually lived, and it might not be; through translingual practices, students may affiliate themselves with language communities which are not based on linguistic inheritance. These networks of affiliation are performed through language use, and through declarations of identity; we suggest that in order to work with our students as they come to our classrooms, and not as we would like them to be, our pedagogical practices need to center "transing" in our discussions of language practices, and teach students different ways to engage, rather than focusing on ideologically constructed end-points (see Chapter 8 for a fuller consideration of these ideas).

Reading Translingual and Transnational Identities: Alexia and Francis

We now move to considering identity performances created by students at Urban College, noting the kind of details to which instructors and scholars need to be attentive as they assign identities to students in their classroom and research. Central to our inquiry is the question "What kind of intersectional identity performances can we understand from examining students' language practices?" As we turn to the students in our own classes, we find complex and sometimes ambivalent networks of connection with multiple sites and cultures. A student at Urban College, Alexia, describes moving to the United States from Haiti; her love for New York, and her longing for Haiti, emerging in her language narrative from the World Englishes class. She writes:

> The earthquake played a good and bad role in my life. A good role because coming here facilitate a lot of things for me such as I was able to finish high school at seventeen, I learned English before going to college, I made friends who went through the same things as me like leaving their county for better education. A bad role because *ma famille me manque*. After five year, we were only able to go back during the summer of 2013 which seemed to have passed so fast. I am reduced to speak on the phone with *ma*. The relationship between us is not as great as it supposed to be. I also missed being Haitian. I missed my culture. I miss what it feels like to enjoy the sun. I miss what it feels like to look at the sky at night, to see the stars and the moon shining so bright that you can literally read under its light (light pollution here, enables me to do so). Most importantly, I miss what it feels like to be free. I don't know how to explain it but freedom here is only an illusion. Other people might not agree but I felt more free and more myself by in Haiti. Enough pondering!

We see in this short passage some examples of code-meshing (Young, 2009) between English and French; Alexia in this passage performs her affiliation with French in italicized text, in what we might consider to be an (ironically) rather standard "translingual" text. Alexia's translinguality also appears at various points in this passage; however, what we want to focus on is her narrative of transnationality as she writes it, and the way in which she integrates her current life in New York City with her love for Haiti and the freedom that she feels in Haiti that she does not feel in New York. Importantly, too, there is no resolution to the longing: it is part of her transnational experience. Our pedagogies and the classroom environments that we create, thus, must become more comfortable with this in-between-ness, this admission of our students' trans-language identities, aspects of which may appear in the various interactions, and, importantly, in the formal texts that they produce. Just as the trans-movement is slowly shifting the responsibility for ensuring "comfort" towards the audience, and away from the performer, so too transing pedagogies and philosophies put the onus on the instructor and the institution to accommodate and embrace the unknowable, and the ever-changing, rather than keeping it on our students. While some of our students are very interested in pursuing an end point to their translingual experience—another student, Nasima, for instance, feels that translanguaging via syntactic fusion, rather than a Bengali word strategically deployed here and there, is a waste of her readers' time. However, others find the opportunity to translanguage in their formal writing in class to be an important way in which to inhabit the indeterminacy that they feel as part of the identity that they wish to perform for their instructors. As Maggie Nelson writes, of being transgender in particular,

> for some, or for some at some times, . . . irresolution is OK—desirable, even (e.g., "gender hackers")—whereas for others, or for others at some times, it stays as a source of conflict or grief? How does one get across the fact that the best way to find out how people feel about their gender or their sexuality—or anything else, really—is to listen to what they tell you, and to try to treat them accordingly, without shellacking over their version of reality with yours.
>
> *(2015, p. 53)*

In this volume, we attempt to occupy this space of irresolution. The challenging part, of course, is to avoid imposing a monolithic idea of how "good students" behave, write, look or sound in favor of acknowledging and accepting who they are and what they bring to our learning environments.

Finally, we turn to an example from another assignment from World Englishes; the videoblog. Because the course explores global English vernaculars, this assignment serves the purpose of foregrounding language as something that we speak and that we hear, alongside something that we read and write, by asking students to perform a text in some English vernacular (from the course text *Rotten English* (Ahmad, 2007), from their own writing, or from another source of their choosing). The videoblog assignment asked students "to perform a creative work in the vernacular in which it is written." In the assignment instructions, Heather ask students to make the connection between vernacular writing and the oral culture that the writing has emerged from, to make the "nation language" live in "total expression," using terms from Kamau Brathwaite's *History of the Voice* (1984) that the class works in the middle of the semester. Because our classes at Urban College are peopled with students with translingual and transnational affiliations, the assignment provides a site where they can recontexualize their non-standardized, or non-American language varieties . . . and so can Heather. Some students also use the assignment to disconnect "language" from "nation" in interesting ways, but for now, we will see in the following example a situation in which "transnational" means performing links between the United States and somewhere else. We suggest that the videoblog, where students (and their instructor, Heather) perform this transnational identity through translingual practice, enacts the mobility that is at the heart of "trans-" and which Blommaert and Horner (2017) identify as so important to recognize in our teaching of academic literacies. It creates a space of movement and connection between students'—and instructors'—classroom identities and language practices and those that we use elsewhere, which are regularly suppressed.

Francis is a Ghanaian immigrant, bilingual in English and Fante. While at Urban College, he was also pharmaceutical sciences major, and took World Englishes to fulfill a general education requirement. Francis chose to frame his videoblog performance as a straight-to-camera recitation of a poem, in his case one written by a Ghanaian poet. Many students chose this format—perhaps because it is videographically simple—but what was different about Francis's performance is that he did it dressed in what Heather interpreted to be "traditional" Ghanaian clothing, standing in front of a Ghanaian flag. Francis used the video blog as an opportunity to perform his Ghanaian identity in the context of his class at Urban College. As he recited the poem, Francis spoke the way he always spoke in class, with a Ghanaian accent. But the backdrop of his performance, and the choice of poem itself, recontextualized his accent and speech patterns: he created a transnational space through visual cues and his language performance. Francis took to heart the instruction from the assignment prompt, which asked students to "Read as though you are performing. It is not enough to read aloud from the book. I need you to practice so that you represent the vernacular accurately and as though it belongs to you." He contextualized the vernacular through the visual element of the videoblog to make it clear where it, and he, belonged. In terms of "trans-," he used the videoblog to cross over into another linguistic space in the context of the World Englishes class. It may also have functioned as an "escape vector": In Francis's other work in this course, a language narrative and an essay responding to the prompt entitled "Resisting Linguistic Imperialism," he expressed many critiques of the linguistic colonization of Ghana, and its consequences for Ghanaians. So perhaps the opportunity to trans- in the videoblog was an opportunity for Francis to make his Ghanaian affiliations—linguistic and national—primary in his identity performance in the context of his U.S. college education.

Other students interpreted the assignment in different ways. By far their favorite poem to perform was Langston Hughes' "Mother to Son" (Hughes, 2007) in a vernacular other than African-American Vernacular English (AAVE). But students' performances of this poem showed them regularly decoupling the vernacular from its social and national context. Students often performed it in AAVE, of course, as it is written, but they have also performed it in Guyanese English and Pakistani English, the latter by a very recent immigrant. While we might argue that rendering "Mother to Son" is a betrayal of what makes the poem important—it is a somewhat rare representation of a raciolinguistically stigmatized variety of English in a famous piece of literature—we suggest that it shows something interesting: that our students have a rather more egalitarian relationship with language than their professors do, perhaps because they are always crossing: they live "trans-" lives. Why should some texts be off limits? Or, more specifically, why should a performance of vernacular writing be off-limits to someone to whom the vernacular doesn't "belong"? A useful next step of this assignment would be a reflection by students on what it means to decouple language and nation, vernacular and lived experience, not instituting a requirement that they work with text in their own "nation" languages. "Mother to Son" was not the only text with which students did this: another student, with a Guyanese Creole language inheritance, decoupled language and nation by performing a poem in Jamaican Creole, and one more, a speaker of AAVE and Standardized English, performed a poem in Spanish which is not a language which she considers "hers" at all. When thinking about these performances, it becomes clear that if we ask our students "where" they are, linguistically, nationally, culturally, even as they do their work for our classes, their answers will be a lot more complex than what we see when we assign only expository writing, where transing becomes an issue of "passing" as a native-speaker of standardized English, or failing to pass.

Pedagogical Implications

These examples show pedagogical contexts in which students can use their already-present translingual and transnational affiliations. As we discuss in the introductory chapter, it is important for us to recognize that students' translingual practice is often unconscious. Furthermore, we suggest that it is our job to take our students beyond that unconscious practice. If the connection between a particular language and a particular context is denaturalized, shown to not be inevitable, then our students from minoritized language backgrounds have more opportunities to explore their sophisticated linguistics repertoires in ways that "count." The videoblog assignment shows students playing with language affiliations and national affiliations: some of them use it to "cross over" into a different set of language-nation connections, ones that are usually marginalized in the U.S. college composition classroom (Matsuda, 2006; Horner & Trimbur, 2002). Other students used the videoblog to disconnect their language use from its usual implied partner, the nation state. Another assignment, the language narrative, also discussed in Chapter 2, creates space for students to explore intersectional identities in an institutionally-sanctioned space: These language narratives are student texts which explore language identity as a dynamic textual negotiation between imposed identities and claimed identities mediated through student agency as writers. In these pieces of writing, students' translingual identities emerge in their infinite variations on the theme of being inside, out of, between, and around languages. The emphasis here is on common linguistic activities—speaking, reading, writing, listening—engaged in routinely and usually with little apparent emotional strain: complex negotiated language practices, mostly in conversation with family members, peers, community, and/or business associates.

Centering translinguality and transnationality in the college classroom means working with context and process and genre and audience in varied ways to help students consider their languaging more imaginatively and critically than a traditional expository essay allows us to do. And understanding context and how writers position themselves is, as Vivette Milson-Whyte argues, at the core of writing in the disciplines. Milson-Whyte (2015) discusses of the challenges that confront "creole-influenced students" at colleges in the Caribbean, and proposes a "transcultural approach to teaching writing," whereby students' cultural affiliations and plural linguistic inheritances and affiliations—commonplace throughout the Caribbean, but also in New York and other metropolitan centers of empire—not only are recognized in our pedagogies, but also form a center to those pedagogies. Milson-Whyte argues that "Creole-influenced students—by their very linguistic/cultural experiences—are advantageously poised to manipulate" the 'multiple tongues' of the university's many disciplines" (p. 191). We conclude this chapter by suggesting that this statement also applies to our transnational, translingual students: if only we can build curricular and pedagogical apparatuses that give them space to trans-.

References

Ahmad, D. (Ed.). (2007). *Rotten Englishes: A literary anthology.* New York: Norton.

Benesch, S. (2008). "Generation 1.5" and its discourses of partiality: A critical analysis. *Journal of Language, Identity and Education,* 7(3–4), 294–311.

Blommaert, J. (2010). *The sociolinguistics of globalization.* Cambridge: Cambridge University Press.

Blommaert, J. (2013). *Citizenship, language and superdiversity: Towards complexity.* Tilburg Papers in Culture Studies, Paper 45.

Blommaert, J., & Backus, A. (2012). Superdiverse repertoires and the individual. *Tilburg Papers in Culture Studies,* Paper 24.

Blommaert, J., & Horner, B. (2017). Mobility and academic literacies: An epistolary conversation. *London Review of Education,* 15(1), 3–20. https://doi.org/10.18546/LRE.15.1.02

Brathwaite, K. (1984). History of the voice: The development of national language in Anglophone Caribbean poetry. In D. Ahmad (Ed.) (2007), *Rotten English* (pp. 459–468). New York: Norton.

Brooke, R. E. (1991). *Writing and sense of self: Identity negotiation in writing workshops.* Urbana, IL: National Council of Teachers of English.
Butler, J. (1988 [2002]). *Gender trouble* (2nd ed.). New York and London: Routledge.
Canagarajah, A. S. (2011). Codemeshing in academic writing: Identifying teachable strategies of translanguaging. *The Modern Language Journal, 95*(3), 401–417.
Chiang, Y.-S. D., & Schmida, M. (1999). Language identity and language ownership: Linguistic conflicts of first year university writing students. In L. Harklau, K. M. Losey, & M. Siegal (Eds.), *Generation 1.5 meets college composition: Issues in the teaching of writing to U.S.-educated learners of ESL* (pp. 81–96). Mahwah, NJ: Erlbaum.
Cox, M., Jordan, J., Ortmeier-Hooper, C., & Gray Schwartz, G. (2010). *Reinventing identities in second language writing.* Urbana, IL: National Council of Teachers of English.
Crenshaw, K. (1990). Mapping the margins: Intersectionality, identity politics, and violence against women of color. *Stanford Law Review, 43,* 1241.
Faez, F. (2011). Reconceptualizing the native/nonnative speaker dichotomy. *Journal of Language, Identity & Education, 10*(4), 231–249. http://doi.org/10.1080/15348458.2011.598127
Garcia, O. (2009). *Bilingual education in the 21st century: A global perspective.* Oxford: Wiley-Blackwell.
Hall, S. (1988). New ethnicities. In A. Rattansi & J. Donald (Eds.), *Race, culture and difference* (pp. 252–259). London: Sage/Open.
Harklau, L. (2003). Changing currents in second language writing research: A colloquium. *Journal of Second Language Writing, 12,* 151–179.
Harklau, L. (2004, October). *From high school to college: English language learners and shifting literacy demands.* Keynote address presented at the 10th Biennial Composition Studies Conference, University of New Hampshire, Durham.
Horner, B., & Trimbur, J. (2002). English only and US college composition. *College Composition and Communication, 53*(2), 594–630.
Hughes, L. (2007). Mother to son. In D. Ahmad (Ed.), *Rotten Englishes: A literary anthology.* New York: Norton.
Jorgensen, N., Karrebaek, M., Madsen, L., & Moller, J. (2011). Polylanguaging in superdiversity. *Diversities, 13*(2), 22–37.
Kanno, Y., & Norton, B. (2003). Imagined communities and educational possibilities: Introduction. *Journal of Language, Identity, and Education, 2*(4), 241–249.
Le Page, R. B., & Tabouret-Keller, A. (1985). *Acts of identity: Creole-based approaches to language and ethnicity.* Cambridge: Cambridge University Press.
Leung, C., Harris, R., & Rampton, B. (1997). The idealized native speaker, reified ethnicities, and classroom realities. *TESOL Quarterly, 31*(3), 543–560.
Matsuda, P. K. (2006). The myth of linguistic homogeneity in college composition. *College English, 68*(6), 637–651.
Milson-Whyte, V. (2015). *Academic writing instruction for Creole-influenced students.* Mona, Jamaica: University of West Indies Press.
Nelson, M. (2015). *The Argonauts.* Minneapolis, MN: Graywolf Press.
Nero, S. J. (2005). Language, identities, and ESL pedagogy. *Language and Education, 19*(3), 194–211.
Norton, B. (1997). Language, identity and the ownership of English. *TESOL Quarterly, 31*(3), 409–429.
Ortmeier-Hooper, C. (2008). English may be my second language, but I'm not "ESL". *College Composition and Communication, 59*(2), 389–419.
Polkinghorne, D. E. (1991). Narrative and self-concept. *Journal of Narrative and Life History, 1*(2), 135–153.

Rampton, B. (1990). Displacing the "native speaker": Expertise, affiliation and inheritance. *ELT Journal, 44*, 97–101.
Rampton, B. (2006). *Language in late modernity.* Cambridge: Cambridge University Press.
Roberge, M. M. (2002). California's Generation 1.5 immigrants: What experiences, characteristics and needs do they bring to our English classes? *The CATESOL Journal, 14*(1), 107–129.
Stryker, S., Currah, P., & Moore, L. J. (2008). Introduction: Trans-, trans, or transgender? *Women's Studies Quarterly, 36*(3/4), 11–22.
Stylize. (2019). In *Oxford English Dictionary.* Retrieved from www-oed-com.york.ezproxy.cuny.edu/view/Entry/192334?redirectedFrom=stylized#eid20351557
West, C. (1992). A matter of life and death. *October, 61*, 20–23.
Young, V. A. (2009). "Nah, we straight": An argument against code switching. *JAC, 29*(1–2), 49–76.

5
ON BECOMING AND BEYOND
My Liminal Identity

Nela Navarro

This chapter has been largely inspired by a work of art called *Collected Letters* by Liu Jianhua in the Asian Art Museum in San Francisco. It is made of porcelain and steel. I was moved by this work of art and impressed by its ability to capture both the fragility and beauty of liminal spaces, a space that I embrace and understand well. The museum description of the work of art inspires me to be open to new ways of interpreting and reading the work that my students create in their learning spaces. It also forced me to rethink my own experiences and roles as reader, writer, and teacher of writing. "Porcelain Western letters and fragments of Chinese characters, suspended in midair, mingle in a silent symphony of symbols, open to interpretation and a new reading" (Asian Art Museum). This artwork embodies the liminal space and identity that many translinguals inhabit and embody in the context of institutions that insist on fixed identities.

Beyond English

I was born in a place in which I heard the Cervantine language of my parents alongside the language of *Os Lusíadas* daily. I also lived in a neighborhood that was predominantly Polish, as a toddler I played with my friends whose mothers called out to them in *Polskie*. My paternal aunt and namesake enjoyed teaching me words from her favorite language, *Française* and observing how entranced I was with the idea that, as she once told me I said, "*Tía* (aunt), there are other words I can use when I grow tired of my own!" My parents cultivated a space in our home in which the many languages that surrounded us became another opportunity to engage with others. As a young girl, I consequently spent a great deal of time listening to, as my mother would say, "the worlds of different languages." I heard, spoke, and played in more than one language, and to me, this was simply ordinary.

There is a photo of me as a five year old on my first trip to the United Nations beaming for the camera, the flags of the world billowing behind me. When my *tía* Nela asked me what I enjoyed the most of our excursion, I supposedly said "I heard so many languages even more than ours." What I meant by "ours" were all the languages I heard in the transcultural, translingual spaces of my home, my neighborhood, my school, and my community.

Mater Lingua/**Mother Tongue**: *español en casa*

My parents spent a great deal of time teaching us to love our home language, *castellano* or *español*. My mom read us stories and poems, she sang songs, and we had nursery rhymes we recited much to her great delight. *Español* was my mother tongue and Colombia was my motherland. My father reminded us that we were fortunate children, with a great bounty, and we had another country and another language, *el inglés*. Both parents also pointed out that our new *herencia* (heritage) included where we lived. After all, we were just minutes away from New York City and my parents felt that we had the privilege of "being of the world," a *cosmopolita*, surrounded by so many other languages "*como un paseo cotidiano por la ONU*" like a quotidian stroll through the UN (United Nations).

Since both my parents were educators, games and toys should, whenever possible, have *un valor educacional*/educational value. Around this time one of my favorite toys was called "flags of the world." It displayed the flags of the world with a tile over the flag. The objective of the game was to name the country. My *Papá* would slide the tile that sat above the illustration of the flag to show the name of the country; to confirm that I had remembered the name and his addition to the game, I also had to name the language of the country. The tiles for me became a fun game of "revealing" and making visible flags and languages that my *papá* reminded me existed in this world, *tus lenguas maternas no son las únicas del mundo*. Your mother tongues are not the only ones in this world, a refrain he often repeated to us. This game delighted me because I could show my parents that not only was I learning to read but that I could do so in both of my languages. This understanding that I was a speaker of more than one language felt like a super power, until one day when it did not.

Either/Or

There are two experiences, or perhaps I could call them incidents, since I associate that word in English with the definition that suggests that something unpleasant has occurred. They are experiences that are indelibly *grabados*/engraved in my *memoria*/memory and in some ways prepared me for the perils and promises of embracing a translingual identity. One day before I started kindergarten, while playing with some children and my mother nearby, I was speaking in English, then *Polskie* to my playmates. My mom called out to me and I responded in Spanish. One of the girls stared at me and asked, what are you? What are you speaking? In English, I heard "what" and to my Spanish sounding ears, even now, it sounded terrible, like I was an alien, a thing. My *Mamá* tells me I ran over to her wanting to go back home. She said that I explained to her what happened, I told her that I had been called a "thing" and it deeply upset me.

I still remember the feeling though, as an adult, I understood it was not intended that way. I was being asked to take on a singular identity claim as well as a singular language claim, but what I heard was the othering effect of the question. My mother attempted to explain to me that my playmate just wanted to know who I was and not "what" I was, that she had misspoken and that I had *malinterpretado* her words and intentions. I adore the word *malinterpretado* in Spanish; it is often understood as not simply a language "mistake" or a misinterpretation, but it can also suggest an unwillingness to understand on the part of the speaker. I remember feeling that there was intent even though my mother explained clearly that it was not the case. I think of the etymology of the word interpret and I choose to ponder on the *inter* (between) and the *mis* (less) and I come to understand that question in a particular way. I see the question as asking me why I seem to be in a space that is "between," fixed, going nowhere and "less" than what is seen as relevant, valuable, and worthy of being visible. It is a question that unmoors me, that forces me to see the aspirational nature of what I call translingual sensibilities, which I envision as purposeful, thoughtful, reflections on one's own (and others) traditions and practices of thinking about language, as a way to cultivate critical, ethical, and just stances on language identity.

Neither/Not

Not long after the "What are you?" experience, my parents witnessed my first assertion of agency and I learned the power of language. My mother, exhausted by the demands of her fourth child, my recently born little brother, was short on patience. I had also entered preschool years in which I relished my independence and consequently took all opportunities available to me to express my desire for self-governance. I manifested this independent streak or, as my parents my say, willfulness, by often refusing to eat for long periods of time. One such day my mother demanded that I sit and that she would feed me using the age old "airplanes food tricks," promises of late bed time, and chocolate as bargaining opportunities to "trick me into eating," but apparently I was not ready to engage. I refused her overtures. In fact at one point I closed my mouth and was content to let my mother's lovingly prepared meal spill down the side of a new dress I was wearing. My mother tried again and, as I squirmed away, the spoon and my mother's large and beautiful ring hit across my lips, scratching me and drawing some blood. It was an accident and my gentle and loving *mamá* was devastated by what had happened, she picked me up, cleaned me up, and consoled me, but I was apparently not too distressed and this relieved her. She put me back in my room with my toys and told me I did not have to eat unless I wanted to do so.

Some time passed and my mother thought she would check in on me and see how I was feeling. She spoke to me in Spanish as always and, much to her surprise, I responded in English, or so she thought. She tried again, an hour later, two hours later, then three.

I continued to avoid speaking to her in Spanish. She finally called my *papá* and related the events that led to my sudden insistence on speaking English, when we only spoke Spanish, and she thought that I knew her English was still quite limited. She implored my father to speak to me and get me to speak to her *en español*. She handed him the phone and I spoke to him. Unfortunately, it was clear to my father that I was not speaking English, he spoke intermediate level English and, according to him, I was not speaking English. My father suggested that I was making up a language. My mother, undeterred, decided to contact our fully bilingual Puerto Rican young neighbor to see if perhaps, because the neighbor was a native speaker of English, she might be able to "translate" what I was saying where perhaps my father had been unable to do so.

The neighbor came over and I remember the smile on her face when she told my mother in Spanish; ¡Su hija está hablando polaco! / Your daughter is speaking Polish! My mother looked incredulous, the neighbor assured my mother she was right because she was dating a Polish young man and she recognized the words. Just to be sure, she called one of our Polish-speaking neighbors, a woman much older than my mom, who confirmed my linguistic transgression. My parents were both so intrigued and confused by this *episidio*/episode that they decided to call a distant relative who was a child psychologist, thinking that something was amiss. They were told that, in fact, I was exercising my right to speak a language that gave me the distance I wanted from that situation, they told my father it might take a few hours for me to revisit my "home languages" and it did in fact take 1–2 days for me to "recover *ingles* y *español*." In that time, I transgressed; I spoke the language of the community, of my playmates, the language that I knew neither of my parents spoke or understood. I claimed the right to express and, in so doing, I also claimed the right to be silent, to be unseen, unheard, to be invisible, to determine how I wanted to "be" in the world.

Beyond the Binary

The "What are you?" question is one that insists on stability, normativity, identifiable markers required to make the speaker feel at ease in the face of their own linguistic identity struggles. It also represents to me an assertion of power on the part of the speaker. I see it as a suggestion that the very question and my answer can bring me back to whatever space and time the speaker wishes for me, while ignoring my translingual identity and the clear claims to an identity that I choose.

My next experience with uncomfortable interrogations about "what am I" came with a second question and around the time of my preschool days. I was in Jackson Heights at my maternal grandmother's house in a neighborhood that was often called *la pequeña Colombia/* Little Colombia because of the growing population of Colombian immigrants. My grandmother, also an educator and a formidable and exacting woman, enjoyed "assessing" our Spanish language skills, asking us questions employing vocabulary that at times was beyond our grade level, esoteric, or just what we now call, academese. She expressed her worry to my parents that we, her grandchildren, must not forget where we came from. Hers was a lexicon of memory and nostalgia. She used expressions, terms, and told stories that evoked a different time, when she was in Colombia living a grand life, with only limited concerns about the implications of political and civil unrest on her own sheltered, privileged life as a mother, wife, and pioneer educator.

My grandmother insisted that we be "fully bilingual" and that we learn other languages as well. She spoke of the ability of language to empower, and of the need to recognize when it was wielded as a weapon to disempower, to propagandize, or to erase. Time spent with my grandmother resembled a *tertulia/*a salon, a place where we spoke about art, music, and most of all of the importance of telling stories, and of the reality that, as she would say, "writing well" enables you to memorialize these stories, to keep them alive, to ensure that it is harder to erase a people and her language.

In that school house that was my grandmother's home sitting outside one summer day, I remember a friend of my aunt's asking me "Which language do you love more, English or *español?*" It was as shocking to me as the "who are you" question and it was disheartening. It had the same impact as the day a misguided, and, I think, inebriated family friend asked me who I loved more my *mamá* or my *papá*. That question was so terrible to hear and it was even worse to think about how to answer it. I recall my parents chastising this friend and assuring me that his question was as limited as his thinking. They told me he did not have a father so he could not imagine loving both a mother and a father. They asked me to remember that his question came from his inability to imagine, *él no lo puede imaginar, no lo culpes, no te enojes*. He can't imagine it, please don't blame him, do not be upset. In some ways the which language do you love question was worse because each one was me, each one enabled me to express myself, each one is/was my identity; I am not two Nelas, I am one who happens to speak more than one language. My aunt stepped in to help me make sense of the neighbor's language questions using the same frame and approach as my parents. She, I think, added to my parent's approach to the earlier question by stating *ella habla lo que quiere*/she speaks what she wants/loves.

That second incident would later mark a lifetime of being asked what language do you really speak? Which is your first language? Which is your second? In which one do you love, dream, imagine? What is your real first language? and so on. The latter question became one that I really learned to resist and still do. It is a violent act of restraint, a neocolonial extension of naming, identifying, and owning. It implies that the speaker already knows what my first language is, has already selected it for me, and it is a rhetorical question that nonetheless they will ask to insert themselves into my narrative, to remind me that they can "write me into existence," that they can and, at times, have also erased me as well.

The question is suffocating, makes me feel schizophrenic, and never felt like a real question, but like an enactment of the speaker's binary understanding and a lack of imagination. In invoking "real" they have rendered me fictional, a figment of their less than creative imagination. They can only see one or possibly two options, but really they only want to see one, they want me to be a mirror that enables them to see themselves, to write their story, and my "beyond binary" stance is a disruption.

Translingual Transitions

Days before I started kindergarten, my father explained to me that I would be using English all the time because I would be going to school. One of the earliest roads that I crossed gingerly and even with awe (so my parents tell me) but also with trepidation, is the one that transported me from ***español*** to ***inglés***. From the bright colors of yellow in my parent's kitchen to the sweet taste of ***dulce de guayaba*** (guava), to the poetic, at times loud, but always comforting sounds of Spanish with its enchanting words like *mija* (this is short for ***mi hija***/my daughter, but it really means something more intimate as it often does in Spanish). This contraction ***mija*** means: my dear daughter. In that brilliant cocoon that my parents recreated from the remnants of desire, loss, and nostalgia, I lived sheltered, and quite differently, yet always in the embrace of the Cervantine language. What I saw, heard in this very Colombian domesticity was very different from what I was plunged into one warm day in September on my first day of kindergarten in New Jersey.

In a small but inviting classroom full of my energetic classmates we were invited to take our naptime. This was a ritual that I refused to accept or understand. How in fact could I simply "stop" my activities to sleep, to close my eyes, to cease my play, my travels, my adventures? I refused to lay my head down in the middle of a brilliant September day (I still resist naps) and so I slept with one eye open. As I watched with my one eye, my teacher and the assistant were preparing our snacks. I noticed that they were pouring milk and taking thin looking sheets from a box. I continued to watch in awe as the lovely white milk was poured in little children mugs in red, orange, and blue. I waited to have my milk and taste the thin sheets they called cookies.

A new road to traverse awaited me when we were allowed to open our eyes. In that Proustian moment when I bit into that "thin sheet" that I learned was a graham cracker, I felt that there, in the classroom, I was one of "them," the *americanos*. I was devouring and embodying, happily the English language, American culture, the world outside my parent's house. I loved not the taste of the cracker or cookie as they called it but the feeling that I was somewhere else. I knew that when I went home for my *merienda*/snack I would have my *dulce de guayaba*. Once again, I would belong to this world, this new place of eating graham crackers. This new place was mine and yet *la casa*/my home was my "place" too. I was elated. In that moment it is clear that I had not yet lost the wonder and possibility that came with having another place to call home. The graham cookie became, what it remains today: a journey from one world to another, but also one journey, mine. The bite of a graham cracker today transports me back to that classroom and to the world of English. I associate that snack and that moment with the entry into my own world, apart from my parents. I still recall it with a bittersweet taste and a sense of inevitability. In that moment when I bit into the graham cracker I was one of "them" as well as one of the "others."

Years later I came to understand that in this world some people prefer that we take single journeys and single paths, while there are other people, I am one of them, who travel many, many roads and some of those roads are challenging and not always encouraging. I would come to understand and expect that I might be asked to choose between the ***dulce de guayaba*** and the graham cracker, but I did not have to choose! To this day when I bite into a graham cracker I feel the urge to pull out my American passport (I was born here, after all), stare out at the NYC skyline near my apartment, and frantically pronounce myself "she who speaks and lives in English." When the "English fever" passes I search for ***español*** and, sometimes, get temporarily but happily lost in the "in between," my beautiful liminal space. I no longer mind the traversing in what others call the "back and forth place" and what I call "moving towards and beyond." Oh, I should tell you that as an adult one of favorite snacks is actually ***dulce de guayaba*** on a graham cracker with green tea.

La Herencia Global Del Quijote or Everyone Reads Don Quijote de la Mancha

In their efforts to ensure that we would be raised with an appreciation of the literary traditions of the Spanish language my parents required that we take Spanish classes in school, that we speak and read in Spanish. We did travel to Colombia often when we were young and, most famously or infamously, we had my mom's after school and summer school programs. She created pedagogical activities all designed to be sure that we did not forget "who we were and where we came from." My dad participated as well. These were educational experiences before and after school and during the weekends and summer at home in what we called "*la escuela de mamá*"/mom's school. We learned about our Spanish-speaking culture especially from literature, music, arts, and dance.

Over the dinner table one day when I was in elementary school and my mom had started reading our children's version of *Don Quijote de la Mancha* my dad pronounced the following with a sense of both joy and gravity: "everyone reads *Don Quijote de la Mancha*, it is one of many things that unites us." With that pronouncement my father *sembró*/cultivated (the same word we use for planting, as in a garden) a lifelong love of texts that are translingual in their very structure and a love of literature for its ability to enable imaginative acts, the kind of engagement that invites us to imagine a place, an experience or a person whose experience is quite different from our own. I was fascinated by the idea that Cervantes insisted on a partly Arabic origin to his most famous work of art. This was especially meaningful given my mother's lessons on the cultural debt we as Spanish-speakers owed to our Pan Arab sisters and brothers whose language and culture had left a deep imprint on our own. "We are Arabs, we are indebted to their culture for our own." My mother's reminders about our shared Arab inheritance is what I think is responsible for my extraordinary love affair with the city of Granada, the seat of the last Arab caliphate of Nasrid/بنو نصر. *Don Quijote de la Mancha* is one of the most translated works of literature in the world, the idea that I could speak about my love of literature across languages and cultures, in a sense going beyond language and culture to another language, the language of great literature, moves me deeply. My dad took me to the New York City Public Library to show me the different translations of *Don Quijote de la Mancha*, different covers, different languages but still the book that I fell in love with as the great novel of modern times.

In high school, years later, I remember my Greek speaking Spanish teacher sharing her joy for this novel, one that she first read in Greek, then in Spanish, and finally in a new English translation. She told the class that those of us who were heritage Spanish speakers had rights as well as responsibility that came with speaking this great Cervantine language. We asked her what she meant and she reminded us that sometimes we were confronted by demands that we "speak English, this is America" and that in fact we had the right to our language, it was not an aspect of who we were, or a tool we used, it **was** who we were. My teacher continued to encourage us to understand that there might come a time when other classmates, who would also be speakers of another language might also need our support and that it would be our responsibility to honor, and come to their assistance if they also faced the same discriminatory attitudes and practices that many of us had faced as speakers of a language other than English. In her class, and later in my English literature class, I learned that language might give us the power to exert our agency and to be heard, for we did have a voice, but often we were simply not heard. As a reader of *Don Quijote de La Mancha*, I felt heard and read. In his world I had the right to dream, to be different, to not have to choose one journey, one adventure, one kind of existence.

In our junior year, I discovered that there were other ways to write essays, other structures, other expectations and other readers. I had just gotten an A on a paper about Jane Eyre. I was proud of my literary incursions and my mastery of the five-page English essay. My teacher pointed to my clearly stated thesis and to my "innovative textual analysis." I was on the edge of my seat, filled with pride and joy that I was learning to write well, something that my parents expected of me and that I expected of myself. At the same time, I was also writing an essay on Cortazar's *Rayuela* in my Spanish literature class. My teacher, the same teacher who reminded me I had rights and responsibilities in my language, admonished me when I submitted my rough draft for the Cortazar essay. She said that I had forgotten the structure and reader expectations, "trampled upon Spanish structure and conventions" and my language was flawless, but I had written an English essay in perfect Spanish. I met with her after school while she painstakingly reminded me that I had included my thesis in my first introductory paragraph and had thus violated the conventions of a good academic writer in Spanish in which, unlike in English, the writer does not "pronounce" their argument and seek to develop it, but rather develops the argument and then, at the end, "arrives" at the main claim/argument or, as the "English speakers," call it, the "thesis." This was stunning, and I went home to get clarity from my parents, who almost word for word repeated my Spanish teacher's lessons. My essay and that of my classmates became a research project for my two teachers and an interesting collaborative effort in which they tried to teach us that writing in another language was also as different as reading, listening, and speaking in another language. This experience inspired my great interest in teaching for and about "writing beyond."

In college I took a class on *Don Quijote de la Mancha*, a seminar on only that text. That year an emerging visiting scholar from Yale University spent the semester showing us what I now recognize were the many translingual reading opportunities this text afforded and it translingual nature as a novel. The following semester I took a survey literature course in which we read excerpts of the latest translation *of Don Quijote de la Mancha*, the professor who was deeply interested in translation theory. He took us away from the classic "equivalence" and prescription approach to translated texts towards a more post-colonial and transformative approach. In that academic year, when I also took French, taught Latin for pocket money, and continued my great interest in Chinese, I saw the richness of a text, an experience and a way of being that did not belong to one language or one people.

Disorientations

In between my undergraduate and graduate days, I continued to nurture a deep love affair with Chinese language and culture. As a ten-year-old girl at a birthday gathering hosted by my parents, wearing a red dress and blowing out the candles of my cake, I made a wish. What was my wish? I wished for the day that I might be able to live in China and walk the Great Wall of China. When I was asked to describe my wish, the room grew uncomfortably silent and then I heard a few laughs. My father stopped the laughing and sternly told our guests that as improbable as that dream sounded to them, for me it was a possibility. He went on to give one of his brief but powerful *discursos*, this word might be translated as "speeches" but it was more like the etymology of the *discurso* in *español* from the Latin, *discursus*, or *expresión oral de razonmiento*/an oral expression of reason. He was reasoning with the guests, asking them to imagine his ten-year-old daughter as a young woman making her dream come true, because as he told them that day, she has already been to China in her books and in her imagination.

Almost twenty years later after that party, I did indeed arrive in Shanghai, China, to become a "foreign expert, visiting faculty" at Shanghai International Studies University, sometimes called the "cradle of diplomacy" because its reputable languages and literatures department had trained so many of China's diplomats in the languages, literatures, and cultures of the world. 中国/ Zhōngguó /China (The Middle Kingdom)/ is humbling, extraordinary, ordinary, beautiful, frightening, and utterly unknowable to me. I found comfort in the fact that the questions about who I was and what I spoke were not even the kinds of questions that I was asked. I felt disoriented, unattached to a predetermined identity; I was "other" in a completely different way, and it was liberating. I was simply "not Chinese." I was and felt extraterrestrial. I was other. I was "Western" and it did not matter that, for example, the United States and Colombia were distinctly different countries and cultures, I was "Western" and therefore "other."

In those days in Shanghai there were very few expatriates. Shanghai was a city with a history of colonial powers vying for control and multiple "foreign concessions or enclaves" of a wide range of nationalities as a consequence of the brutal colonial enterprise otherwise known as the Opium Wars. It was a port city with people from around the world and around China trying to make a life. I met with a young American couple who had recently lived in China and they described Shanghai as "New York on speed," a place that moved quickly, changed quickly, but also in some ways stayed the same. My attempts to speak Mandarin were met with a combination of horror, admiration, pity, concern, pride, and humor. I was supposed to speak Shanghainese and although I knew this before I arrived, my tutor back in New York City had insisted that I focus on Mandarin. In this way, I became a language learner, once again forced to recall my language learning journeys in Latin, Russian, French, and Arabic.

Shanghai became a place that enabled me to rethink my language identity and my assumptions about China and 普通话 Pǔtōnghuà/Mandarin. Most of my understandings were subverted, my western centric preoccupations, values, and beliefs upended. China seemed to demand that I recognize where I was, that I was in their land, speaking their language, reading their history, and enjoying their culture. I embraced the disorientations and dislocations happily, it offered me a blank canvas onto which I could create and paint my own sense of self, something that had eluded me in many ways when I was home in the United States. Learning Mandarin was humbling, the silence and feeling of demarcations and limitations that come with struggling to speak and be heard in a new language was in a strange way an opportunity to reclaim and reassert the "me" that often got lost at home with two languages that were "my own." In Mandarin I could experiment, I could live in that "between liminal space" that I saw not as the "place in the middle," the place of refuse, and rejection, but a space that was at once becoming and beyond, dynamic, complex, and transformative, much like China herself.

Toward a Translingual Sensibility

Al regresar de la China, sentí la nostalgia de mis padres por aquellos días de ayer y anteayer. De cierta forma lo de hoy y mañana en Estados Unidos generaba desanimo y desorientación. After a long, bittersweet, and anxious plane ride, I landed in JFK airport on my return home from living in China with my husband; no one was there to greet us, they had misunderstood the time change, return date, and we were now in the airport, at home in NYC, with no sign of family, no rituals of return, and no sense of "the familiar." It was a transformative moment, and I recall feeling a level of culture shock that I was intellectually familiar with, on the one hand, but whose intensity, on the other, shook me to the core. This did not feel "familiar" or like "home." I had been dislocated somewhere between the "going to" and the "coming from." I was expecting with some joy this day, a day of speaking my languages, affirming my identities, welcoming the sense of belonging. I wanted to speak English and Spanish, or so I thought. At the baggage claim, the announcements were of course in English, and a confused baggage claim attendant responded to my query about the baggage from Shanghai (上海的行李在哪里, please, gracias?) the attendant replied with a terse question, "What are you speaking?" and then with an impatient command, "Try it again!" and then again with another command, go over there, he added, "The luggage from Shanghai is arriving now." This exchange has come to embody my life-long adventure, and resistance to assumptions about my language identity. I realize now that in that exchange, I did understand that I had to "try it again," but I did not have to and in a sense I think I knew it. He understood part of my message; he had negotiated meaning with me, the exhausted traveller.

I have come to reassert for myself the idea that many of the social and deeply ideological approaches to language differences are invented, constructed, and therefore can and should be deconstructed, interrogated, and rethought. I embrace a "trans" approach to understanding and negotiating these cultural differences. I am especially interested in the "going through, going beyond," and transformative (as the etymology of the word "trans" suggests) aspect of a "trans" frame. I do so because it is this approach that signals hybridization, critical cultural, and language awareness, life in the "neither/not," progressive, postmodern, transnational, and decolonial stances. These are stances that are more likely to promote a culture of language identity rights and to prevent monolingual paradigms from maintaining their longstanding dominant positions.

What am I speaking? I speak the languages of my translingual, transcultural experiences; I speak the languages of those who are often forgotten, deliberately misunderstood, sometimes silenced and erased. I do not speak *for* an identity. I express my identity. I am both becoming and beyond, deeply aware of the liminal spaces I inhabit.

6
LANGUAGE AFFILIATION AND IDENTITY PERFORMANCE AMONG TRANSNATIONAL STUDENTS

The challenges that face international students in U.S. universities are well-known and formidable. Students whose prior education has taken place in a language other than English confront expectations of fast adjustment to English-medium instruction and to extensive reading and writing in disciplinary genres and discourses. They also often quickly discover that their need to seek out, use, and develop support systems is not always matched by the availability or accessibility of these systems at their U.S. institutions (e.g. Shang-Butler, 2015; Angelova & Riazantseva, 1999; Sharma, 2019; Ravichandran, Kretovics, Kirby, & Ghosh, 2017). Although the (trans)linguistic and transcultural experiences of the students whose narratives we read, and who we interviewed at State University, illustrate these well-known challenges and also the well-known trajectory of academic success for international students (intense early difficulties, the development of coping strategies, and successful immersion in and practice of academic discourses in English), in this chapter we focus on students' emerging and existing language affiliations, highlighting some students' growing engagements and connections with the linguistic community in the United States, while showing that, for some students, the expected trajectories of improvement, immersion, and affiliation do not emerge and, rather, their continued progress in U.S. educational institutions may well solidify their feelings of being "other" with respect to academic, professional, and social English, and with respect to the American cultures that they encounter in that country.

Extant narratives of these challenges, while offering crucial insights for those faculty and staff who work with international students, still often reinforce a reified understanding of international students' language identities. Using the framework for language identity developed in Rampton (1990) and Leung, Harris, and Rampton (1997), and which we also explore in Chapter 4, we offer a perspective that intervenes in these identity assignments. That is, rather than focusing on students' language inheritance and the development of their language expertise, we focus on students' narratives of their language affiliation, as they recount them in in-depth interviews and in biographical writing assignments and literacy narratives. We consider, too, these students' linguistic performances, acknowledging that in written work and interviews, students are constructing particular personae of themselves as students and sometimes, for the graduate students, as professionals. The students' linguistic affiliations come out via these performances.

By focusing on linguistic performance and linguistic affiliation, rather than expertise and inheritance, we position students as agents in their own linguistic identity development, whose identity is not necessarily bound to their linguistic expertise and inheritance, even when their administrative status as international students keeps them contained in terms of their nationality and so-called native language. Such a perspective is essential: as Sharma (2019) writes with respect to international graduate students,

> Especially given the lack of established formal support structures that (when used) benefit international graduate students, research on these students must focus on their agency. As it is problematic to 'assume' that these students need no support or attention just because they are talented or mature, it is similarly problematic to assume that they are powerless, helpless, or deficient.
>
> (v)

A focus only on students' language competence and inheritance is therefore problematic because it removes any agency that students might assume in their linguistic, professional, and academic trajectories; a focus on how they affiliate themselves with U.S. based linguistic communities, whether they are disciplinary or social, shows how students negotiate their new environment, rather than focusing on what they bring from their "old" ones.

This chapter brings together both groups of international students whose narratives we are exploring in this book, highlighting the connections between undergraduate and graduate students' linguistic identity formation, as well as exploring the ways in which their developmental and experiential trajectories differ throughout their time at State University. Thus, we work with biographical essays, literacy narratives, and reflective essays from five undergraduate students, written in the context of their English for Academic Purposes (EAP II) course, alongside interview responses and "intellectual autobiographies" from two students enrolled in different graduate programs at State University: one in the mathematical finance PhD program, and one in the violin performance PhD program. All students are international students whose origin is identified by the university as China or Taiwan. These students, furthermore, have all been classified as "English Language Learners," and were required to take the TOEFL exam as a requirement for entry into State University. We meet these participants as Nela's students, either in one section of EAP II, or as students enrolled in the Graduate Academic Success Program (GASP), in which the faculty work as instructors in academic discourse, test preparation (for department-level English fluency exams), advocates for and liaisons between students and their academic departments, and as allies and participants in the students' support networks.

Language Affiliation, Linguistic Performance, and Agency

Leung et al. (1997) offer the language affiliation-expertise-inheritance model of language identity in order to counter the binary of "native-speaker" and "non-native speaker," which they show to be too reductive to account for the lived experience of high school students from immigrant families in England. The students in Leung et al. (1997) study are routinely raciolinguistically profiled (Flores & Rosa, 2015) in their schools and in the broader English culture, and are often assigned "non-native speaker" identities because of what Leung et al. (1997) refer to as "reified ethnicities"; that is, their ethnicity is assumed to provide all the information that instructors need to understand what the students can do linguistically. As the authors write, "there is an abstracted notion of an idealised native speaker of English from which ethnic and linguistic minorities are automatically excluded" (p. 546). Leung et al. (1997) show, however, that focusing on students' ethnicities and the languages that their families speak paints a very incomplete picture of the students' language identities; hence, the authors, following Rampton (1990), developed a tripartite model of language identity, as follows (also discussed in Chapter 4):

> In a slight reworking of Rampton's original formulation, the term *language expertise* refers to how proficient people are in a language; *language affiliation* refers to the attachment or identification they feel for a language whether or not they nominally belong to the social group customarily associated with it; and *language inheritance* refers to the ways in which individuals can be born into a language tradition that is prominent within the family and community setting whether or not they claim expertise in or affiliation to that language.
>
> *(p. 555)*

Previous studies which focus on international graduate students often emphasize these students' existing language expertise, and strategies to help students develop this expertise in academic English, especially in writing. Studies such as those reported in Chang and Kanno (2010) and Shang-Butler (2015) show that, over time, international students' use of disciplinary academic English develops to a very high level, but that this expertise can vary widely depending on the student's discipline. Furthermore, students' levels of expertise in disciplinary English can differ greatly from their expertise in the use of English within the broader U.S. community; indeed, as we discuss in Chapter 13, there is little space in many academic disciplines for transnational students to connect their proficiency in disciplinary discourses with their need and desire to use English as an everyday language. Certainly, the challenges that international students face with respect to the acquisition of academic English should not be minimized, even as most studies narrate a trajectory of improvement, describing, in effect, how students get their English wings (e.g. Shang-Butler, 2015; Eldaba & Isbell, 2018; Shuck, 2010). Other studies show that the demands of disciplinary English vary widely from discipline to discipline (e.g. Chang & Kanno, 2010), and others still connect this developmental trajectory to a broader engagement with the requirements and structures of U.S. academic culture, of which disciplinary writing is only one piece (e.g. Angelova & Riazantseva, 1999; Shang-Butler, 2015; Ravichandran, Kretovics, Kirby, & Ghosh, 2017).

These studies, too, often focus on students' language inheritance, emphasizing the transient identities assigned to international students by their visa status, and thus denying the possibility that these students might consider themselves to have a more "global" identity, part of which originated in early English instruction, and/or ignoring the possibility that students might have ambitions to stay in the United States or countries other than their "home" after they complete their degrees. While it does no good at all to deny the linguistic challenges that many international students face as they confront discourse expectations in their graduate programs, the emphasis of this chapter will be an assertion that their language expertise and language inheritance are not all that international students are, and that considering their dynamic linguistic affiliations are a helpful way for faculty and staff and institutions to consider and support not only what students "are," but what they have decided to "become." Thus, in this chapter we explore instances of international students owning their transnational and translingual identities, as they describe their linguistic performances and their affiliations with English and a variety of other languages, including, but not limited to Mandarin, the official language of China. In order to frame these narratives as performances, we refer throughout to students' linguistic agency. Following Alessandro Duranti's framework of linguistic agency (Duranti, 2004), we offer the following definition of agency: "The property of those entities (i) that have some degree of control over their own behavior, (ii) whose actions in the world affect other entities (and sometimes their own), and (iii) whose actions are the object of evaluation" (p. 453).

Ahearn (2001), similarly, sums up agency as referring to "the socioculturally mediated capacity to act" (p. 112). Other researchers into students'—particularly so-called "second language," multilingual and international students—identities have focused on agency as vital to any discussion of these students' linguistic and writing practices, since the institutional "processing" of students assigned to these categories tends to remove much of their agency as drivers of their own educational experiences (see in particular Shuck, 2010; Ortmeier-Hooper, 2008; Shapiro, Cox, Shuck, & Simnitt, 2016). We focus on how the students depicted in this chapter "engage in the exercise of power in the sense of the ability to bring about effects and to (re)constitute the world" (Karp, 1986, p. 137); that is, how the students place themselves in their narratives of language and literacy acquisition, and how they connect this acquisition process to their broader narratives of becoming State University students, in the case of the undergraduates, and of becoming members of their disciplinary communities, in the case of the graduate students. In particular, we suggest that the students focus on a trajectory of development in terms of social and individual agency, which they reveal as a particularly American kind of agency that they have to develop, and which they discuss particularly in the context of their relationship with English.

We begin with five undergraduate students from one of Nela's recent EAP II classes. Nela asks students to write, as their initial assignment, a short autobiographical essay followed by a brief literacy narrative, framed by a series of questions about their language identity and their identities as students at State University and in the United States. The questions are provided in Appendix B. As their final assignment, students write a reflection about their development as readers and writers over the course of the semester in EAP II. In this chapter, we will see that these two pieces of writing, which are used as part of the students' portfolios for assessment, also frame their identities as transnational, translingual students at State University.

Before going into their narratives in depth, we note that none of the students discussed in this chapter are novices—either in English, or as students. All of the undergraduate students have been at State University for at least one semester, and are enrolled in their second semester in the EAP sequence. Furthermore, the students do not perform the identity of novices, even if performing such an identity might be an effective way to show a willingness to accept academic support: one student writes, for example, "I am still not fluent in English though I have been at [State University] for one semester." The students' narratives, moreover, demonstrate what seem to be efforts to contain their English language deficits: the students identify specific areas of improvement such as "vocabulary" and "grammar" and avoiding "translation," while simultaneously expressing feelings about learning English such as amazement, feeling that it is magical. However, even as students describe experiences of emerging into the wonder of English, they still strongly affiliate themselves with Chinese logics, which we take to show an investment in a Chinese intellectual identity, even though only one student primarily affiliates themself with the Chinese language. We see how these negotiations and affiliations emerge in the following.

"Amazing," "Magical," "Terrible"

The first student we meet among the State University undergraduates from EAP II is **Cheng-Chih**. In his biography, Cheng-Chih writes,

> As a Chinese, Chinese is my native language. And you know I also speak English and learn it nearly 9 years. The first time I attach English I remember I felt it is pretty interesting because I am interested the new things. Except that, I have to study the way that how English speakers state their perspectives and it is totally different from Chinese logic. The process that I learn English just like a process exploring a new land and makes me feel amazing and believe language is magical. However, I also meet some problems from the vocabulary when I studying English my remembrance is not good and I forget the words that I learned in the class after half a day. And vocabulary problem also affects my writing.

Cheng-Chih's discussion here is in many ways typical of the way the Chinese students in this section of EAP II present themselves. The fact that Cheng-Chih has been learning English for many years mirrors the experience of most of the graduate and undergraduate students in this study. Furthermore, many of the undergraduate students are highly complementary of English, like Cheng-Chih is—they call English, and the process of learning it, "amazing," "magical," "comfortable," "beautiful," and "like music." Several students also note that writing in English changes the way they think: sometimes the change in logic slows their thinking down in ways that they don't like, but many also describe the necessity of learning to think in English, rather than translating from "Chinese" to English. Even within this context of changed—some students even say reversed—logic, though, when asked about specific areas they want to work on, the students tend, like Cheng-Chih, to be very specific, and contain their areas of perceived deficiency into "vocabulary," "grammar," and avoiding translation, apparently echoing the focus of their English instruction in China and Taiwan, which many students describe as emphasizing these areas, rather than discourse-level communicative goals. In his reflection, Cheng-Chih narrates a trajectory that moves from discomfort to enjoyment over the course of EAP II, but a continuing struggle with the logics of U.S.-based academic discourse, with its requirements of up-front theses and deep reading. His advice to other EAP II students is as follows: "students need to read more news in the daily life that can help you deepen the perspectives."

This final recommendation reflects an awareness of the need to connect not only with academic discourses, but also the broader culture, which the former discourses reflect and analyze. It is as though Cheng-Chih is in the process of figuring out not only the "connective thinking" that is an integral part of the State University writing pedagogy, but also how this kind of connective thinking can help him find a place in the United States.

We can read **Yang**'s rather short biography as expanding on the perspectives that Cheng-Chih offers. Yang writes that he started learning English at the age about five, and that "the most difficult thing for me is that to speak or write English changes the way I think. There is always an extra step to think about how to express my opinions in English, so it sometimes makes my mind less sharp." However, Yang seems rather sanguine about the time it will take to learn the U.S. academic writing processes and logics that EAP II emphasizes, writing that "as a student, [he is] always willing to learn new things and devote efforts to it. Time management is what [he] am trying to improve." However, in another student's—Amy's—biography, which we discuss later, we see a picture of serious struggle with the process of learning to write in English, which is connected to a perceived lack of proficiency in writing in Chinese as well. In contrast to his brief biography, though, Yang is voluble in his final reflection, especially in the way he has managed the logics of U.S. academic discourses. He writes,

> My writing process changed a lot this semester. I used to write directly from I just think of rather than a clear and specific outline. Now, I draft a basic but clear outline about what I am going to argue. Whenever I come up with new ideas, I write it down immediately. After gathering some ideas, I list and organize them in a logical way on the outline. Then I will check if they are all connected to both texts and if I can find quotes. This change is revolutionary to me. It saves me plenty of time.

Remembering that one of the major challenges that Yang identified at the beginning of this semester was with thinking in English ways, his description here of finding a way to manage his writing process is a major achievement in understanding how to perform academic English—"revolutionary," as he describes it. However, this trajectory towards English logics, which Cheng-Chih and Yang both narrate, is not shared by all of the students in EAP II.

Amy occupies a very negative space when considering her expertise in and affiliation with English, and this does not change, even when she shows, in her final reflection, that she has internalized the processes of writing in English that will lead to success in EAP II. While, in this biography, Amy describes her extended English study and the ways in which she has learned Korean, she expresses a wish that "everyone can speak Chinese," flipping the trope that learning English is the only avenue to transnational access and success that is at least implicit in all of the other student narratives: "Sometimes, I hope everyone can speak Chinese, so that we can communicate without any barrier."

Among all the students, Amy is the only one who strongly affiliates with only Chinese, even as she describes her long-term study of English (since kindergarten) and her efforts to learn Korean so as to understand the Korean dramas that she likes to watch. Unlike the other students, too, Amy goes into detail about her perceived failures and weaknesses in her narrative, rather than containing them as the other students tend to do: she itemizes them after briefly presenting her strengths, as follows:

> As a student, I think I'm good at doing homework and self-study. I like doing homework because I can more deep understand the theory of math and give me more think about the theory. Oppositely, I should admit that I'm not good guy who is active to talk with others, and because that kind of characteristic, I missed a lot good opportunity. The hard thing when I write in English is not to translation. You know I try to be like American writer and use their expression and sentence construction. The first reaction when I'm writing and speaking is in Chinese and then I need translate in English in my brain. The easy part is the English alphabet is not hard to write as Chinese. To be honest, the two terrible things in my life are writing and speaking English. Even in Chinese writing, I still not have good grade.

In this narrative, she targets as her weakness the specific social-educational behaviors that are a hallmark of U.S. classrooms, and which are often extremely challenging to international students (e.g. Andrade, 2006): participating in whole-class and group discussions, which would make her a "good guy," mimicking the style of American writers, and writing and speaking in English. Just as the genre of literacy narrative has been critiqued as an enforced "coming out" into the light from darkness (Inayatulla, 2013), so Amy's narrative challenges the expectations of a narrative of improvement and optimism, which other students' biographies inscribe. In her reflection, Amy does relate a developing understanding of the requirements of the academic discourses circulating at State University; however, the reflection resists any interpretation of Amy's increasing comfort and enjoyment of writing and reading in English. She writes,

> Of course, writing should include some key term like thesis and topic sentence, but the idea and writing style should not be limited. Whatever you writing should clearly express what's your meaning, and specify your idea. The one of most important reminder is the writing is not math, we cannot follow the formula to write the essay.

Given that Amy's preferred discourses are mathematical—in her biography, she writes that she chose mechanical engineering as her major "because I prefer at math and physics as well as this kind of logical subject, not lots of things need to remember"—Amy's reflection reveals that while she has learnt the expectations of EAP II, she remains unconvinced of their usefulness to her in terms of her interests and her ways of thinking. Her declaration at the end of the quotation, that "writing is not math" could well be read as a source of disappointment, rather than of enlightenment, given her expression of her affiliation with the ways of thinking that she can engage in in physics and mathematics.

Amy's narrative reminds us of the seriously difficult and at times daunting nature of the task faced by international students who are moving to English medium instruction and assessment, and of the possibility of rejecting translingual and transnational language affiliations, which tends to be erased in students' narratives of coming to U.S. institutions in order to participate in global educational, social, and financial economies.

But, of course, other students challenge Amy's performance of studenthood at State University. **Jared**, on the other hand, feels much more comfortable in a U.S. classroom, gladly claiming English as one of his languages alongside Cantonese and Mandarin, and describing how three years in a "small private Catholic boy[s] school" in California has set up his decision to study Statistics at State University. He writes, "I love adventure and believe moving to the east coast would give me a better understanding of America as culture and as geography country."

For Jared, moving to the east coast was an adventure that would help him in his immersion in U.S. culture. Jared, in the starkest contrast to Amy's narrative, also writes that he

> loves to share [his] opinion in the classroom; expressing my experience in California. As a writer, seeking for some good ideas is not the hard part for me, but looking for the right words to express in formal and organized language. I can easily find the main ideas for the essay in classes, however it spent me days to try to write down what I wanted. And few more days to make it more organize. And also, I am a bad reader, in order to understanding the passage in the first essay in [EAP II] I read it three times just to get the basic understanding of the main idea. The academic way to expression is the hard part when I read something. And my vocabularies is what I have to improve in the [EAP II] this year, I sometime used the same words times just because I don't know the other way to say it.

Jared actually seems to have developed good study skills that help him to cope with the demands of studying in what he identifies as his third language. His experience reflects that of many other non-native-English-speaking students in U.S. institutions (e.g. Chang & Kanno, 2010), who must put in significantly more time with their reading and writing in order to do the same things that so-called domestic students do. Again, his persona as a student somewhat mirrors Cheng-Chih's, in his frank and unemotional discussion of what he is "bad" at, and of his containment of his limited vocabulary in the way he describes his weaknesses.

Interestingly, in his final reflection, Jared writes his experiences in EAP II challenged his conception of his identity as a STEM student. Finding a strong analogy between his work as an emerging statistician, and the critical thinking processes that Nela asked him to engage in for EAP II, he writes,

> Writing class teach me as a writer write more logically so I can change my idea to a logical essay. And with the same critical thinking of logic is not necessary to be the fact, it links back to my academic career as a stats student, what the data shows is not always the correct result. But to consider the different various variables that can affect the result. To questioning the science systems, we have and create something new within it.

This connection between Jared's academic identity and his work in EAP is significant, we suggest, because it offers a route to affiliation with English-language academic logics through an existing engagement in the logics of statistics, with which Jared is strongly affiliated. This affiliation is clearly supporting Jared's trajectory through the State University curriculum and, importantly, gives Jared a way to measure his success in writing in English that goes beyond the grades that he earns—even though he is justifiably proud of his success in this area, mentioning his EAP I grade in both his initial biography and this reflection.

The final student whose biography and reflection we explore is **Winnie**. Like Jared, Winnie attended a U.S. high school for three years before coming to State University. Winnie's major is as yet undeclared—like many so-called domestic students at the end of the first year of college, she feels that she has time to decide. We highlight Winnie's biography because it shows linguistic affiliations that go beyond what we might expect from "international students." For instance, while Winnie identifies as a native speaker of Chinese, but still shows a strong pragmatic affiliation with English. Spanish, she says, she takes as her "third language," and says about it,

> I truly enjoyed learning another language other than Chinese and English. It is a challenge for me. Spanish, in my opinion, is not that hard, I felt is much easier than English, maybe it is because Spanish and English has lot of commons. But I was shocked by the conjugation, one single verb in present has six transforms in regular way and irregular way.

And she returns to her love of Spanish later in the biography:

> Then, when I started to learn Spanish, I found out that language is so fascinating and full with magic. Each language is unique and beautiful. I enjoyed learning new words every day and I was so proud of myself after I read a short Spanish paragraph at the first time.

Furthermore, alone among the students whose biographies we examined, Winnie expresses a nostalgia for Chinese, writing, "I was regretted that I did not figure out the value of the Chinese before and I really missed my Chinese class when I came to America."

This nostalgia seems to locate Chinese as something from the past—an inheritance, but not a particularly salient part of her present. She writes, as what we see as an indication of her primary affiliation with English at this point, the following:

> I also found out the importance to using not only one language when I am in the United States. All the people around me are speaking and writing in English. I felt how important to know the language well, cause it really makes your life much convenience when your are in other countries.

Winnie performs an identity which embraces the use of English as "convenient," and which is nostalgic for Chinese—but it is Spanish that has shown her, she writes, that language could be "so fascinating and full with magic." The ways in which Winnie writes about language demonstrates a strong affiliation not only with English, but with the United States as her present home. In this way, her narrative contrasts with Amy's, and with Cheng-Chih's, who are both much more tentative, or even reject affiliations with the U.S. and with English.

Linguistic Affiliations, Disciplinary Affiliations

We turn now to the interview responses from the graduate students with whom we spoke, to fill out our picture of ways in which Chinese international students at State University affiliate themselves with English, Chinese, and their other languages. Yi-fen, a PhD student in mathematical finance, described the most complex set of affiliations with Chinese languages. Yi-fen is from Shanghai, which is of course China's most international and prosperous city, blooming with rapid growth, filled with foreigners. Yi-fen identifies as a speaker of Shanghainese, a language that he describes as being for speaking and listening, not writing and reading, and which is not mutually intelligible with Mandarin. As Yi-fen describes it, Shanghainese is the language,

> for the local Shanghai people speak and listen to each other. It's international big city many like outcomers, but they don't really know each other. So that's why how show I was Shanghai native . . . whenever you like buy something at some local shop. If you say Shanghainese, you will get a low price.

His facility with and use of the local language allows him to claim an identity that is situated not only geographically or linguistically, but also as part of various social networks. As his education progressed, and he became more comfortable with Putonghua (Mandarin, or official "standard" Chinese), he sometimes experienced moments of conflict between his use of the official standard language and the expectations of his family and their circle: "so there will be cases when like I met up with some friends of my parents and after I start with Putonghua my parents will say, oh don't say that. Oh don't be so formal formal. Be careful. We are friends."

Yi-fen's detailed discussion of Shanghainese resists the linguistic and cultural totalization that students from China often experience when they study at U.S. educational institutions. Indeed, Heather, who grew up among friends who identified as speakers of Mandarin and Cantonese, and whose families had immigrated to Sydney from Hong Kong, Malaysia, and Singapore as well as mainland China, was surprised to hear faculty members in the Linguistics Department at State University referring to the language "Chinese"—she had never heard of such a language. For Yi-Fen, the use of Shanghainese and Mandarin affiliate him with quite different social groups, as we see in the earlier passage.

Similarly, Yi-fen's use of English clearly affiliates him with a professional, disciplinary community. When asked about whether he could give a presentation in his field of Mathematical finance in Mandarin, Yi-fen laughed and said, "That's much difficult. Yes because I know this word like a stochastic calculus in English, but sometimes it's difficult to translate into Chinese."

This response reflects a feeling narrated by many multilingual speakers: that their disciplinary expertise does not translate. In some ways we can draw a connecting line between the technical, grammar-and-vocabulary focused English that Yi-fen reports having been taught over many years in China, and this discipline-limited English in mathematical finance. Yi-fen relates a story about the relative uselessness of his Chinese English instruction for actually functioning in the United States; his example centers around the word "stationery":

> For example, like the Chinese we have we have been we have been told of English words, which is called the stationery which is weak which represent like those books like those notebooks pencils pens and rulers or something like that but in check but in America when I was trying to get myself a pen and I asked someone to say that if there's some stores around ourselves stationery and they do not know this word.

Heather notes that the term "stationery" is much more commonly used in the Commonwealth than it is in the U.S., so Yi-fen's experience in some ways mimics hers: even "knowing" a language does not mean being able to use it in a specific local context. Nonetheless, Yi-fen now feels affiliated with the U.S. and his English performance demonstrates as much: he has worked on his facility with everyday English and can now, for instance, conduct major transactions like buying cars, as well as giving presentations in "stochastic calculus."

And, finally, Yi-fen is strongly considering continuing in the United States after he finishes his graduate degree, noting that he has been on a transnational track from an early age:

> Most of my friends are in the U.S. now. Oh, that's my high school kind of they have like separate program for the for high school students, like preparing SAT, sometimes you've like that and so they choose they pay more money to choose that road.

Yi-fen gives us a picture of a transnational, translingual, professionalized student, who not only understands the roles that each of his main languages play in his life, but can also discuss how they complement each other, and indeed occupy different spheres. It is clear that Yi-fen struggles much less to perform a transnational, translingual identity than some of the undergraduate students we discussed previously, and than the graduate student, Qianqian, whose interview responses we explore later. Furthermore, Yi-fen's responses suggest that he is working within the context of significant family resources, supporting him on his transnational and translingual path for many years. Access to money, however, may be assumed of many Chinese international students, but it is not a universal experience by any means.

Qianqian, for instance, reports experiences that are framed not only by hardship based on poverty—graduate student stipends tend not to provide very much money to live on without supplementation from other sources—but also by long-term challenges with learning English, and limited social connections with the broader U.S. culture. We see in her interview responses something of a performance of a translingual, transnational identity, but it is much more tenuous, colored by the difficulties she has experienced as she has tried to "cross" into English, even as she now declares English as "her friend" in her intellectual autobiography, written in Nela's course in the Graduate Academic Success Program (GASP).

Of the students who were interviewed, Qianqian, a violin performance PhD student originally from Taiwan, described the most difficulties with her immersion in academic English. Before coming to State University, Qianqian had completed her masters degree at a university in a southern U.S. state. She recounted, in her intellectual autobiography, that before she was accepted at this southern university, her applications to study at many other U.S. institutions had been rejected because of "her English." She experienced a great deal of anxiety about her use of English, saying in her interview that:

> [Although I wanted to come to the U.S.,] I delayed applying for a few years because I am afraid of English actually my biggest fear like that time. I don't think I have any issue for like perform in front of people. I have issues use English. So when I decide like really come to America and I still struggle with English and still but I mean now I can talk. I

still remember I have worked for years ago. When I first speak English just sounds like so ridiculous. Like I only use a single word trying to put things together trying to express myself very hard.

However, in her intellectual autobiography, Qianqian writes that after participating in two U.S. graduate programs, she "I started to be the friend with English." Certainly, Qianqian's responses in the interview, and most of her intellectual autobiography goes into detail about the difficulties she has had in her acquisition of English that she is comfortable with and confident in using. But these eight words—"I started to be the friend with English"—narrate a current language affiliation that differs from a difficult past. Indeed, even when Qianqian said that "I still struggle with English" in the interview, she ends that sentence with "but I mean now I can talk." Qianqian claims an affiliation with English in her interview and intellectual autobiography, even as her narrative shows a struggle to affiliate. While she exerts agency over her linguistic performance, it is the product of much exertion—she seems to want a connection with English in order to fulfill her professional goals, but these goals are not supported by English affiliation in other areas of her life. We note, too, that her description here focuses on speech, and talking, which Nela suggests is often a neglected part of international students' professional development: after all, they not only need to be able to write and perform in their disciplines, they need to be able to talk in them too.

Qianqian relates a strong cultural connection to the United States in her love of Disney movies, out of which she also finds a connection with English, and which also allows her to make social connections too: "I love to watch Disney cartoons Hollywood of mine. Okay, when I got here that kind [of] topic become the connection between me and my friend here. So I realized oh, I actually connect with English more than I thought."

However, despite the connection she claims, integrating all the different English-oriented parts of her life is challenging. She says:

> Outside the classroom my social life here is pretty small. But I mean I have to make regular contact with one of my American friend here. This one Chinese friend, one Korean friends, but mostly I will hang out with my church friends. They're all Taiwanese.

Nonetheless, while Qianqian does intend to return to Taiwan, she sees a place for herself in the United States in the immediate future after she completes her graduate program: "Long-term goal that I want to go back to Taiwan to help our education, but short term goal want to stay here for the new year what could experience it become an educator and performer."

This gesture towards the future, like Yi-fen's, are important because they show deliberate transnational affiliations. The plans that Qianqian is making contextualize the linguistic work that she is doing, suggesting why she still exerts herself in her struggle with talking, when, as students such as those in Chang and Kanno (2010) indicate that for certain disciplines, an engagement with everyday English is not really necessary for disciplinary success in some PhD programs.

These two graduate students, unlike the undergraduates, exhibit the results of the pressure to perform expertise—in English and in their disciplines—while the undergraduates have more space to perform studentness, and being on a learning trajectory. But more than anything else, what these narratives demonstrate to us is that just as there is no one language that is "Chinese," there is no one "Chinese" international student. This observation may seem obvious, but institutional policies, even the most well-intentioned, tend to totalize international students from non-English speaking countries, and Chinese students in particular. The students whose narratives we explore in this chapter relate a wide variety of relationships to their "Chinese(s)," to English, and to other languages. Some are confident in their relationships with and affiliation to English; others narrate a rather more tentative trajectory of improvement, and one, Amy, describes reading and writing in English as a terrible thing in her life—but also indicates that reading and writing was not a successful endeavor for her in Chinese either. In several ways, these reflections confound our expectations of a linear trajectory of improvement, showing what we might call a spiral trajectory instead. We can draw some connections between individual international students—Winnie and Qianqian and Jared all describe long-term mobility in the United States, Qianqian and Amy describe social and linguistic isolation; Yi-fen and Winnie and Yang describe language affiliations that stretch far beyond English and Mandarin. Amy and Yi-fen describe an affinity for technical, disciplinary discourses rather than "everyday" English, and Cheng-Chih and Yang describe how, for them, English fuddles their minds. But in this chapter we can offer no real summing up of the identity of international students, and so, rather, we end with an entreaty, which is: support for international students needs to be an encompassing effort, perhaps starting with English proficiency and support for students' immersion into English-medium academic discourses and into English-medium reading and writing. But it should also address students' professional and psychosocial development, even, and perhaps because, international students look administratively like sojourners in the United States, but who, in their ambitions and those of their families, may well be on their way to integrated transnational and translingual lives in the United States.

References

Ahearn, L. M. (2001). Language and agency. *Annual Review of Anthropology, 30*, 109–137.
Andrade, M. S. (2006). International students in English-speaking universities: Adjustment factors. *Journal of Research in International Education, 5*(2), 131–154.

Angelova, M., & Riazantseva, A. (1999). "If you don't tell me, how can I know?" A case study of four international students learning to write the US way. *Written Communication, 16*(4), 491–525.

Chang, Y. J., & Kanno, Y. (2010). NNES doctoral students in English-speaking academe: The nexus between language and discipline. *Applied Linguistics, 31*(5), 671–692.

Duranti, A. (2004). Agency in language. In *A companion to linguistic anthropology* (pp. 451–473). Oxford and Malden, MA: Blackwells.

EAP II. (2019). *State University course catalog*. Retrieved from https://wp.rutgers.edu/academics/undergraduate/courses/630-356-156-ead-ii

Eldaba, A. A., & Isbell, J. K. (2018). Writing gravity: International female graduate students' academic writing experiences. *Journal of International Students, 8*(4), 1879–1890.

Flores, N., & Rosa, J. (2015). Undoing appropriateness: Raciolinguistic ideologies and language diversity in education. *Harvard Educational Review, 85*(2), 149–171.

Inayatulla, S. A. (2013). Beyond the dark closet: Reconsidering literacy narratives as performative artifacts. *Journal of Basic Writing, 32*(2), 5–27.

Karp, I. (1986). Agency and social theory: A review of Anthony Giddens. *American Ethnologist, 13*(1), 131–137.

Leung, C., Harris, R., & Rampton, B. (1997). The idealized native speaker, reified ethnicities, and classroom realities. *TESOL Quarterly, 31*(3), 543–560.

Ortmeier-Hooper, C. (2008). English may be my second language, but I'm not "ESL". *College Composition and Communication, 59*(3), 389–419.

Rampton, B. (1990). Displacing the "native speaker": Expertise, affiliation and inheritance. *ELT Journal, 44*, 97–101.

Ravichandran, S., Kretovics, M., Kirby, K., & Ghosh, A. (2017). Strategies to address English language writing challenges faced by international graduate students in the US. *Journal of International Students, 7*(3), 3–7.

Shang-Butler, H. (2015). *Great expectations: A qualitative study of how Chinese graduate students navigate academic writing expectations in US higher education*. Unpublished doctoral dissertation. University of Rochester.

Shapiro, S., Cox, M., Shuck, G., & Simnitt, E. (2016). Teaching for agency: From appreciating linguistic diversity to empowering student writers. *Composition Studies, 44*(1), 31.

Sharma, S. (2019). Focusing on graduate international students. *Journal of International Students, 9*(3), i–xi.

Shuck, G. (2010). Language identity, agency, and context: The shifting meanings of "multilingual". In M. Cox, J. Jordan, C. Ortmeier-Hooper, & G. Gray-Schwartz (Eds.), *Reinventing identities in second language writing* (pp. 117–138). Urbana, IL: NCTE.

7

CONFESSIONS OF A (RECOVERING) MONOLINGUAL

Translingual Moments and Excursions in Language Ideology

Jonathan Hall

1

Everybody wants to talk English. In many countries around the world, it is becoming imperative for almost everyone to know at least enough English to pass an exam, or to communicate in certain situations. As a "native" English speaker, whenever I travel abroad I sometimes find myself in the role of an ambivalent ambassador of the language, a walking opportunity for practice, an involuntary representative of linguistic colonialism, all of which heightens my sense of my own language identity, sometimes in uncomfortable ways.

Often people want to talk English in the sense that they want to "talk about" English, what it means in their lives. And I guess that my status as a "native speaker" gives me a certain air of authority about it, plus of course I have a professional interest in understanding the ways in which students in my classes and millions like them function across multiple languages at once, transing the interstices between languages.

I call myself a "recovering monolingual" in the same half-ironic way that I call myself a "recovering Catholic": in both cases I have been exposed from the earliest portion of my life to an extremely powerful and pervasive ideology that has exerted, and continues to exert, systematic pressure in both conscious and unconscious ways. For a middle-class white man like me, in the case of monolingualist ideology, much of the catechism is conveyed through unspoken assumptions, woven throughout our educational, economic, and political systems. It's regarded as natural that one person speaks only one language, and that one language defines a national identity. "Foreign" languages are just that: foreign, not part of "us," not that important, at best a nice "accomplishment" to have, like playing the piano. Though I use the metaphor of "recovery," monolingualism is not a disease, nor an addiction, but it is definitely a condition, one that I, along with so many in the United States and elsewhere, acquired simply from living in the culture.

I would like to share a few signposts in my own language-learning journey, as well as some of the translingual moments that have, for me, shined a faint light into the complex experiences of people I have met along the way. I make no claim to fully understand the experience of systemic monolingualism for those who do not share the privilege of a white U.S. middle-class English "native speaker," but here are some of the excursions into language ideology that have helped me come to some kind of preliminary understanding. None of these vignettes are earth-shaking or dramatic—but that's really the point. Translinguality is not something weird and rare; it is not (usually) something self-consciously transgressive or provocative; rather, it's a routine, everyday experience for millions of people all over the world. It's only a recovering monolingual like me who has to get on a plane in search of it.

2

I've been trying to learn Spanish for over fifty years now, on and off—mostly off. It started with a one-year teaser in second grade, when a harried-looking woman would stop in for about half an hour two or three times a week before running off to her next class in the next-door classroom or in the next school in the district of the suburb of Rochester, New York where I grew up. The next year the budget didn't pass, and foreign language wasn't like schoolbus transportation or sports, something that people cared about and that might get voted back in on a supplemental referendum, and so my first Spanish teacher was out of a job, and I was out of Spanish until high school. Did that one year of haphazard instruction, albeit during the "critical period" for language learning, perhaps help me with my pronunciation later on? Who knows?

So began my lifelong wrestling match with Spanish, which is really a grudge match with myself, which continues to this day. This novel of education mostly consists of non-education, mostly failure, especially in the early going, though recently things have been going much better as I think I've finally figured out how to learn a language. I'll take my share of the responsibility: I know at times I didn't take it seriously. Through four years of high school Spanish (only two, I believe, were required) I did my workbook grammar exercises, learned some factoids about Simon Bolivar and El Cid, wrote a paper about Fidel Castro, one page of which had to be in Spanish. I got some high school credits for it, and then in my first semester in college I tried to take a course that involved reading Latin American short stories. I'll always be glad that it introduced me to Borges and Cortazar, among others, but I only had a general sense of what was going on in those stories, even with the vocabulary apparatus provided.

So I failed to really learn Spanish. My early failures, though, I will contend, are not only mine alone. Not many people of my generation or my children's generation or now my grandchildren's generation are, in the United States, very likely at all to make the transition from monolingual English speakers to speakers of multiple languages. And that's a scandal. And it's also deliberate. "They don't speak English" has been something to hit immigrants over the head with since the nineteenth century. One nation, one language. One person, one language. It sounds almost democratic, this declaration of monolingualist ideology, but it's actually quite the opposite. And it's a powerful ideology, deeply entrenched in U.S. culture, not easy to shake off or transcend. Recovering Catholic, recovering monolingual, that's me.

3

Audrey was working as a bartender in an "Irish" bar in Buenos Aires. French by birth, she first worked in Barcelona for six months (in an "Australian" bar, her English already her meal ticket) and then three months here in Argentina, but she's still far more comfortable in English than in Spanish, and it's her command of English that continues to be her meal ticket, even in two Spanish-speaking countries. When I ordered my drink in Spanish, she was efficient but not communicative—I thought she didn't want to talk. But then I overheard her talking to her (Argentinian) colleague in English about a table of Europeans who had ordered expensive champagne and then Red Bull to put into it. I made a comment and we were off to the races.

Among other things she told me about a bunch of French guys who had come into the bar, already somewhat drunk, behaving rather obnoxiously so she decided not to address them in French, which would have necessitated a conversation she didn't want to have. They proceeded to talk among themselves, during the course of which conversation they made disparaging remarks about the bar, the wait staff, and Argentina in general, and they spoke loudly in French, confident that they were protected by the mask of their language. As they were paying at the end, she addressed them in French, and they profusely apologized.

"The French," Audrey remarked about her countrymen, "are like Americans." She meant that they are insular, and believe that anything that is not like it is at home is by definition inferior.

But the story's protagonists could not have been Americans at this point in time, though perhaps it could have been fifty years ago. Americans are very much aware that it's very likely the Spanish-speaking bartender also speaks English, or at least that somebody within earshot does; it's no longer possible to use English as a kind of insider code to exclude eavesdroppers.

4

If I'm still wrestling with Spanish after all this time, it's partly a matter of unfinished business: like many people, I studied Spanish for four years back in the 1970s, took one course at university level—and then concluded it was too hard.

As an undergraduate I decided to start over and studied German at college level, including a study abroad for six months in Heidelberg at a small English-medium college there. But just as the Spanish didn't take the first time around, neither did the German. I ended up hanging out at the Bier Bretzel drinking Weisenbier with my friend from Long Island, pretending to throw in German words whenever we could.

I also had a German friend named Manfred who I met at the mensa, the university cafeteria where you could get really cheap blutwurst, who, because he was my friend, would put up with speaking to me in German for a few minutes at a time, so I could practice, but then we would switch to English, which he was much better at, so we could actually talk. Even when speaking to a German it was hard to learn German, so far had English already penetrated, and this was in 1979.

5

Edson, an earnest young Brazilian, has a college degree in history. But now he is managing his family's bakery business in a provincial Brazilian city. He's not simply on vacation, he told me, but is rather on a mission to "get ideas" for running his business. "The world is big," he said, referring to an epiphany he'd had on an earlier trip to Peru. We spoke in English, though I offered to speak in Spanish. He said he hardly knew any Spanish at all, though I had naively assumed that beginning from a native Romance language like Portuguese, it would have been a fairly easy step to learn Spanish, and with his country literally surrounded by Spanish-speaking ones, that he would have practical motivation to do so.

But no: English is his traveling language. And a large part of his home life as well: he said that a lot of his knowledge of English came from watching English-language movies (mostly U.S.), and listening to music with English lyrics. So for Edson, English does serve as a lingua franca when traveling abroad, but it is also much more than that to him: it is an important part of his cultural life. He feels connected not only (and perhaps not even principally) to the U.S. per se, which he has never visited, though he did express curiosity about various cities. Rather, his shared experience of English language cultural products connects him with a common consciousness of people around the world, especially young people around the world, watching movies in English and singing along to English-language pop hits. Edson practically ached to be connected to the world, plugged in to something bigger, beyond his small Brazilian city.

One would think that if there were any business that could escape the juggernaut of globalization, it would be the bakery business. Its products are swiftly perishable, susceptible to local tastes and expectations, and they must be made daily. It is in no danger of being outsourced offshore. And yet clearly Edson did not think that way: he firmly believed, in a somewhat inchoate and yet fervent manner, that the success of his business—and his growth as a person—depended on plugging into a global consciousness, and that English was the wire that would make it possible for that crucial life-giving electricity to flow. "English," he said, "is the future."

6

In my mid-fifties, I decided to try Spanish again. My motivations for re-entering the fray of language learning are perhaps as murky as my reasons for giving up on it before. Or perhaps not. Some of them are probably personal to me—I don't like to fail at things, I was at a crossroads in my private life—but there are also professional reasons. My research has increasingly focused on multilingual students, especially their struggles and their triumphs in our writing courses on U.S. campuses. But I was always looking at it from the outside in, as a "native" U.S. English speaker trying to find ways to connect pedagogically with the experiences of the largely immigrant or domestic translingual student bodies with which I have been working for the past two decades on two different urban university campuses. Perhaps struggling (again) with learning another language might give me some faint idea of the much higher stakes language project that my students are pursuing?

Through my Spanish-learning trips, first to Guatemala and later to Argentina and to the Dominican Republic, I can't claim that I have experienced even an echo of what my students are going through as they work toward acquisition of various registers of academic English. But my hope is that the translingual pedagogy we explore in this book will help *them* to understand what they are going through, to give them the tools to work through the various levels of translingual experience, and that is more important than anything I come to comprehend.

7

A Dublin-born bartender in an "Irish" bar in Buenos Aires reproved me for ordering my drink in Spanish. "You're a Yank, aren't you? Why're you speaking Spanish?"

But still, when he told me the price of my beer, it was "Veintiocho pesos." He'd clearly memorized the prices in Spanish, the local language of commerce.

He was born in Ireland but he'd lived for ten years in the Bronx, and was planning to return to New York City, so we talked subways for a while.

When I told him that I was an English teacher, he skeptically remarked, in an exaggerated Irish brogue, "Imagine that! An American teaching English!"

8

So when I went to Guatemala several years ago for a language-learning visit of a few weeks, I thought that I would be starting over from scratch. I wasn't sure that I would remember anything at all. I had arranged to take Spanish lessons in the city of Antigua, Guatemala, for four hours a day for two weeks, and I figured that I would be back to square one.

On the ride from the airport in Guatemala City to Antigua, I managed, after greatly prolonged anxious hesitation, to ask the driver a carefully-rehearsed question about how far it was, even though I already knew the answer because I had looked it up online. But when I was actually able to ask the question, and to understand the answer, I was ecstatic, and it didn't even matter that neither the driver, not a chatty type, nor I, having shot my one shot, said another word during the entire 45-minute trip.

The main thing I discovered in the course of those Spanish lessons, and my evenings at the table of my homestay family, was that I knew a lot more Spanish than I thought I had. It wasn't like starting over from scratch, not at all, even though it had been thirty-five years since my last Spanish lesson. There's something odd about language: I studied calculus at the same time, and I seriously doubt that I would be able to recover my knowledge of that subject in two weeks to the extent that I activated my Spanish.

People sometimes say something like entiendo mas que puedo hablar. And they say that they learn from television programs, but that I don't understand at all. The hardest part of learning another language for me is listening, especially if people aren't speaking directly to me—a television program, an overheard conversation. That's hopeless for me. But if it's written down, if there are closed captions in Spanish, I understand everything. Sometimes if I can read it I can even begin to hear it. One time I had the English lyrics for a song in Spanish—and then I began to hear the Spanish words.

I remember one Monday morning's lesson in Guatemala, when my instructor in my one-on-one class tried to get me to narrate my weekend trip to Lake Atitlan, a famously scenic lake in the crater of a volcano. I had enjoyed my trip, and thought I had something to say about it, but I was incoherent when I tried to speak. So she had me write about it, and although there was nothing special about what I wrote that day—I still have it and I re-read it in preparation for writing this—I nevertheless found out its value that same evening when, at my homestay table, I was asked the same question: how was your weekend?

And then all of a sudden the floodgates opened and I was able to talk about it with some degree of coherence—because I had already written about it.

That's the story of my life right there.

9

They've got English on their minds.
They've got English in their minds.

No, this isn't an ELL exercise about preposition use. Rather, both propositions are true, and the first one is true, in part, because the second one is true. Everyone is wondering where all this is going. Will their other languages get completely swallowed up by English? Will their grandchildren or great-grandchildren all over the world speak nothing but English? What does it mean today to participate in the worldwide conversation that is going on in English 24 hours a day in every country, on the Internet, inside music headphones, in movie theaters, in classrooms, in bedrooms, inside everybody's head?

Does English become the language in which you do most of your thinking? Does English become the language in which you make love, in which you fantasize? In what language do you call out in celebration of a sports victory? In what language do you dream? If the whole world dreams in one language, does that mean that at some level they share the same dreams? Or, as Oscar Wilde once said of Britain and the United States, will we become billions of individuals, all separated from each other by a common language?

10

Gary, a U.S. expatriate I met in the same Irish bar, had taught EFL in Spain for twenty years, now retired to Buenos Aires. He was very much attached to the traditional mode under which the "native speaker" is the standard and the ideal and the judge of what is to be considered "proper English." Gary was very vehement in defending the rights of native speakers to ownership of English. "It's our language."

Without a TESOL degree nor indeed any particular training in the teaching of language, Gary's status as a native speaker had been his principal asset in his profession, and he was not interested in any of my theories about how English belongs to everyone now, that more people speak English as a second language than as a first, etc.

"No," he stoutly insisted, "It's our language. It's our language."

11

Antigua, Guatemala is a tourist magnet: we come for the ruins of the Spanish eighteenth-century city, destroyed by a massive earthquake in 1776, and we stay for the touristic infrastructure, the efficient transport to volcanos, lakes, and beaches, and for its many language schools. The Spanish spoken is laid back—the locals tend to speak slowly, pronounce all their consonants, which makes it an excellent place to learn Spanish.

Antigua also attracts, of course, entrepreneurs who want to profit from the tourist trade. Among these was a new café that had recently opened near my language school, and where I had gone for coffee a couple of times. The place was run, I soon learned, by a U.S. expatriate couple who had recently arrived in Antigua after ten years running a similar establishment in Honduras, on the Atlantic English-speaking islands. They were friendly, their coffee was good, so on my last day of class I invited my teacher, with whom I had shared four hours a day for two weeks, to go to the café. She blanched visibly when she saw the Starbucks-like prices, but I assured her that it was my treat, so she went up to the counter and tried to order some tea, in Spanish of course.

"Uh oh!" That was the reaction from the woman behind the counter. She wasn't used to anybody using Spanish in her business, and she clearly had not learned any even in her 10 years living abroad. I helped my teacher get what she wanted, and suggested, perhaps a little insolently, that there was an excellent Spanish language school just down the street.

12

It was the last night of a two and a half week trip to Northern Italy, and I was ordering my dinner at an outdoor table of a restaurant in a pedestrian street in Firenze. I ordered my meal and then added, "y una birra alla spina tambíen." I was a little proud of myself for having learned the "birra alla spina" meant draft beer.

Then two women seated at the next table asked, "Do you speak English?" That was definitely the first time I'd been asked that question, especially after they had heard me say something. "Do you mind if we smoke?"

I agreed, and then one of the women confessed that they had thought that I might have been from Spain because I had added the Spanish "tambíen" instead of the Italian "anche" (which, I have since learned, would have properly gone at the beginning of the clause instead of at the end).

It turns out that the women were from Germany. German is my third-best language—that is, my worst by a mile. Nevertheless, I probably would have understood if they had asked me in German: I do remember the word "rauchen" for "to smoke" and I would have figured out the rest from the context—especially since they already had their lighters and packs of cigarettes out on the table in front of them! But, of course, they never considered addressing me in German: I've heard it said that you can tell a German—or at least a German can spot a German—from a distance, just by the way they walk or sit. More to the point, especially if they thought that I was Spanish, the most likely common language would be, of course, English.

Clearly they had *some* Spanish, though, as they recognized my translingual mixing of Italian and Spanish. My pronunciation of tambíen must have been good enough to fool—well, to fool what were obviously two non-native speakers of Spanish. So, not to get too carried away, what I was proudest of was that they were, at least momentarily, in some doubt about whether I spoke English.

And of course they did speak English themselves. Perfectly. I told them about my experiences in Germany, back in 1979. And so we talked in English, and as soon as they found out I was from the U.S., of course the only topic of conversation, this being 2016, quickly became Donald Trump. This, of course, I was unable to explain in any language.

13

The persistence of monolingualism as an ideology in the U.S.: it's obviously getting more virulent, as incidents of people challenging the rights of others to speak Spanish in public places are all over the Internet these days.

I don't want to portray myself as a big world traveler. I know people who have been to exponentially more places than I have. But part of my motivation for traveling was to learn a language. And the hardest people to explain *that* to are those in my own country.

"Why would you want to do that? Can't you just go talk to the people at your corner bodega?" This from people who ought to know better, colleagues, educated people.

Well, first of all, the person at the local bodega probably speaks English. I remember one time standing in line at a sandwich place where one customer ordered in Spanish and chatted with the sandwich-making guy. The woman in line ahead of me then tried to order her sandwich in labored, high-school Spanish. The response, of course, was, "so do you want mayo or not?"

We're so attuned to the expectation of monolingualism in the U.S. that if somebody speaks Spanish we assume that they can't speak English. This is obviously untrue if you think about it for two seconds, but that's still the cultural belief. And probably the guy who ordered the sandwich in Spanish could have ordered it in English. Why did he not? Because speaking Spanish with another native Spanish speaker is a mark of identity, of continued cultural belonging. Because it would seem weird not to. As much as I want to practice my Spanish, if I meet another American or a Brit abroad, I'm going to speak English with them, even if they speak Spanish. Same when two native Spanish speakers, or two speakers of Caribbean Englishes, interact in New York. This seems pretty basic to me, but I have had to explain it to people, which is why I mention it here.

14

The restaurant in Milan was almost empty at dinner time, but close by at the next table was a middle-aged French couple, the man with about three buttons of his shirt unbuttoned revealing a hairy chest, his wife, sitting next to me on the banquette, was more formally put together. They didn't talk too much to each other, except about the menu, and the woman didn't say more than a few words to me—her English, it seemed, was not as active as his, or maybe she was just shy. But eventually, after hearing me order my dinner in really broken

Italian—this was my second night in Italy—from a waiter who didn't speak English, the man asked me, in English of course, "Do you speak Italian?"

"No," I admitted.

"Why not?" Well, that would be a long story, such as the one that I'm telling now, but as this was only my second brief trip to Italy in my life, it's unlikely that I would put in the effort to learn that language specifically.

But as the question seemed somewhat accusatory, I did feel the impulse to defend myself a bit. "I do speak Spanish," I insisted, "and sometimes I can get by using the Spanish word."

This seemed sufficient to modify his opinion of me, as he leaned back in his chair, and his tone was less accusatory, perhaps because he realized that I was not as stereotypically monolingual as Americans are generally thought to be. "Yes, that can work." He played a little with the wine list in front of him. "We do the same thing. We use the French word but pronounce it in the Italian manner. That works most of the time."

After we talked a little while, it turned out that although they were French they were actually living in Munich, because of his job, which, fortunately, took place mainly in an English-speaking workplace. Even with having studied German as a third language in school, he found the local Bairisch dialect nearly impenetrable.

15

Everyone wants to *talk English:* let's take that as an example of a frequently used but not fully "correct"—yet completely understandable—phrase, the kind of linguistic "mistake" often made by "non-native" English speakers—though even in "native speaker" English the distinction between *to speak* and to *talk* is porous.

And here's the thing for us, in our involuntary roles as "native" English speakers: if it bothers us, and we feel the impulse to want to make sure that the person saying it is made to understand that they really should say "*speak* English," then: here's another translingual moment. Presumably we understand the speaker's meaning. How will we respond? Will we stop the conversation to "correct" the person saying *talk English*? Or will we continue and, well, talk English with that person?

8
TRANSING PEDAGOGY

Introduction

In this chapter, we consider what a pedagogy that embraces trans-[1] might look like in the U.S. college classroom, going beyond the specific instantiations of transing—translinguality and transnationality—that we explore elsewhere in this volume. We explore the possibilities that transing pedagogy offers, and we outline the challenges and contradictions that coexist between the idea of transing pedagogy and an educational system that privileges and fosters normativity and an orientation towards "polished" final products, seeking to respond to Deborah Britzman's question, "Can pedagogy provide ethical responses that can bear to refuse the normalizing terms of origin and of fundamentalism, those that refuse subjection?" (2012, p. 293). We offer some specific methodologies to incorporate into classroom practice, which exemplify transing pedagogy in the ways in which they invite and encourage instructors and students to occupy a middle and liminal space, to chart a course between and through the normative categories that inhere in higher education more broadly, and the teaching of writing in particular. We interrogate and challenge power dynamics between programmatic imperatives and pedagogical possibilities, between instructors and students in our classrooms. We encourage writing to cultivate change, transform, interrogate, and disrupt at the programmatic as well as the course level. We envision transing pedagogy as the means by which we co-construct teaching and learning spaces, in which students are free to think and build a network between their experiences and their peers, their course materials and the possibilities for language use—normative and nonnormative—that are available to them. Transing pedagogy is comprised of two components: changing our habits of mind with respect to the ways in which we ask our students to approach their work, and committing to a socially-just stance which rejects fixity, stability, homogeneity, and monodirectionality in terms of the practices, positionalities, and "products" that we expect students to engage in and generate in our classrooms, the processes by which they approach these products, and the languages and identities they construct in the midst of enacting these processes. Transing pedagogy is a methodology or approach, not necessarily a content-level preoccupation with language and mobility, though these can be understood as important areas of exploration for a transing classroom. Perhaps most importantly, in our efforts to trans- pedagogy, we embrace the positionality offered by Maggie Nelson in The Argonauts, investigating "How to explain, in a culture frantic for resolution, that sometimes the shit stays messy" (2015, p. 53).

Transing Pedagogy: Transing as Method

Transing pedagogy is a methodology: there is no "transed" final product that occurs at the end of our classes. Indeed, a "transed" final product is antithetical to our project here, which focuses on continual negotiation. A final essay might look very similar to what comes out at the end of another class, but the process of getting there is rather different. Readers might indeed ask how transing pedagogy is distinct from enacting a general process pedagogy as in those advocated in the teaching of composition almost since the inception of the field. We would suggest that further theorizing and articulation of the processes of our pedagogy is still critical, especially when we consider the reality that the messiness that process pedagogy embraces tends not to have been permitted in contexts where black and brown, multilingual and transnational students are enrolled in classes, as even so-called progressive educators such as Peter Elbow show in their insistence on white English in the final product of a writing class (Elbow, 2012). Moreover, Lee (2017) notes that scholarship in applied linguistics and composition still "tends to be overly fixated on understanding how to improve students' proficiency in English" (p. 144), and we note that our disciplinary writing practices still reify binary distinctions such as formal and informal, reading and writing, writing and editing, student and writer, as though all these elements of the writing process were not mutually constitutive and in continual shifting relationship to one another. Stacey Waite writes,

> I think our teaching of composition asks us . . . to help our students "come into being through language" (Alexander & Gibson, 2004, p. 8) and to come into being means, in part, to become embodied, to appear as a body, to let Ben Franklin appear, to let your authorial hands appear. . . . Our teaching of composition asks us to engage with paradox, with difficulty, with failure, with the ambiguous blurs of articulation; it asks us to give new names to the interpretative and writerly moves we make, to revise those names when they fail us, or, as Bornstein (2013) puts it,

"every time we discover that the names . . . are somehow keeping us less than free"; it asks us, as teachers, to "decenter" our practices, and this might mean collaborating with our students, this might mean temporarily moving out from the center of our classrooms, it might mean generating new languages with each class rather than providing the language our students should use to talk about form.

(2017, p. 67)

With the conceptualization offered by Stacey Waite in mind, we reconsider some of the categories that structure college writing instruction. Some foundational ideas:

- Writing pedagogy is recursive, creating networks of ideas and language in which any singular goal is a contingent object, *even and especially as this makes assessment and evaluation more complex.*
- Genuine entanglements with subject matter knowledge are important, and so our current iterative models of college composition, where students apply rules with the expectation of a certain end point being achieved within the course of a semester, changing topics and practicing the same skills in discrete paper assignments, do not give students the opportunity to build the networks that, we suggest, we should offer them practice in building. This network building is the methodology that composition can transfer to other disciplines, but which we cannot enact if we treat content as incidental to our teaching practices.
- We challenge writing programs and other assessors and evaluators to create institutional structures that provide students with space to trans-. Doing so is particularly important because of the large and increasing numbers of contingent faculty who teach writing, who both need to be efficient and also promote "correctness" so they can be evaluated as "good teachers" who teach "transferrable skills" and thus who can be rehired. The adjunctification of writing programs across the U.S. shrinks the space available for pedagogical risk-taking. When instructors cannot take risks, students certainly cannot take risks.
- We ask instructors and program directors to not take any of our discipline's structuring terms for granted, in a challenge to what we consider to be composition pedagogy's normalizing tendencies.

Writing programs in the U.S. are often enmeshed within a neoliberal institutional context that emphasizes a bureaucratic conception of "assessment," that privileges achievement of known and limited goals over discovery and transcendence, that articulates learning objectives as measurable and unmoving destinations, that conceptualizes learning as linear movement along a predictable path toward a predetermined goal. Writing instructors in the post-modern university engage, on the one hand, with increasing student diversity of every kind within the same classroom, while, on the other hand, they experience relentless pressures toward standardization and reproducibility of learning results. It is within this context of contradictory forces impinging on classroom practices that the paradoxical space of transing pedagogy may open up. Pulled in opposite directions by the diversity of student identities and institutional demands for pedagogical homogenization, instructors may find transing pedagogy an impossible dream of reconciling incommensurable realities, or, on the contrary, a source of hope of finding a new praxis through embracing the liminal space between and beyond common assessment models and supposedly fixed identities of "instructor" and "student."

Transing

In the Introduction and in Chapter 4 of this volume, we offered Stryker, Currah, and Moore's conceptualization of trans- as a framework: "'Trans-' thus becomes the capillary space of connection and circulation between the macro- and micro-political registers through which the lives of bodies become enmeshed in the lives of nations, states, and capital-formations" (2008, p. 14). With this framework in mind, we consider transing pedagogy to be a methodology or set of methodologies by which we build our capacities to teach in this "capillary space of connection and circulation." We politically implicate our pedagogy as a way to equip students as they become "enmeshed in the lives of nations, states and captial-formations," while resisting the normativizing pressures of our educational institutions and the place that is continually being carved out for them in our late capitalist, globalized economies. As such, in our conception, transing pedagogy creates a space for students' and instructors' embodied identities realities even as these positions, these approaches are "self-conscious, web-like and fragmentary" (Waite, 2017, p. 15). We consider transing pedagogy as the building of a network of knowledge and skills in the classroom context that contingently connects instructor and student and text and language; as Perry and Medina (2011) discuss, learning is about movement and becoming. They write,

> Many poststructural theorists have taken up this notion of becoming, to replace the more traditional focus on *being* (Davies et al., 2001; Knight, 2009). Applying this to education, Ellsworth calls for a pedagogy that "address[es] a student that is not coincident with herself, but only with her change . . . a learning self that is in motion.
>
> *(2005, p. 7)*

Both of these conceptions of learning inform the ways in which we envision transing pedagogy, and its focus on movement. Transing rejects notions of stability and progress towards a defined goal, and strives instead to create networks of understanding, centering student performance and practices rather than "authentic" representation, and admitting, acknowledging, and perhaps embracing contradiction all as part of our understanding of student identities. Transing pedagogy includes creating and cultivating spaces in which students are encouraged and supported to think beyond boundaries, across disciplines, and toward transformative positions and practices, and contends with the normalizing systems of education that are imposed from day-to-day in our institutions. Rather than only fostering student agency on the individual level without challenging these systems, a transing pedagogy focuses *politically* on the system that students must engage with, particularly those from linguistically minoritized backgrounds, and endeavors to change it. In this political focus, it combines aspects of culturally-sustaining pedagogy (Paris, 2012), translanguaging pedagogy (Lee, 2017), decolonized pedagogies (e.g. McGregor, 2012; Kanu, 2011), and queer pedagogy (Waite, 2017).

We suggest, in fact, translinguality and transnationality are like the multitudes of gender expression and sexualities among our students, and faculty and staff: things that we always must recognize and contend with in their pervasiveness and which, as such, are everywhere and ordinary. But being ordinary is different from being normative, and transing pedagogy must not engage in the "flattening of language difference," Gilyard (2016, p. 284), or what Vivette Milson-Whyte describes as "ignoring sameness and difference while attempting to address difference" (2013, p. 121). There is, indeed, a difference between "normative and peripheralized Englishes" (Lee, 2017), just as there is a difference between queer and straight, white and black and brown. Ellen Cushman suggests what a trans- approach to composition teaching and scholarship could afford, via her consideration of the decolonizing potential of translingualism:

> Translingualism could also help the process of decolonizing thought and everyday languaging practices in composition scholarship and classrooms by helping scholars, teachers, and students dwell in the borders of colonial difference by using multiple scripts, media, languages, and English(es) as routine and integral parts of the teaching, learning, and knowledge making activities of universities.
> *(Cushman, 2016, p. 240)*

One critical understanding that we wish to highlight is that students' transnational and translingual affiliations are already, as Cushman puts it, "routine and integral parts of the teaching, learning, and knowledge making activities" of our students, but our institutional systems and structures severely limit what is "acceptable" in these ways. These limitations are adopted by our students, especially those who do not come from backgrounds of linguistic and educational privilege: as Vivette Milson-Whyte writes, "Teachers have to be prepared to have students decline invitations to code-mesh or disregard translingualism because these students live/operate in situations where languages are still treated as discrete systems" (2013, p. 121). Despite the best intentions of many faculty, for many students, declining such invitations seems like the safest option, in an educational system that upholds middle-class, metropolitan, white Englishes as not only the "standard," but the only "appropriate" Englishes for the higher education context (see Chapter 11 for further discussion). It is for these reasons that, from the outset, within our existing higher education structures, transing pedagogy may seem impossible.

The Contradictions of Transing Pedagogy

As we explored in the previous sections, we understand trans- to mean a repudiation of the destination, of directionality; instead, we take it to be an embrace of movement, of a middle and indeterminate space, of moving beyond. However, we recognize that education is usually a directional project: the descriptions of students' movement through the system that we use, officially and unofficially, tend to be built upon concepts such as progress, momentum, improvement, and development. These words imply a fixed endpoint, which is agreed upon by all parties involved: students, instructors, institutions. But nonetheless, as we illustrate in Chapter 11, this agreement is an enforced, hierarchical one, with aspects of it built upon raciolinguistic ideologies (Flores & Rosa, 2015) and the prioritization of the White gaze, and White ways of knowing. So in this chapter we propose a pedagogy that resists this enforced agreement by focusing on movement, and resisting normative expectations of linguistic and identity and performance, and supporting students' exploration of their raciolinguistic identities in a way that helps them to succeed while challenging hegemonic linguistic, cultural, and educational structures for the ways in which we define success.

In this way, transing pedagogy requires a different idea of the goals of teaching and of pedagogy, centered not so much on "improvement" and "achievement' but on movement between spaces which may not "belong," thus building on Ben Rampton's idea of language crossing (1993, 1995). Language crossing, Rampton writes,

> involves code alternation by people who are not accepted members of the group associated with the second language that they are using (code switching into varieties that are not generally thought to belong to them). This kind of switching involves a distinct sense of movement across social or ethnic boundaries and it raises issues of legitimacy which, in one way or another, participants need to negotiate in the course of their encounter.
>
> *(1995, p. 485)*

As David Bartholomae suggests in "Inventing the University," for many of our students, a foray into higher education is a crossing into these spaces where they are shown that their multiple languages and ways of knowing do not belong. Thus, we think of transing pedagogy as a pedagogical approach which facilitates this crossing, partially by de-emphasizing arrival, and focusing instead on, as Lee (2017) suggests, the approach students take to their work, rather than their achievement of a particular target. By doing so, we hope to challenge what the "targets" for higher education are, and render them multiple.

Transing Pedagogy's Antecedents

Several authors have considered the possibilities for a pedagogy that refers to or embraces trans- as a framing idea. In considering a pedagogy that builds on trans- particularly as a gender identity, s.j. miller writes,

> for new knowledges to emerge, classrooms must be thought of and taught rhizomatically, or as a networked space where relationships intersect, are concentric, do not intersect, can be parallel, nonparallel, perpendicular, obtuse and fragmented. Taken together, a theory of trans*+ness becomes a critical consciousness about how we read and are read by the world and a refusal for essentializations.
>
> *(2016, p. 3)*

In this chapter, we build on this concept of the classroom as a "networked space," particularly as one where relationships between texts and ideas can follow many paths, and where transing in the classroom centers on reading and being read. We also embrace the political aspects of "transpedagogies," articulated by Francisco J. Galarte who, in turn, builds on the definition of this term that was coined and conceptualized by Vic Muñoz and Ednie Kaeh Garrison. He writes,

> In a transpedagogical approach, processes of learning become political mechanisms through which identities can be shaped and desires mobilized and through which the experience of bodily materiality and everyday life can take form and acquire meaning. . . . Transpedagogies should offer students the tools they need to participate in the political and economic power structures that shape the boundaries of gender categories, with the goal of changing those structures in ways that create greater freedom. In a transpedagogical approach, processes of learning become political mechanisms through which identities can be shaped and desires mobilized and through which the experience of bodily materiality and everyday life can take form and acquire meaning.
>
> *(2014, pp. 146–147)*

Galarte's focus on mobilizing desire is particularly important here: in Chapter 4, we examine how identity formation can be thought of as being developed out of a network of desires. We seek to mobilize these desires in a teaching and learning space, where students use them to make meaning within, and exceeding, the frameworks of our courses. In developing an approach to transing pedagogies, we create room for this excess and these desires, as we see in many of our chapters, where we describe ways to create spaces for students to write how they want to. Stacey Waite describes queer pedagogy as a methodology that fosters particular habits of mind, rather than being a focus on a particular content or a particular kind of queer or queered product emanating from our writing classrooms. Waite writes that queer pedagogy is a site where we as instructors ask students to "inhabit positions" where they embrace "uncertainty, confusion, fluidity, self-reflexivity, multiplicity [and] embodiment" (Waite, 2017, p. 100), even as we know we and they will fail to keep them up. Just as queer is a resistance in the face of heteronormativity, so too is transing a resistance in the face of monolingualism, citizenship-based pedagogy and normativitized student-writer identities. Instead of telling students what they ought to become in educational spaces, transing pedagogies create room for us to negotiate with students about what and how they might perform in our courses, contending with the issues of legitimacy that Rampton suggests participants negotiate in instances of language crossing.

As we turn now more specifically to translinguality and translanguaging, Ellen Cushman offers what she sees as the wide range of possibilities afforded by translingual approaches to composition: "Translingual approaches can also work at the level of pedagogy wherein students' languages and categories of understanding can be expressed in the classroom in ways that allow these knowledges and practices to persevere" (Cushman, 2016, p. 235). The outcome of translingual approaches that Cushman suggests is important in the ways in which students' "languages and categories of understanding" are centered and negotiated in a sustaining way in the classroom. Jerry Won Lee, too, explores what he calls "translanguaging pedagogy," with a specific focus on the implications of translanguaging for evaluation and assessment. He writes

> Guided by a desire to promote linguistic social justice, translanguaging pedagogy emphasizes the negotiability of linguistic, cultural, and institutional expertise, and considers the inadequacy of universal evaluative criteria, while problematizing the translingual-monolingual binary. Translanguaging pedagogy decentralizes the instructor by not limiting students' language resources to those the instructor has prior competency in and does not position the instructor as the dominant interlocutor who solely determines what constitutes "effective" language use. Rather than reducing assessment to a determination of "how well a student writes," translanguaging pedagogy confronts the inequitable power

relations specifically in the classroom by understanding that different students have different objectives for English learning and instruction, and being taught how to produce a predetermined type of English, whether "monolingual" or "translingual," may or may not meet the varied needs of all students.

(Lee, 2017, p. 145)

In our conceptualization of what transing pedagogy might look like, we build on the ideas outlined previously. Miller's ideas about the networked space are similar to those that we put forward here, and their idea about "trans*+ness" being about reading and being read in the world is particularly important for our formulation of transing pedagogy in the writing classroom, as is the renegotiation of our "categories of understanding" suggested by Ellen Cushman, and a decentering of the instructor and institution in determining "effective language use," as described by Jerry Won Lee.

What Are the Possibilities of Transing Pedagogy?

Even as we draw on the perspectives on queer, trans- and translanguaging pedagogies outlined in the previous section, we question whether transing pedagogy is possible. Certainly, those who try to articulate "alternative" pedagogies, such as Stacey Waite and Jerry Won Lee, are tentative and somewhat reluctant in offering their own conceptualizations of queer pedagogy and translanguaging pedagogy respectively as transferrable to other instructors' classrooms, or as fully imagined "classroom ecologies" (Lee, 2017). In its focus on embodiment, movement and process, transing pedagogy operates in contradiction to the institutional structures, and focuses on forward momentum, distinct and polished products, and so on, which preoccupy higher education. Because of the connection that we see between queer and trans-, it seems to us that trans-, like queer, may well be one of "composition's impossible subjects" (Alexander & Rhodes, 2011, p. 179). Composition, and higher education more generally, in their "focus on a fetishized final product" (McRuer, 2004, p. 151), seem antithetical to the spirit and practice of transing, with its possibility of unending movement, and the necessity, within transing, for contingency. Furthermore, as Perriton and Reynolds (2004) discuss in the context of critical management education, but whose perspective is readily transferrable to other disciplinary teaching areas,

> the problem with any progressive pedagogical practice or theory is that it can maintain and in fact reify power differences between students and teachers, because the teachers give 'permission' for radical acts, because instructors are avatars and beneficiaries of the hegemonic system.
>
> *(Perriton & Reynolds, 2004, pp. 67–68)*

This reification of power is a concern for many scholars who consider and attempt translingual and queer pedagogies; they risk turning themselves into "the colonizer who refuses" (Memmi, 1965), "an individual who is employed to further the aims of colonialism, while refusing to believe in it" (Perriton & Reynolds, 2004, p. 72). Thus, the implementation of transing pedagogy must occur at the level of program and curriculum, rather than being left to individual instructors to attempt to enact, to make it an effective intervention in the perpetuation of higher education's normativizing categories.

And yet, the challenges that it poses are, in fact, the primary reasons that it is important to try transing pedagogy. Alexander and Rhodes (2011) write that

> grappling with the incommensurable spaces in composition allows us to approach our work not only with greater subtlety and sophistication, but with a greater understanding of the complexities—and impossibilities—inherent in any democratic project that wants to make a space for different voices, different views.
>
> (p. 154)

Transing pedagogy, and its methodology focused on developing habits of mind and habits of writing in students and instructors, rather than on the unattainable perfect final paper, admits the possibility of education being a negotiation between instructor and student, of student and institution, individualized rather than massified or industrialized. As the diversity of our institutions comes to better reflect the diversity of the population, the white straight citizenly ways of knowing on which the academy is built become more and more untenable. Transing pedagogy is necessary to avoid the traps either of "linguistic tourism" (Matsuda, 2014) and/or the consumption of transnational, translingual student writing as "a fashionable commodity" (Kubota, 2014, p. 487) that, nonetheless, has no currency, no force, beyond the composition classroom. Hence, we embark on an effort to see transing as a way to address real-life problems in the U.S. college classroom, now moving to center our discussion on our structuring terms (long challenged in composition) but with a particular focus on how these structuring terms cause problems for instructor engagement with transing students. Notably, we do not want student identities, assigned and performed, to be our only object of inquiry in our classrooms; they are not the content of our courses, but rather the context in which we always work. And we suggest that we need to push towards "seeing" and "hearing" authors, even as we reckon with their illegibility, their inscrutability in the context of our institutions (cf. Lee, 2017), rather than participating in the globalizing superconformity (Holborow, 2013) which invisibilizes the authors who are writing, in favor of a supposedly neutral "clear and concise language," which conforms to the linguistic norms of white, upper-middle class speakers and writers in Great Britain and North America (see also Hartse & Kubota, 2014).

Thus, transing pedagogy may be challenging, but it is urgent, especially in an educational environment where one extremely popular textbook for first year composition is entitled *They Say, I Say* (Graff & Birkenstein, 2018), setting students up in a binary relationship with published authors, and where students construct an argument via alignment or disagreement with singular positions taken in these texts. These alignments and disagreements happen one by one. Transing pedagogy, on the other hand, means charting a course through a network of ideas, and acknowledging that this course amounts to a performance, rather than a solid argument. Students can then be assessed on their work in approaching, rather than achieving the final product that instructors imagine when they develop a class assignment. As teachers, then, our responsibility is to understand the contingencies that inhere in a student's charting of a particular course on a particular day.

Transing Our Terms of Engagement

In this section, we challenge the existing schemas that prevail in dominant notions of the teaching of writing. Our concept of transing pedagogy as network-building forces us to reconsider our relationships with the normalizing centers of writing pedagogy, where pre-writing and "brainstorming" are separated from writing, where revision and editing is confounded with proof-reading, where class discussion often led by the instructor is offered as a precursor to writing and yet whose modes of engagement are often precluded from being included in students' writing. In these conceptualizations of what transing pedagogy might look like, then, we find spaces to occupy between these normalizing centers. Our first suggestion travels in the spaces between and beyond pre-writing and drafting; the second between revision and conversation, and the third between revision and editing. We do not claim that the ideas that we present here are revolutionary or even loudly disruptive. Rather, we want to offer generative frameworks and networks for repositioning students as writers, for renegotiating the student-instructor binary in our academic writing classrooms, and for engaging with the political problematics of higher education that disproportionately affect linguistically, racially, and raciolinguistically marginalized students.

Between Pre-Writing and Drafting

In our conceptualizations of pre-writing and drafting, we draw on Ben Rampton's sense of language crossing as going into and between spaces that aren't "ours" (1995). Transing these processes means rejecting clearly delineated lines between low stakes and high stakes, formal and informal, between what happens before writing, and when the writing happens. When we write, the stakes are simultaneously high and low—every encounter with text, someone else's or our own, is important in building a network, even if the thing that we have encountered does not make it as part of the final route that we map. But this takes time; and, instead, our institutions push us to make college writing urgent at the expense of making it meaningful. In the approach we suggest here, we seek to encourage our students to try out the networking, crossing model that experienced writers, like us, practice when we write, of charting courses between languages, experiences, identities, and texts, all the while knowing that while we design one particular route, there are several others available to us. We reject the word brainstorming because it obscures that groundwork, the connectedness that writing is built out of, and suggests that writing emerges out of some cataclysmic internal event, rather than as a careful performance of what we know and wish to express.

Furthermore, we build on Deborah Britzman's exploration of reading practices in the context of queer pedagogy, connecting reading with self and with language in the network we build in writing. She asks the following question:

> What if one thought about reading practices as problems of opening identifications, of working the capacity to imagine oneself differently precisely with respect to how one encounters another, and in how one encounters the self? What if how one reads the world turned upon the interest in thinking against one's thoughts, of creating a queer space where old certainties made no sense?
>
> *(Britzman, 2012, p. 297)*

We envision drafting to be the process in which students do their thinking in whatever language the idea emerges in, and in the language that enables them to express this idea as they wish to see it expressed. To enact these possibilities, we suggest the following as steps along the way of students' network-building:

Virtual writing alongside class discussion: Blogs and other virtual writing spaces offer a place for reflective engagement in writing with texts and framing ideas. Blogs can be graded, which sets aside the need for students to perform intrinsic motivation to begin engaging with the texts of the class, and the framing of themes and ideas. Or these virtual writing spaces can simply exist as an integral part of the process of generating ideas, as records and extensions of class discussions, or as sites where students can write themselves into ideas, Furthermore, blogging, or writing reading journals in electronic spaces, means that students already have writing that can be easily moved, rather than requiring students to translate and copy out their ideas and their words as they transfer them from classroom to paper to screen. Many composition instructors, in our experience, fetishize the use of paper for "free writing," "journalling," and drafting. We suggest exploring the fullness of electronic writing spaces as a way to facilitate students' network building in writing; virtual spaces can be sites of power for voices that are often silenced in class discussions and other modes of student interaction that draw on western models of argument and engagement.

No devil's advocate: Transing pedagogy suggests creating spaces for students to develop personal investments in engaging the ideas that we are introducing in our courses. Disengaged intellectual arguments have no place as we work on transing pedagogy. If students cannot find a personal—emotional/intellectual—investment in a writing project, that writing project solidifies the message that higher education is not for them. Hence, we suggest that it is critical to find ways for students to write themselves into some kind of personal investment in the intellectual work of reading. It is our responsibility to help students discover why and how they might want to engage with a particular reading—or where their antipathy to a text or a topic comes from, and thus how that engagement or lack of engagement might inform the network that they are building. Choosing texts from beyond the canons of the readings that circulate in composition textbooks—works in translation, works by non-Western and/or non-European authors—can support this network-building. It is also important that we find ways to help students write about personal experience in intellectually-engaged ways: autoethnography, for instance, builds a network between the "academic" and the personal in ways that provide affordances for students to care. Autoethnography, as a genre for writing and for reading, is also important in the work that it does to center the voices of writers and academics who are marginalized in the academy.[2]

Collecting quotations: We suggest that students collect quotations as nodes in the network that they are beginning to build, selecting parts of the texts that "speak" to them, rather than parts of the text that "speak" to the essay that must be written. Paraphrase and summary, which have been considered to be important skills for students to develop in their academic writing classes, sometimes make the building of networks unnecessarily complicated for novice writers to handle, because they obscure the distinction between the "normalizing centers" of the networks that we are asking our students to build, and our students' ideas (and thus incidentally create situations where unintended plagiarism occurs). Having students select quotations for their potential, rather than their functionality, within an already fixed framework (including "quotations" from their own experience), and write themselves into connections between these quotations as they build their networks: collecting quotations delineates a clear space of engagement. We imagine a network, after all, as being made up of distinct lines of connection, even as these distinctions can become hard to see as the network becomes more and more complex.

Recognized genres: We advocate for imagining projects for students to complete which occupy recognized genres beyond academic writing; that is, we encourage instructors to have students write in genres other than the "paper." We take as an interesting example the films that Michelle Cox describes her students making in Shapiro, Cox, Shuck, and Simnitt (2016). Cox writes that she

> sought to create optimal conditions for agency by inviting students into the academic conversation on second language writing, equipping students with the same literature and tools that academics have access to, and providing a venue for self-positioning as international students at Dartmouth.
>
> *(Shapiro et al., 2016, p. 43)*

We see "equipping students with the same literature and tools that academics have access to" as crucial to the project of transing pedagogy, as it disrupts the identity of "student" and offers a project that students might invest in.

Assignments that invite transing: What are the conditions that create opportunities for students to own their writing assignments? Can the structure of the assignment make transing more likely to occur, less a rarity and more an omnipresent possibility, for *more* students, ideally for *all* students? In answer to these questions, we suggest the following heuristics:

- There has to be some *space* in the assignment, some room for *choice*, some requirement that the student bring something to the assignment that is not just given to them.
- And yet: assignments have to offer structures within which students can begin their writing. These limitations may be liberating: good assignments force improvisation within a given key and a given rhythm, creating the context within which the student can take off on a solo.
- Assignments that invite transing call upon something that students bring from themselves, from their lives. But these assignments, in most subjects, will not be purely autobiographical: rather, they will require engagement with something beyond the self, with something unfamiliar, with something foreign and new. Transing assignments require that students can go beyond themselves and their own experiences, and bring in something from outside, and that students can transcend the strangeness of outside material by finding something familiar in it. They make space for students within the institutional structures that the assignment enacts, a place for authentic encounters between students and the materials of instruction.

Between and Beyond Revision and Conversation

Response and re-vision: One particularly vexed site of engagement between instructors and students is that of revision, and its ancillary apparatuses: instructor comments, peer review, conferencing, and assigning multiple drafts. Our goal in teaching revision is to have students to read their own writing, re-seeing it, and indeed, many institutions offer extra-curricular support structures to help with just this, studio courses and tutoring services being two particular interventions in the drafting and revision process that our field and our colleges and universities often invest in. In order, then, to trans- the ways in which we perform and teach response and revision, we consider ways in which to focus on connections between students and instructors, and students and their own writing, in such a way that they are fully present as embodied readers who seek to understand, rather than disembodied readers who read to react.

Embodied engagement: Academic English is well-known to be something of a disembodied discourse: "accents" and other characteristics that identify the author are supposed to be (i.e. should be and are imagined to be) erased in academic writing, *pace* the reality that Flores and Rosa (2015) articulate, that raciolinguistically profiled speakers and writers will be deemed to be not writing "appropriately" or "correctly" even when their speech and writing are objectively identical to that of white hegemonic speakers and writers. Furthermore, Hartse and Kubota (2014) discuss the tensions that arise between these expectations of "clean" academic English in published works from translingual and transnational scholars, and the desire to preserve authorial voices in their writing. It is against this backdrop that we suggest a practice of embodied engagement, where students' and instructors' literal voices and bodies become part of the teaching process.

Kazan (2005) writes, "Institutional spaces discourage us from thinking about ourselves as bodies. Teachers need to be aware of these erasures; otherwise, we condone them" (p. 394). Focusing on the need for awareness that Kazan articulates, we suggest that transing pedagogy means being aware of not just teaching "what" and "that" (Conquergood, 2002), but also being actively aware of "how" we teach and learn, and who is doing the teaching and learning. For example, Jonathan sees one-on-one student conferencing as the most important part of his pedagogy over the course of the semester, providing a space in which the instructor and student can see each other as people, and negotiate the terms of engagement between writer and audience. We might indeed see conferences with students as performative moments, in which we must be aware of the space that we and our students occupy, as described in Perry and Medina (2011): even where we stand or sit, whether we move or stay still, who talks first, and so on, are ways in which we construct relationships of power, and thus set the terms of negotiation in a conference setting.

But embodied engagement goes beyond seeing and knowing "how" and "who" in pedagogical spaces, and means also having instructors—and most specifically white instructors whose authority and right to be in the role of "teacher" tends to be uncontested (see Wagner & Shahjahan, 2015, p. 246)—initiate conversations about racial and raciolinguistic dynamics in our classrooms or in student-instructor interactions on a personal level. We particularly encourage white instructors to address their own whiteness and the privilege that accompanies it, and to acknowledge and address racial difference and how racial difference impacts linguistic prestige and acceptance. Acknowledging racial and raciolinguistic difference is often—perhaps surprisingly—hard for white instructors, who may adopt a "color-blind" positionality in their teaching, but which can mean that their syllabi and text selections are also "color-blind," which, in turn, manifests itself as white, and/or whitemale, as Toni Morrison puts it (Morrison, 1988). As bell hooks has written, it is only the most privileged who have the option of denying their bodies (hooks, 1994). So, for instructors, especially white cisgender so-called "native English speaking" instructors, acting as though we have bodies and also that we can see students as people rather than as students would go a long way to transing our pedagogies.[3]

Between and Beyond Revision and Editing

Editing is often conflated with proof-reading in our classroom contexts, rather than being seen as either a negotiation that is part of revision, and which is deeply connected to students navigating what are effective uses of language for their purposes in what they are writing. Indeed, editing, as engagement at the sentence-level, has often been centered as a project on making the writer as an embodied person disappear; as our undergraduate student writers in Chapter 6 describe, for example, that at the beginning of the semester, their focus tends to be on vocabulary and grammar, and "fixing" the Chinese logics of their writing so that it conforms to the rubric which defines the space in which they are working in EAP. Since editing, even more than drafting, is about the assertion and negotiation of power over singular text, whereas drafting is often about generating connections between multiple texts, and so admits a certain amount of being "out of control," editing can reify hierarchical relationships, especially between student writers and editor/instructors. We suggest that writers have to have power to be "edited" effectively; that is, they need to be able to negotiate with their editor, rather than just submit to them. Thus, we seek to trans- the idea and the processing of "editing" in instructional contexts, reframing editing as "effective use of language" which is not just a euphemism for "correcting" writing. Indeed, a focus on the effective use of language goes far beyond—indeed, it transes—discussions of form and function and focuses on context, audience, project goal, and engages students in the practice of negotiating meaning. Other authors have discussed how using a focus on the sentence-level can be a site of engagement with audience and purpose (e.g. Kolln & Gray, 2007; Micciche, 2004, Larsen-Freeman, 2001). But all of these frameworks, of course, do little to challenge ideas of "appropriateness" in academic contexts; appropriateness, as Flores and Rosa (2015) demonstrate, can be used as a cover for the perpetuation of raciolinguistic ideologies in the academy.

Conclusion: Transing Pedagogy, Diversifying Meanings

In his essay, "Translingual English," Alastair Pennycook describes Indian English as "chimerical," emerging from an "unimaginable community" that is an insecure notion of "nation-India" (Pennycook, 2008, 30.2, citing Krishnaswamy & Burde, 1998, p. 63). In this chapter, we have suggested that we might think of academic writing as the same kind of chimera, emerging from an "unimaginable community" that is built on insecure and shifting foundations, despite the strong push in academia towards normalization and totalization. Such an approach focuses on the communicative effectiveness of the academic writings that emerge from classrooms in which we trans- our pedagogy, rather than comparing these writings to programmatic standards, or student learning outcomes. It might indeed make assessment and evaluation more challenging, but we hope that these challenges help us to rethink our expectations and the ways in which we write our learning outcomes, rather than placing the responsibility for change only on our students.

In our discussion of transing pedagogy, we offer a model of teaching similar to that which Kramsch imagines for English language teachers, in which they "diversify meanings, point to meanings not chosen, and bring to light other possible meanings that have been forgotten by history or covered up by politics" (2006, p. 103). This approach centers the negotiation of meaning through language use, involving instructor and students in that negotiation and framing the instructor's role as one of helping students think through the consequences of their decisions, and then supporting students in following through on those choices rather than sanctioning and limiting the choices that we "allow" our students to make. And finally, we suggest that we consider academic writing as a lingua franca, rather than a reified product governed only by top-down conventions: as Canagarajah (2007) suggests for lingua franca English (LFE), in academic writing "there is no meaning for form, grammar, of language ability outside the realm of practice. LFE is not a product located in the mind of the speaker; it is a social process constantly reconstructed in sensitivity to environmental factors" (p. 94). Transing pedagogy highlights the localities in which our student writers are embedded, and focuses on pedagogical interactions in which we start from the premise that what instructors and students have to offer in classroom contexts are of equal value.

Notes

1. In this chapter, we refer to trans- either as such, with the hyphen suggesting a readiness to be appended to another noun, or as transing. We avoid "trans-ed" and "transness," as they suggest static states, where at the core of what we want to suggest about trans- and transing is a dynamic readiness for movement, or a state of being in motion, with all the discomforts that that might bring. The term "trans*+ness" comes from s.j. miller, and appears later in this chapter.

2. See Canagarajah (2012), Inayatulla and Robinson (2019), Griffin (2012) for discussions of autoethnography as particularly important for people whose identities tend to be marginalized in academic contexts. See also Gunzenhauser and Gerstl-Pepin (2006) and their discussion of students' "life-projects," and our further discussion of Intellectual Autobiographies in Chapters 6 and 13.
3. For further discussion, we refer the reader to Wagner and Shahjahan (2015), Perry and Medina (2011), Lugo-Lugo (2012), Kazan (2005), Nguyen and Larson (2015), Swan (2005), Wilcox (2009), Knoblauch (2012) and references therein.

References

Alexander, J., & Gibson, M. (2004). Queer composition (s): Queer theory in the writing classroom. *JAC, 24*(1), 1–21.

Alexander, J., & Rhodes, J. (2011). Queer: An impossible subject for composition. *JAC, 31*(2), 177–206.

Bornstein, K. (2013). *Gender outlaw: On men, women and the rest of us.* New York and London: Routledge.

Britzman, D. P. (2012). Queer pedagogy and its strange techniques. *Counterpoints, 367,* 292–308.

Canagarajah, A. S. (2007). The ecology of global English. *International Multilingual Research Journal, 1*(2), 89–100.

Canagarajah, A. S. (2012). Teacher development in a global profession: An autoethnography. *TESOL Quarterly, 46*(2), 258–279.

Conquergood, D. (2002). Performance studies: Interventions and radical research. *TDR: The Drama Review, 46,* 145–156.

Cushman, E. (2016). Translingual and decolonial approaches to meaning making. *College English, 78*(3), 234.

Davies, B., Dormer, S., Gannon, S., Laws, C., Rocco, S., Taguchi, H. L., & McCann, H. (2001). Becoming schoolgirls: The ambivalent project of subjectification. *Gender & Education, 13*(2), 167–182.

Elbow, P. (2012). *Vernacular eloquence: What speech can bring to writing.* Oxford: Oxford University Press.

Ellsworth, E. (2005). *Places of learning: Media, architecture, pedagogy.* New York and London: Routledge.

Flores, N., & Rosa, J. (2015). Undoing appropriateness: Raciolinguistic ideologies and language diversity in education. *Harvard Educational Review, 85*(2), 149–301.

Galarte, F. J. (2014). Pedagogy. *Transgender Studies Quarterly, 1*(1–2), 145–148.

Gilyard, K. (2016). The rhetoric of translingualism. *College English, 78*(3), 284.

Graff, G., & Birkenstein, C. (2018). *They say, I say: The moves that matter in academic writing* (4th ed.). New York: W. W. Norton & Company.

Griffin, R. A. (2012). I AM an angry Black woman: Black feminist autoethnography, voice, and resistance. *Womens Studies in Communication, 35*(2), 138–157.

Gunzenhauser, M. G., & Gerstl-Pepin, C. I. (2006). Engaging graduate education: A pedagogy for epistemological and theoretical diversity. *The Review of Higher Education, 29*(3), 319–346.

Hartse, J. H., & Kubota, R. (2014). Pluralizing English? Variation in high-stakes academic texts and challenges of copyediting. *Journal of Second Language Writing, 24,* 71–82.

Holborow, M. (2013). *Applied linguistics and the neoliberal university: American Association of Applied Linguistics Presentation.* Dallas Sheraton, Dallas, TX, 17 March 2013. Invited Colloquium.

hooks, b. (1994). *Teaching to transgress*. New York: Routledge.
Inayatulla, S., & Robinson, H. (2019). "Backwards and in High Heels": The invisibility and underrepresentation of femme(inist) administrative labor in academia. *Administrative Theory & Praxis*, 1–21. https://doi.org/10.1080/10841806.2019.1659045
Kanu, Y. (2011). *Integrating aboriginal perspectives into the school curriculum: Purposes, possibilities, and challenges*. Toronto, ON: University of Toronto Press.
Kazan, T. (2005). Dancing bodies in the classroom: Moving toward an embodied pedagogy. *Pedagogy*, *5*(3), 379–408.
Knight, L. (2009). Dreaming of other spaces: What do we think about when we draw? *Psychology of Education Review*, *33*(1), 10–17.
Knoblauch, A. A. (2012). Bodies of knowledge: Definitions, delineations, and implications of embodied writing in the academy. *Composition Studies*, *40*(2), 50–65.
Kolln, M., & Gray, L. S. (2007). *Rhetorical grammar: Grammatical choices, rhetorical effects*. New York: Pearson Education.
Kramsch, C. (2006). The traffic in meaning. *Asia Pacific Journal of Education*, *26*(1), 99–104.
Krishnaswamy, N., & Burde, A. S. (1998). *The politics of Indians' English: Linguistic colonialism and the expanding English empire*. Oxford: Oxford University Press.
Kubota, R. (2014). The multi/plural turn, postcolonial theory, and neoliberal multiculturalism: Complicities and implications for applied linguistics. *Applied Linguistics*, *37*, 474–494.
Larsen-Freeman, D. (2001). Teaching grammar. *Teaching English as a Second or Foreign Language*, *3*, 251–266.
Lee, J. W. (2017). *The politics of translingualism: After Englishes*. New York: Routledge.
Lugo-Lugo, C. (2012). A prostitute, a servant and a customer service representative: A Latina in academia. In G. Gutierrez, Y. Niemann, C. Gonzalez, & A. Harris (Eds.), *Presumed incompetent: The intersections of race and class for women in academia* (pp. 40–49). Boulder, CO: University Press of Colorado.
Matsuda, P. K. (2014). The lure of translingual writing. *PMLA*, *129*(3), 478–483.
McGregor, H. (2012). *Decolonizing pedagogies teacher reference booklet*. Aboriginal Focus School, Vancouver School Board.
McRuer, R. (2004). Composing bodies; or, de-composition: Queer theory, disability studies, and alternative corporealities. *JAC*, *24*(1), 47–78.
Memmi, A. (1965). *The colonizer and the colonized*. Boston: Beacon Press.
Micciche, L. R. (2004). Making a case for rhetorical grammar. *College Composition and Communication*, *55*(4), 716–737.
Miller, S. J. (2016). Trans*+ ing classrooms: The pedagogy of refusal as mediator for learning. *Social Sciences*, *5*(3), 1–17.
Milson-Whyte, V. (2013). Pedagogical and socio-political implications of code-meshing in classrooms: Some considerations for a translingual orientation to writing. In A. S. Canagarajah (Ed.), *Literacy as translingual practice: Between communities and classrooms* (pp. 115–127). Routledge.
Morrison, T. (1988). *Unspeakable things unspoken: The Afro-American presence in American literature*. Tanner Lectures on Human Values, University of Michigan, 7 October 1988.
Nelson, M. (2015). *The Argonauts*. Minneapolis, MN: Graywolf Press.
Nguyen, D. J., & Larson, J. B. (2015). Don't forget about the body: Exploring the curricular possibilities of embodied pedagogy. *Innovative Higher Education*, *40*(4), 331–344.

Paris, D. (2012). Culturally sustaining pedagogy: A needed change in stance, terminology, and practice. *Educational Researcher*, *41*(3), 93–97.

Pennycook, A. (2008). Translingual English. *Australian Review of Applied Linguistics*, *31*(3), 30–31.

Perriton, L., & Reynolds, M. (2004). Critical management education: From pedagogy of possibility to pedagogy of refusal? *Management Learning*, *35*(1), 61–77.

Perry, M., & Medina, C. (2011). Embodiment and performance in pedagogy research: Investigating the possibility of the body in curriculum experience. *Journal of Curriculum Theorizing*, *27*(3), 62–75.

Rampton, B. (1993 [2018]). *Crossing: Language and ethnicity among adolescents* (3rd ed.). New York and London: Routledge.

Rampton, B. (1995). Language crossing and the problematisation of ethnicity and socialisation. *Pragmatics: Quarterly Publication of the International Pragmatics Association (IPrA)*, *5*(4), 485–513.

Shapiro, S., Cox, M., Shuck, G., & Simnitt, E. (2016). Teaching for agency: From appreciating linguistic diversity to empowering student writers. *Composition Studies*, *44*(1), 31.

Stryker, S., Currah, P., & Moore, L. J. (2008). Introduction: Trans-, trans, or transgender? *Women's Studies Quarterly*, *36*(3/4), 11–22.

Swan, E. (2005). On bodies, rhinestones, and pleasures: Women teaching managers. *Management Learning*, *36*(3), 317–333.

Wagner, A. E., & Shahjahan, R. A. (2015). Centering embodied learning in anti-oppressive pedagogy. *Teaching in Higher Education*, *20*(3), 244–254. http://doi.org/10.1080/13562517.2014.993963

Waite, S. (2017). *Teaching queer*. Pittsburgh, PA: University of Pittsburgh Press.

Wilcox, H. N. (2009). Embodied ways of knowing, pedagogies, and social justice: Inclusive science and beyond. *Feminist Formations*, *21*(2), 104–120.

PART II
Translingual Transnational Literacies

9
TRANSLANGUAGING, PERFORMANCE, AND THE ART OF NEGOTIATION

Heather Robinson

Part of the goal of a translingual pedagogy is to help students integrate their multiple language identities, and to create a classroom space in which students can perform these identities—*if they want to*. Translingual pedagogy asks instructors to provide students with the tools to articulate the relationships between, or to negotiate between, the components of their linguistic identities and help them see their plural linguistic expertise as a resource in an educational context. That is the goal. But we also seek translingual pedagogies that are not tokenistic and which neither marginalize nor patronize vernacular writing, nor require disclosures and demonstrations of an "authentic" linguistic identity. Hence, a pedagogy of translingual performance is important because it creates a space in which to approach translingual writing as a project in which we can teach students to think like authors of fiction, and so negotiate with an audience, rather than exposing themselves to their teachers and classmates without allowing them creative space to choose how any revelations or disclosures might happen. And, of course, our students are often already adept performers, because their educational success depends on it: as Inayatulla (2013) argues, "Playing to an audience's desires can be a profoundly useful skill. And without doubt, a student's ability to do this may be their key to success in a system where they are earning a grade" (p. 22). Our goal in implementing translingual pedagogies is to harness this skill into writing that expresses a student's linguistic identity as they want to construct it, not as it "ought" to be.

This chapter explores translanguaging in student writing, considering what kinds of writing assignments might encourage translingual writing among students, and what kinds of philosophical approaches to these translingual assignments instructors might best adopt. I begin by discussing the kinds of translanguaging that students at Urban College do on a regular basis, and the reasons behind this translanguaging. I move on to discuss how translingual writing can be incorporated into core pedagogies in the classroom—including formal assignments—considering the kinds of assignments that might give students space to perform translingually without requiring them to "out" themselves as translingual. Finally, I move on to explore the work of specific students, all from different linguistic backgrounds, but who are all adept translingual writers though their facility, as I will show, comes from different places.

What Is Translanguaging?

As we have discussed throughout this book, translanguaging, as Suresh Canagarajah puts it, refers to the "communicative competence of multilinguals" (2011, p. 403). Translanguaging, as we have argued, is an everyday practice for many, if not most, English speakers; it not only describes the back-and-forth between languages that multilingual speakers negotiate in their day to day interactions, but also the shifting between varieties of the same language that many speakers of the imperial colonial languages—English, Spanish, French, Portuguese— might produce as they engage with speakers from different geographical or socioeconomic backgrounds. For instance, I, as an Australian who has lived in the United States for 20 years, might speak in a more Australian version of English as I talk to my mum early in the morning, before she goes to bed. As I speak with the members of my department, I might later in the morning use a standardized version of educated American English, using a U.S. vocabulary (papers, grades, schedules-pronounced-skedules) and syntax, and then later, in my World Englishes class, I might go through a list of sentences that are or are not grammatical sentences in New York City, African-American English, and share, with my students, reliable grammaticality judgments for the sentences in our list.

Translanguaging is, according to Canagarajah (2011), "enacted in text by code-meshing" (p. 403). Code-meshing, a term coined by Young (2004), describes incorporating forms and structures from at least two languages or varieties of a language, sometimes alongside other systems of communication in text, such as non-textual symbols, and typographic variations, into the same text; for instance, standardized and non-standardized forms of English being included in the same sentence, both, together, being used to express an idea. We consider translanguaging and code-meshing as being separate from code-switching, where a speaker or writer keeps languages or varieties separate, usually in separate conversations, or separate texts. We might also consider code-switching to describe the narrative technique adopted by authors such as Zora Neale Hurston, who has her narrators "speak" in standardized English, but whose characters use a vernacular English in their dialogue with each other. As Canagarajah describes it, "whereas codeswitching treats language alternation as involving bilingual competence and switches between two different systems, codemeshing treats the languages as part of a single integrated system" (2011, p. 403).

I add to this discussion of translanguaging in writing the technique of "vernacular transcription," which Ashcroft, Griffiths, and Tiffin (2002) describe as a core characteristic of post-colonial writing. The act of writing down vernaculars to be read and interpreted by readers is a translingual act, as it requires the integration of a writer's spoken and written codes. Vernacular transcription differs from code-meshing in that it constitutes a sustained written engagement with a non-standardized, non-imperial variety of a language, foregrounding the primacy of spoken interaction in most human communities. And, importantly, it requires significant negotiation with an imagined audience, and with how easy the author wants to make comprehension for that audience. As I will discuss in more detail later, translanguaging—and code-meshing and vernacular transcription in particular—are linguistic techniques through which authors negotiate how much access they want to grant their audience to the cultural references that their writing encodes. As we see later, the degree to which the author grants this access can vary significantly from text to text, depending on the author's stance towards and their imagining of the audience for which the piece is intended.

Translingual pedagogies, as we discussed in the introduction, are particularly important given the linguistic diversity among students which is becoming the norm in higher education in the United States, and which is, indeed, becoming the norm in many areas of the country. The linguistic profile of the students of Urban College can, as Shondel Nero has shown (Nero, 2016), be directly mapped onto the linguistic profile of the metropolis where Urban College resides. In Chapter 2, we offered a nuanced look at how students at Urban College perceive their linguistic affiliations; we repeat some of that data in Table 9.1 to re-paint that picture of a group of students who are multilingual, and, as is most relevant for the present chapter, who speak several varieties of English. We note (again) that the total does not equal thirty-two, the

TABLE 9.1 What Englishes Do You Speak?

What Englishes do you speak?	N		N
Standard/Standardized	21	Dominican	2
American	10	Caribbean/West Indian	2
Ebonics/AAVE	9	Jamaican	2
Broken	8	Jargon	2
Creolese/Guyanese	6	Borough	2
Slang	4	Spanglish	2
Patois	4	British	1
Metropolitan	3	Trinidadian	1
Chicano	2		

number of respondents, because several students described more speaking than one variety of English.

There are a few points to note in Table 9.1. To begin, almost two-thirds of the students in the class identified as speakers of Standardized English; another ten described themselves as speaking "American English." Other students expressed an affiliation with Englishes associated with various national origins; others with different geographical origins. I note too, the use of the term, by the students, of "Ebonics," rather than AAVE, an acronym which in my experience students are familiar with. To explore students' preferences for "Ebonics" over "AAVE" is beyond the scope of this chapter, but nonetheless it is an interesting reclamation of a term that was the subject of so much controversy in the mid-1990s. But of course, many of these students were small children or not yet born at this time, and/or did not live in the United States. We also see significant numbers of responses that seem to offer a somewhat pejorative view of the Englishes that the students speak: they describe their Englishes as "Broken" (8) or "Slang" (4). Students who recorded these responses generally also described themselves as speaking standardized English as well. In fact, most students' responses to this question offered multiple Englishes: the following responses were typical:

- AAVE, American English.
- I don't know what to call them, but I would say that I speak slang, Spanglish, and the English of a person from Brooklyn as well as standard English when I need to.
- Standard, Ebonics, Broken Guyanese, Trinidadian, Jamaican (Caribbean) English.
- Standardize [sic], patois, ebonics/slang.

Importantly, these descriptions show that affiliations with various varieties of English do not always have to do with citizenship status in the various countries. Several students whose language inheritance (Rampton, 1990) is in the Anglophone Caribbean or in Africa identify as speaking AAVE; the one student who identified as a speaker of British English is almost certainly from the Caribbean. Our students' linguistic identities are intersectional (Crenshaw, 1990), just as their gender, racial, and national identities are. This flexibility and intersectionality of linguistic affiliation is extremely important when considering translanguaging in the classroom: a student's racial, ethnic or national identity may not provide any kind of accurate picture of what a student can do, linguistically, as Leung, Harris, and Rampton (1997) discuss eloquently.

Translanguaging Is a Part of Life

The monolingualist assumptions that tend to govern the U.S. college classroom, as Matsuda (2006) has shown, obscure an important aspect of the lived reality of students who come from underrepresented linguistic groups: that most people are active translanguagers, switching their language practices to suit the context throughout the day, every day. The difference with the students at Urban College is that they are often conscious of doing so. In the same survey from which the data in Table 9.1 is taken, students wrote, when asked how they changed their speech in response to the linguistic and social context, about the changes they made in terms of what each of their languages or varieties was for, as well as how their language use changed:

- Standard English is used to gain access to corporate America. Caribbean English is used around native and Caribbean Americans. Ebonics is used in various neighborhoods. I change it by switching words and dialects.
- Speak clearer and slower than when I'm talking to friends and family; my speech changes with tone, the speed at which my words are spoken; I may speak clearer, slower and often times when changing my speech, I change my posture by standing right, shoulders even; instead of using words or phrases like bed, word, bruh, fam, I would say words like sir, miss, yes, friend, etc.
- Depending on who I'm talking to and how comfortable I am with them. I change it by speaking slang instead of proper English; I pronounce things clearly and avoid slang words in professional settings. At home and with friends, I do not bother to completely pronounce words right or speak grammatically correct.

They also discuss the reasoning behind switching between languages and varieties:

- So they can understand better; because I've been told it's difficult to comprehend. For my and listener's comfort.
- I change it because I was taught to have manners. If I am at work, I am less likely to use patois or slang terms because it is not appropriate. Once home, I am more relaxed so there is no need to speak professionally.
- I change it because it is something everyone is expected to do. As a child, you noticed that your parents spoke freely at home, but on the phone, at the doctor's office, or at school, they spoke differently. I learned it through observation and it became routine.
- I was told to.
- Survival.

These responses show what people from the linguistic majority—and, indeed, most white people—take for granted: that standardized forms of English are associated with comfort, politeness for others, and with survival but also with strictures for translingual speakers. These responses also suggest just how adept and successful Urban College's students are as translanguagers, adapting their language to their audience as it changes, when it changes. They negotiate with their audience to achieve the results that they, the speakers, want to achieve. As Canagarajah (2006) puts it: "What they choose to display varies according to diverse contexts in order to achieve their interests" (p. 602). The negotiation in the traditional U.S. college classroom is, however, rather one sided: since the power resides on the side of the instructor, and of standardized English, the colonial language in a very literal sense, since many of the students at Urban College are immigrants or the children of immigrants from the former British colonies in the Caribbean, South Asia, and Africa (see Robinson (2019) for further discussion of the Urban College in its Caribbean linguistic context). Students find that they need to respond to the monolingualist requirements of classroom and institution, making choices about when the risks of using non-standardized Englishes outweigh the loss of "comfort" and instead the assumption of linguistic strictures that accompany using a standardized form of the language. For some students, avoiding risk is equivalent to maintaining comfort, and so they use standardized English at all times in an educational context. So, in the next section, I move on to theorize a pedagogy by means of which instructors can make the negotiation two-sided, where the risk of using non-standardized forms is reduced and/or made worth taking, and the real rewards attached to expressing a more integrated linguistic identity than has traditionally been allowed for students who are multilingual or speak multiple varieties of English.

Translanguaging and the Art of Negotiation

A "negotiation model" of linguistic research and the study of student writing is described in Canagarajah (2006), as a gesture towards changing the way instructors approach linguistic variation in student writing. He writes:

> Rather than studying multilingual writing as static, locating the writer within a language, we would study the movement of the writer between languages; rather than studying the product for descriptions of writing competence, we would study the process of composing in multiple languages; rather than studying the writer's stability in specific forms of linguistic or cultural competence, we would analyze his or her versatility (for example, life between multiple languages and cultures); rather than treating language or culture as the main variable, we would focus more on the changing contexts of communication, perhaps treating context as the main variable as writers switch their languages, discourses, and identities in response to this contextual change; rather than treating writers as passive, conditioned by their language and culture, we would treat them

as agentive, shuttling creatively between discourses to achieve their communicative objectives. As a precondition for conducting this inquiry, we have to stop treating any textual difference as an unconscious error. We must consider it as a strategic and creative choice by the author to attain his or her rhetorical objectives.

(pp. 590–591)

Here, Canagarajah outlines multiple ways in which a negotiation model would require repositioning how we read and evaluate multilingual student writing. Of particular importance in the passage is his emphasis on "the changing contexts of communication," whereby students and instructors would "treat context as the main variable as writers switch their languages, discourses, and identities in response to this contextual change," rather than "treating language and culture as the main variable." That is, teaching translingually requires a pedagogy in which instructors explicitly discuss and foreground context—genre and audience, authorial stance, and intent (and their perceived risks and consequences), for instance. It also requires incorporating translingual textual practice—writing—into the sentence level, and into formal writing assignments. This requires instructors to, as Canagarajah (2006) states, reorient themselves with respect to what they perceive to be error, and consider the purpose of every variation that a writer incorporates. Such a re-orientation pushes us to create new spaces for vernaculars in student writing, and so acknowledge students' agency in creating different stances, and their use of language to create different effects, in their school writing, along with reflection on the linguistic negotiation that vernacular writing requires.

Students' rhetorical objectives, as Canagarajah (2006) discusses, deserve more consideration as well. Traditionally, the objectives for any piece of writing that students complete in a classroom context are defined by the instructor. Furthermore, genres that are frequently assigned to students from underrepresented language backgrounds, such as literacy narratives, often ask—or even require—them to reveal details about their linguistic histories, and so ask them to trace what Inayatulla (2013) describes as "dark-to-light trajectories" as they move from primarily using their vernacular languages into proficiency in the standardized variety of English, if they ask them to explore their linguistic identities at all. As the multidirectional model of translanguaging (Canagarajah, 2015) implies, we need, rather, a model that builds in recursivity and creativity rather than revelation, outing, and transcription of "real" life.

When students are asked to write about their identities in either informal or formal writing, instructors often assume—and perhaps require—that students offer authentic disclosures of their linguistic identities. As Baillif (1997) discusses, while self-disclosure has been considered to be empowering for students, assignments that ask for self-disclosure come with a set of problematic assumptions:

> To suggest that a student is "empowered" through the act of disclosing that which has been suppressed or repressed is to presuppose an either/or "world of discourse divided between accepted discourse and excluded discourse" rather than constituted "as a multiplicity of discursive elements that can come into play in various strategies."
> (Foucault, 1980, p. 100, cited in Baillif, 1997, p. 79)

The problem with requiring authenticity from students from underrepresented groups is that it can lead to exoticizing or fetishizing their difference, their otherness, their non-standardness, while relegating it to a past that is disconnected from their standardized English-wielding future—because the presumption is that standardized English inscribes the only path to success at college. Requiring students to trace these dark-to-light trajectories ensures that, in academic contexts, their vernaculars and their standardized forms of English must be separated; that students' cultures and languages cannot mix. It also reinforces the idea that academic spaces are white spaces, where Brown and Black and immigrant students must be outsiders because their languages are the languages of outside, and if they want to be insiders, they must conform to the linguistic standards that are already in place.

Rather, and in development of the ideas in Chapter 4 and 8, I suggest that, to teach translingually, we also need to teach writing and identity work—especially where they intersect—as performance. Teaching a performative approach to writing can mean that students can choose a linguistic identity to express in their writing *even if they do not affiliate themselves with that language or variety in their everyday life.*

Creative Writing Assignments as Translingual Spaces

Creative writing assignments are useful replacements of or extensions for "literacy/language narrative" assignments, because they get us away from the "authenticity problem" of the literacy narrative and other personal writing. Language and literacy narratives can of course fuse the "authentic" and the "creative," but most of the models that we have of such pieces of writing—and those that are frequently assigned in composition and composition-like classes—are truly assigned as personal, "true" narratives. In my own experience, it is very hard for students to conceive of language narratives as "stories," rather than as "papers." For every one story that performs *some* narrative voice that may or may not be the student's, there are ten whose narrative voice is unequivocally that of the student writer. The presupposition of a requirement of disclosure limits the way that students imagine their audience:

while they are used to having to reveal themselves to their instructors, they may not be as comfortable doing so for their fellow students, and the idea of the assignment as story suggests that there will be an audience that is broader than the expected singular instructor. Thus, incorporating creative writing assignments that explore identity into a composition course, or into an English literature and language course can require that instructors work to overcome students' quite reasonable presumption that they are expected to write themselves. Creative writing assignments that ask students to use language that they would not normally use in their academic work, however, creates a space for them to write narrators and characters who are explicitly not them, and so opens up a space for a performance. Furthermore, students who write in the vernacular often have a stake in creating a good representation of the vernacular, but the distance that such writing can create between the instructor and the student can help to create an authorial persona because the student has to actively decide how much help they want to give their instructor in understanding the text. As we will see, students' decisions about that particular question can have many different forms, but in all cases vernacular writing helps students to take an authorial stance, and to decide what their use of the vernacular is for, because it always turns out to have a purpose beyond getting a good grade.

As such, creative writing is a type of writing that is well-suited to a translingual pedagogy, in that it provides a space designed for performance, and thus helps students work with language as a means of creative expression, rather than, necessarily, of "authentic" self-revelation. Because of our ever-growing transnational and translingual populations in institutions of higher education, creative writing forms a useful part of many curricula because it provides a kind of writing that is formal and thus can be graded (contra Elbow's (2002) imaginings of the place of vernaculars as being limited to journaling or free-writing, low stakes assignments, which must be eventually "translated" into a standardized variety of English). Creative writing has a valuable and assessable place in most college curricula, and can be effectively incorporated into composition and language classes as a generic pedagogical tool. Inayatulla (2013) writes, in the context of her discussion of basic writers' composition of literacy narratives, "performance becomes a tool for leveling or renegotiating an uneven playing field—one in which readers cannot gloss over the multiple or intersecting identities present on the pages of a narrative and in the unknowable, uncodable, behind-the-scenes space" (p. 24). Teaching translingual performance means treating the classroom as a space for negotiation, of making overt the assumptions that undergird not just our pedagogies and our relations with students, but also the unspoken, monolingualist contract between instructor and student that assumes that academic writing takes the same form, and makes the same sounds, in every classroom. Teaching performance makes instructors work harder because it makes us think about ourselves as audiences, rather than as consumers of the kind of work that our colleagues have prepared our students to produce before arriving in our classrooms.

Translanguaging in creative writing requires a critical engagement with language. But, as teachers of creative writing already know, it also requires critical engagement with other authors and other texts. A translingual pedagogy also provides models of what translingual writing might look like, through which students might imagine models for their own writing, and thence adopt and adapt those models as a foundation for their own construction of authority in writing. In creative writing, student writers must consciously adopt a persona, or develop characters, who speak in a certain way. In fact, most renditions of vernaculars that we see are performative, ornamental, in that they represent accent rather than syntactic variation. But when we see syntactic variation in student writing, it is important, as it signifies an understanding in the student writer that linguistic variation is not just about accent. Further, it contributes significantly to the creation of characters, or, indeed, the creation of a narrative voice for the student writer, which may not be the same as the student's.

Translanguaging as Performance

In the section which follows, I will discuss three examples of student writing taken from the World Englishes course that I teach at Urban College, and reflections on and descriptions of their language identities and motivations for writing taken from interviews and other writing done in class. We will see, in the first paper, a model of translingual performance that claims to follow the lead of Zora Neale Hurston and her linguistic separation of narrator and character in terms of their use of black English, but in fact shows vernacular transcription as an accomplished performance of a linguistic identity. The next student writer shows how translingual writing constructs and challenges its audience by code-meshing two languages, Urdu and English, in ways that make the text inaccessible to a monolingual English speaking reader. And the third example shows how an accomplished translingual writer can embrace a monolingual Anglophone audience while asserting a plurilingual identity in their writing and connecting with others from their linguistic community, again through strategic vernacular transcription.

Not every multidialectal or multilingual person is also a "natural translanguager." In the World Englishes class, many students have kept their languages and language codes strictly separate, and so do not construct their linguistic identities by code-meshing. Thus, when asked to incorporate vernaculars into their writing for class, learning to translanguage—whether by code-switching in the same text or by code-meshing—does not necessarily come easily. Choosing an "authorial," rather than a personal, stance can be a gateway into translanguaging for students who generally perform monolingual, monodialectal linguistic identities or who, alternatively, are adept code- and language-switchers and who keep those linguistic identities deliberately separate. Mimicking the translingual practices of authors of fiction or poetry that they have read in class helps them to translanguage successfully, and to find a stance from which to negotiate successfully with the audience. More generally, too, writing from the point of view of a narrator who is not the author provides students a resource to use in order to present linguistic variation positively. We see this linguistic separation between "character" and "narrator" in many of the short stories written by students in the World Englishes' classes. Susan Sniader Lanser explains a possible motivation for maintaining such a separation:

> Any project to authorize characters outside the social hegemony is already undermined by the conventions of narrative form. As Judy Grahn observes, "an outside and all-knowing narrator . . . speaks standard English while quoting characters who speak what is called 'dialect' or slang, or people's English . . . [as if to say] that the occupation of writer belongs only to the upper class and those who can *pass* by using its standards; no one else need apply—except as a *character*, an object to be quoted and described, an in effect, looked down upon from a class distance" (1978, pp. 10–11). The containment of black vernacular . . . to orthographically marked and framed "dialect" is an emblem of a larger containment of folk cultures in novelistic worlds where social and textual success is measured by educated white standards. Such a practice leaves formally unchallenged the implied race and class of realism's "generic" voice, the overarching consciousness that adopts an authorized language in order to forge a collusion between narrator and narratee.
>
> *(Lanser, 1992, p. 215)*

On the other hand, though, as Lanser writes, there is another stance to take, in which the author decides not to "negotiate" with the audience—which primarily means the professor in the context under discussion in this chapter but tells the story that she wants to tell without accommodating the professor's linguistic "needs." Lanser writes of Toni Morrison,

> One sees [in Morrison's] refusal [to explain anything in her novels] as well in a gradual decrease in her novels of the kind of Western intertext . . . Morrison . . . mak[ing] her work less bicultural, giving white readers less and less familiar material on which to ground readings that would assimilate her novels to a white tradition and "universalize" what is historically particular. . . . If *Sula* provides the white narratee a space in which race is not central, *Beloved's* narrator denies its narratee any such space, any location outside the anguished memories of slavery; the multiplicity of perspectives filtered as free indirect discourse through the narrative voice

disallows the safety of distance, while narrative comments make clear who is responsible for the horrors the novel represents.

(1992, p. 138)

This is the core choice that we see students making: accommodation of their readers' linguistic limitations, in mimicry of the language work that they feel they have had to do throughout their education; or, for the students who identify as more bilingual or bicultural, an emphasis on the non-white, non-dominant culture through a more seamless use of the author's vernacular in the language of both narrator and character. I will return to these contrasts in my discussion of the students' writing in the following paragraphs.

Brittany: I Only Speak Standard English

The author of the following writing assignment, Brittany, speaks Standardized American English. In the survey that she completed at the beginning the semester, she writes, "I USED to code-switch from standard to slang, depending on the groups of people was surrounded by" (emphasis Brittany's). She writes, "I am older now, and prefer to communicate in standard English at all times." In her responses to the interview questions, she writes again about how she consciously "gave up utilizing AAVE" in her teens. Brittany's kind of disaffiliation with AAVE seems to be somewhat widespread among students who have community and family connections to AAVE. However, where the World Englishes class opened up a set of new possibilities for acknowledging AAVE as a part of many students' linguistic identity, Brittany's responses and writing suggest that she was aware as a teenager that she was multidialectal and decided not to be. This is the reverse of the performances that we might often see, where students perform multiple linguistic identities through their language varieties: Brittany, instead, performs what she considers to be a singular linguistic identity no matter what the context. Other students who I have spoken with, of African-American or Afro-Caribbean descent, take a similar stance towards their own linguistic identity performances, whereby they claim only one language variety—standardized English—and view any suggestion that they might still be speaking a variety of African-American English, even one associated with a middle-class African-American community, as contradictory to their experience. For instance, another student, Danielle, writes:

> Being that I was always strived to be an excellent student, I always tried to stay away from using Ebonics so that I wouldn't get it mixed up with my Standard American English. It wasn't until my "blackness" got called into question that I started using Ebonics.

Unlike Danielle, Brittany does not see a need to assert her blackness by using AAVE. She identifies as speaking only standardized American English.

However, in the piece of writing that follows, Brittany writes her story entirely in African-American English. In her commentary on her writing, despite her declared mono-lingual, mono-dialectal linguistic affiliation, Brittany claims an affiliation and expertise in AAVE:

> I chose to use African American Vernacular English because it is my linguistic expertise, alongside Standard American English. Throughout middle school and my first two years of high school, AAVE was the language my friends and I used as our primary method of communication.
>
> (p. 5)

In these words, we see Brittany adapting Rampton's (1990) terms for describing linguistic identity, which students had read about in class.

The linguistic affiliation with standardized English that Brittany claims is supported by the challenges she experienced in crafting a piece of vernacular writing. In her first draft she transliterated almost every word into a phonemic spelling of the African-American vernacular that her characters and narrator were speaking in the story. Transliterations are not negotiations or performances: they are "faithful" renderings and as such do not have space in them for the author's voice; the creativity behind the rendering is obscured. So too with Brittany's first draft, the story was almost completely incomprehensible because it was a minutely-detailed rendering in writing of a particular variety of English, rather than a visual representation of that variety. In her revision she demonstrated a very competent performance of negotiating audience expectations and representing the vernacular of her characters. Even though Brittany, by the account offered earlier, has code-switched permanently into Standardized American English, her story shows an expert vernacular transcription of African-American Vernacular English, with extra flourishes in spelling and other presentation. It is a performance of African-American English.

> "Hello?" *said a voice on the other line.*
>
> "Yo Mya, I can't find nothin to wear. You need to come through asap!" "Damn girl. You can't do nothin without my help," *Mya laughed.*
>
> "Jus shut up and come quick." "Alright, be there in 20."
>
> *About 20 minutes later, Cali heard the doorbell ring. She ran down the stairs and opened the door; it was none other than Mya. Together, the girls went up the stairs of Cali's parents Rosedale crib to Cali's room. Mya always loved bein in her room; it had pink walls and leopard print EVERYTHANGGG. There was a king-sized bed with the softest comforter anyone done ever felt and sat on, a love seat in the corner by the window, a dope ass 42in screen tv that hung on a wall, a brown wooden computer desk that held a silver Apple laptop and a closet filled with flee clothes and kicks. But today, it looked like a hurricane hit.*
>
> "Damn Cali, what's goin on here?"
>
> "I tol you I can't find nothin good to wear."

> "You buggin. I could go through that closet and throw together like mad outfits real quick."
> "Go ahead. I'm jus tryin to look cute tonight, you know, find me a man or somethin."
> "Matter of fact, there is someone I've been wantin you to meet for a minute now." "You for real?" Cali asked, surprised.
> "Yessss girl!"
> "Yo, what have you been waitin for? Why you aint hook me up then?" "Don't worry, I got you tonight."

We can see in the passage that follows Brittany's description of her authorial identity being a role that she inhabited while writing this piece:

> Many features of pronunciation are disregarded by my characters and idiomatic speech is utilized as a natural part of the English language. I wanted to incorporate more distinct features of my characters' speech, but as a writer, it was crucial that I kept my readers in mind. Using the vernacular profusely, and transcribing every written word how an AAVE user would speak it, would have contributed to my readers having difficulties interpreting the text. Nonetheless, I feel I effectively showcase the written vernacular as it is commonly spoken by primary AAVE users.

Despite a semester of language variation pedagogy, Brittany still characterizes AAVE speakers as coming from a place of linguistic deficit: "Many features of pronunciation are disregarded by my characters." She imagines a reader who is not part of the AAVE speaking community, despite the fact that most students in the class—and most people in the metropolis where Urban College is located—have at least a working knowledge of this language variety. Translingual pedagogies can only work from a position of a language variation, and even then, translanguaging is not always something that students celebrate, even if they can perform it well. Brittany's steadfast rejection of AAVE as her current linguistic affiliation, contrasted with her facility at writing in that vernacular—and thus performing that linguistic affiliation—are important elements of her linguistic identity. Brittany's linguistic *identity* is not clearly translingual and yet she is adept at negotiating AAVE and her audience's expectations in her story, because she approaches it as a writer who is making a case for a language marking her narrator's and her characters' identities. For Brittany, translanguaging is an appropriate authorial performance, but it is too limiting for, as she puts it, "the outside world."

Hina: Trilingual, not Translingual

Our second student writer, Hina, is a self-identified trilingual speaker of Urdu, Punjabi, and English, who emigrated to Urban College's metropolis with her family when she was six years old. Hina writes that she has "mastered" Standard American English during her education. Her pride in this mastery comes through in her language narrative, in which she writes,

> Someone once said to me, "Hina, do you ever say anything out of the normal English?" I thought this was a funny question since I realized that what is considered "normal" English is the Standard American English. I was actually quite pleased to then think about how I am able to speak a language that I had to acquire throughout time with such perfection.
>
> (p. 2)

Hina, like many multilingual speakers, keeps her languages completely separate; she sees them as fulfilling very different functions in her life. She writes, "I have always been able to distinguish the difference between my 'school' and 'home' cultures so much so that there is a specific way for me to categorize them in terms of the languages I speak in both environments" (p. 3).

Despite—or perhaps because of—her studied separation of English, Punjabi, and Urdu into different spheres of her life, Hina chose the creative writing option on the final paper, writing a short story in a code-meshed combination of English and Urdu, about a young girl meeting her future husband for the first time. Hina does not negotiate with her instructor-audience very much: her story is very difficult to understand, although, like Brittany's second draft, the version that I present here, the second draft, is easier for a non-Urdu speaker than the original draft was. The story starts off fairly clearly, but as it progresses, instead of getting easier, becomes harder to understand, at least in my (Heather's) experience. The passage that follows is the beginning of the central event of the story, and is mostly quite separate (in terms of the introduction of vocabulary) from the first page in which she introduced her main character, Aliyah. We know from the context in the preceding passage what "kamra" means (room), but other words such as "maine," which have appeared before, still do not help to reveal what is happening.

> *Chand din later, Ami came to Aliyah's kamra. "Aliyah, maine tumse important talk karni hai" "Ami, kya hua? Boliye" replied Aliyah.*
>
> *"Beta, I think ab you should have your shadi done. If your Abu was zinda, he would have wanted your shadi to be done jald az possible."*
>
> *"Ami, I know aap ka kya meaning hai. I agree with aap ki baat"*
>
> *"Good, beta. MashaAllah. I knew ke my daughter meri talk listen karay gi."*

Unlike in Brittany's writing, where she was systematic about the words that she rendered in the vernacular and in which variation is mostly phonemic with some syntactic flourishes, Hina's codemeshing infuses syntax and vocabulary, but not in a predictable way. That is, Hina does not use her writing to teach her English-speaking reader Urdu, by gradually introducing more Urdu vocabulary into English syntactic structures; nor does she use Urdu syntax with English vocabulary. For instance, her syntax and vocabulary in the last line of the passage previously mentioned is almost entirely Urdu, with English words occurring in these sentences in a way in which it is difficult to identify a pattern. In the line, "I knew ke my daughter meri talk listen karay gi," it seems that Hina has translated the function words—the complementizer and the auxiliary from English to Urdu, and has used Urdu syntax. She follows what I take to be the auxiliary, *meri*, with what we might take to be a serial verb construction, which Hina would *not* use if she was speaking English. This example shows Hina combining translation with transliteration, which complicates the reading process.

The payoff for Hina's story occurs in the passage that follows.

> *"I sent him into the kamra first"* said Umar. *"Maine wanted to see how you would react to him saying to you ke you have no husn. But you kept your anger inside. Your andhar ki beauty is strong I have realized"*
>
> Aliyah just kept staring.
>
> Umar gave a musskurahatt now. His teeth showed.
>
> Fezan was laughing. *"I'm sorry Baji. Bhai wanted to test you. I was just an actor"* Fezan then left the kamra. Aliyah was still staring at Umar.
>
> *"Aliyah . . . this is the first time main see you in real life. I only saw you in the picture Ami showed me. I am very picky about husn and being pretty. But now I realized that what matters is andhar ki beauty. You really are beautiful andhar se and from outside. You did not cry or yell when mera brother said that to you. It was a test for me to see how much you cared about husn or being pretty."*

The passage is mostly English, but the nouns that make the whole pay-off make sense are in Urdu, and as Hina has not taught us these words earlier in the passage, the reading experience (for me, her instructor, at least) is no less difficult, even though there is more English. These nouns are deliberately rendered in Urdu, with no translation, introduction or glossing. In her commentary, Hina discusses the ending of her story at some length:

> I chose to include words in the last part of the story that really brought out the personalities of both Aliyah and Umar, and did not define them because I believe that the real connection to my culture was through the use of these words, which would have definitely been lost or made less significant had I provided the meaning as well.

Hina's use of the word "husn" in the passage is indicative of Hina's non-negotiation with her audience. While the term was introduced about a page before the passage, in the sentence that follows, the set-up does not really help the reader understand that, in fact, "husn" is beauty, as Hina explains in her commentary on the story, especially since the English word beauty is used in the text adjacent to *husn*. Code-meshing can be a negotiation, but Hina's stance is didactic, not translingual, and so she is not really working with her reader but rather asking them to work with her, so that they can learn about Pakistani culture. We see this demand in her discussion of her use of the word "husn."

> In my own short story, this is the reason why I chose to repeat the usage of the word "husn" because I did not feel as though the part about a girl having "beauty" would have been deemed as important had I used an English word. At first, I had the reader understand the meaning of this word because I wrote "beauty" right before it. For the rest of the story, however, I wrote "husn" because it is something that the Pakistani people are prideful for. Beauty is indeed something that is considered very important when it comes to marriage. Therefore, just like Malkani,[1] I used an Urdu word instead of an English one so that my readers understand its importance in the Pakistani culture.

Hina accommodates her professor-reader by writing this section mostly in English, and then strategically uses Urdu words to draw the English speaker in to Pakistani culture. But the work is on the side of the reader; we could see Hina, in her demanding prose, echoing her own pride in her trilingualism and biculturalism by showing what is easy for her, acknowledging what is hard for her audience, and making them do the work anyway. Hina is, after all, a teacher in her day job too (she graduated with a degree in English Education, and is now teaching elementary school students in Queens). She is used to playing this role.

But though a ready interpretation of the story is not available for a reader who does not speak Urdu, we cannot assume that Hina did not do this on purpose: we cannot assume that her story is difficult to understand because she is a novice translanguager. Rather, we might consider the fact that the professor was not, after all, the main audience for this piece of writing. Such a suggestion emerges when we consider the follow-up interview Heather and Jonathan did with Hina in April 2016, in which she describes giving the story to her Urdu-English bilingual friends before submitting it to be graded. The friends, she relates, read it easily, and laughed at it—they understood the story, and knew that it was an artificial confection of Urdu and English, and one which would not occur amongst the bilingual Urdu-English language community of which Hina is a part. According to Hina's interview responses, code-meshed Urdu and English doesn't exist in their experience, but only they can get the full meaning—and entertainment—from it, when they read it.

Like in Brittany's story, there is no separation between the characters' and the narrators' language and voices in Hina's story. It's a more confident use of the vernacular, and has the effect described of Morrison's work—it's not really bicultural, and "gives white readers less and less familiar material on which to ground readings." (Lanser, 1992, p. 138). The privileged readers are her bilingual friends. The effect is powerful. "Hina's own voice is authorized through this US Pakistani community," in a paraphrase of Morrison's description of her work being authorized through the African-American community.

Hina's story is a performance of mastery: "mastery," after all, is the language that she used in her language narrative to describe her relationship with all her languages, but particularly English. Hina's essay is as performative as Brittany's, but her performance is didactic, and so does not accommodate a two-way communication between her and the audience. Hina's linguistic performance, too, contrasts with Canagarajah's student Buthainah's gradual "toe-in-the-water" approach to code-meshing, in which Buthainah gauges and re-gauges how her audience is responding to her code-meshing, and introduces more and more features (Canagarajah, 2011). Hina tempered her code-meshing between drafts, trying to imagine her audience's needs after some prompting from her instructor, but her purposes—teaching about Pakistani culture through the Urdu language—are primary. Hina, like Brittany, provides examples of students who live in a cultural context in which we might expect translanguaging to emerge spontaneously and often, but it seems that both of these women's academic success has relied (at least in their own perceptions) on building clear separations between their linguistic inheritances and their linguistic affiliations, depending on the context. The aspiration of a translingual pedagogy, of course, is that they should not have to be separate at all, but we cannot and should not discount our students' lived experience that tells them that they *must* be. Hence the focus on the pedagogy of performance, which gives students space to trans- between their identities as successful students (and as such, often, as proficient users of standardized Englishes) and as members of multilingual, multivarietal language communities.

Sharon: An Ignorant Muchachita

The third author whose work we will look at is Sharon, who again wrote a short story in the first person. Sharon is a Spanish-English bilingual speaker who grew up in New York City, and identifies as a speaker of English, Spanish, and Spanglish. In her story, she writes in the latter, a hybrid of English and Spanish.

Sharon's story occupies a third space alongside Brittany and Hina's pieces, in her use of the first-person narration—a narrative strategy which Lanser (1992) argues signals the writer occupying a position of authority which doesn't require dialect to be contained—and in using an orthographic representation of the vernacular which transcribes non-essential points of variation, such as the use of the—za ending rather than the —er in "regista", in order to indicate "non-standardness," as well as such features of pronunciation such as the unfricated "d" in *the, those*, etc. But the site of Sharon's most effective translanguaging is in the syntax itself, where she blends English vocabulary and Spanish syntax, and vice versa. She also incorporates the distinctive cadences of a teenager from the outer boroughs of the metropolis, in a performance that transcends language variation and moves firmly into register. Sharon's is a confident performance of the translingual identity that she explicitly assigns to her narrator, as we see in the excerpt that follows.

> *Let me tell you how rude these customerz were to me tho. So listen, one day, a lady walked by my regista wit her cart fulluv groceriez. She wuz a chunky, dark woman. I culd tell she wanted to ax me a question, so I smiled at her. I wuz always polite . . . til dey were rude to me. She axed me, "Where de codfish?" Now, remember, I was jus a muchachita. I didn know what codfish wuz back then. I wuz confused. So I axed her "I'm sorry, what did you ask?" And she yells, "Codfish!!! Where de codfish?" I wuz so confused. I was like, "What's that?" She looked mad at dis point, so I wuz gonna turn n ask a coworker if dey know what dat is. Den she yells "Bacalao! You dunno wat bacalao is? You dun speak English?" Now I know wutz bacalao. My mom makes bacalao wit white rice, onions, tomato and yuca on the side wit guineos verdes and den we throw olive oil all ova it. Its delicious but I didn know dat codfish wuz bacalao. So I got mad.*
>
> *Mind you, I wuz jus a muchacha so I yell back, "You da one that don't speak English with your heavy accent!"*

Sharon's writing is easy to read—identifying as a writer, her engagement with the audience in her code-meshed text is much more sophisticated than Hina's, at least partly, I believe, because she is a more experienced creative writer than Hina. She writes to represent metropolitan Latinx culture, and in this effort to represent, she uses mostly English with Spanish vocabulary, pronunciation and syntax functioning emblematically. In her commentary, she writes,

> [M. NourbeSe Philip,[2] . . . uses the word "i-mage" discusses the struggle of a Caribbean person being able to represent themselves and create in their own i-mage. She states, "The excitement for me as a writer comes in the confrontation between the formal and the demotic within the text itself' (2007, p. 492). This very confrontation is occurring in my story. The "demotic," which is the variety of English used, is the vernacular used by ordinary people. However, the formal confronts the demotic in different ways; one being with this very commentary which is written in

Standard English. Another way is the use of the demotic in an occasion in which it is rare. Literature usually consists of the "formal," canonical texts and scholarly texts are usually written in Standard English. However, my story is a vernacular transcription. It is created in my i-mage and represents people who use the demotic when speaking.

(pp. 5–6)

This passage shows us that like Hina, and unlike Brittany, Sharon seeks to represent herself in her story, though this is not to say that either Hina or Sharon should be thought to be the narrator in their stories. Rather, Sharon tells us that her story is her creation: she has invented it. We see the performative stance that Inayatulla (2013) recognizes as being so important to cultivate amongst college students, so that they have space to exert the power of their i-mage (Philip, 2007) [1993] without a requirement of disclosure.

Linguistically, what is important—from a translanguaging perspective—is that Sharon's rendering of her narrator skillfully immerses her reader in the culture of the story through the use of the vernacular. Her sentence, "now, I know wutz bacalao," from the earlier passage, shows us the type of translanguaging she does, to create this immersive experience: the spelling of "what's" as *wutz* signals that she is writing in the vernacular, rather than making mistakes, and so the vernacular Spanglish syntax, with the auxiliary verb coming before the noun *bacalao* is read as a deliberate performance.

What is also notable about Sharon's story is her direct engagement with the issues of language difference that her narrator encounters as a speaker of Spanish in the metropolis. Her narrator describes the differences between the Spanishes of that city—differences to which monolingual English-speaking readers would perhaps be oblivious. Sharon's narrator, in the passage that follows, describes in detail the differences, from her perspective, between Dominican and Puerto Rican Spanishes:

> But it wuz hard to understan some of da people when dey talked to me. Wuz bad enuff I culd barely understan my coworkers. They wuz all Dominican n I wuz the only Boricua. If you not from dese places, you think whats da difference? But we talk completely different. Dem Dominicans talk so fast! N we talk fast, trust me I know! But dem? They sound like dey singing a whiny song supa loud n fast. Son unos llorones. Askin for change wuz always confusin cuzl wuld say I need fichas or pecetas. Dey wuld ignore me cuz they didn know what I meant. In Puerto-Rico, we use American money n in DR, dey got deir own money so dey didn't have any Spanish wordz for da money or change.

The tone of the narrator here is important, too: she is a speaker inside a culture and, like Hina's narrator, is teaching her audience. Perhaps this is still an indicator of the student writer: there must still be some accommodation of the Anglo reader—the professor—but the stance is one of teaching the professor. Sharon's story provokes many questions. When she is writing outside the classroom context, does she still engage the reader in this way? What would happen to her story if she wrote it in Spanglish, and not in dialect, following Morrison's model, as Lanser describes it:

> Instead of opposing 'dialect' and 'white English,' Morrison's narrators adopt a vernacular that is neither dialect nor white; "black language," Morrison has said, means for her "not so much the use of non-standard grammar" as "the manipulation of metaphor." (Morrison and McKay, 1983, p. 427). While some of Morrison's characters do use vernacular grammatical and lexical forms that the narrator herself does not employ, the novels do not translate the inflections of spoken Black English into a deviant typography, eliminating a visual class distinction between narrator and characters.
>
> *(1992, p. 129)*

As Sharon's work shows, a translingual writing performance can combine superficial markers of "otherness"—the "z" endings, "the" spelt "da," and so on, with a deeper rendering of a vernacular sound. She at once lets her reader in, and creates a space that is not entirely for them.

In the three excerpts from student writing, we have seen a variety of ways of approaching translingual writing. One is a code-meshed text, two are vernacular transcriptions, but with different levels of variation at the syntactic, rather than the graphic level (i.e. Brittany's story incorporates more aspects of AAVE into the actual structure of the sentences, making the syntax sound different, than Sharon's does.) Both are decoratively translingual in the ways that they mark otherness through spelling and textual presentation.

All three, however, close the space between narrator and characters, while maintaining the distance between the writer and the story. That is, these stories are not acts of disclosure about the students' linguistic identities; they are creative pieces where the writers perform different linguistic affiliations that they may or may not perform in their day-to-day lives. None of these stories depicts the writer, and yet, as Sharon explains, they are written in the writers' "i-mage," connecting the writer to some aspect of their linguistic inheritance. These stories, and the accompanying commentaries, show the linguistic control and the sensitivity to linguistic context that our plurilingual students live every day. The linguistic identities portrayed by the narrators and characters in these stories are recognizable to speakers and readers within the linguistic communities with which the authors are affiliated, but also show the writers participating simultaneously in multiple linguistic communities and, particularly, in the linguistic community of academic English, this community from which students from underrepresented linguistic backgrounds are often systematically excluded, and yet for whom membership is required if they want to be perceived as successful college students.

Notes

1. Gautam Malkani, *Londonstani*, (Ahmad, 2007) which students read for the course. Unlike Hina's story, however, this novel is predominantly written in, roughly, Cockney English, with Urdu individual words—often quite vulgar ones—occurring within the London vernacular. There are some full and sentences in Urdu, but the experience of immersion is within the Hounslow vernacular, rather than Urdu.
2. M. NourbeSe Philip, The absence of writing, or how I almost became a spy, in Ahmad D. (Ed). (2007) *Rotten English*.

References

Ahmad, D. (Ed.). (2007). *Rotten Englishes: A literary anthology*. New York: Norton.

Ashcroft, B., Griffiths, G., & Tiffin, H. (2002). *The empire writes back: Theory and practice in post-colonial literatures* (2nd ed.). New York: Routledge.

Baillif, M. (1997). Seducing composition: A challenge to identity-disclosing pedagogies. *Rhetoric Review, 16*(1), 76–91.

Canagarajah, A. S. (2006). Toward a writing pedagogy of shuttling between languages: Learning from multilingual writers. *College English, 68*(6), 589–604.

Canagarajah, A. S. (2011). Codemeshing in academic writing: Identifying teachable strategies of translanguaging. *Modern Language Journal, 95*(3), 401–417.

Canagarajah, A. S. (2015). Clarifying the relationship between translingual practice and L2 writing: Addressing learner identities. *Applied Linguistics Review, 6*(4), 415–440.

Crenshaw, K. (1990). Mapping the margins: Intersectionality, identity politics, and violence against women of color. *Stanford Law Review, 43*, 1241.

Elbow, P. (2002). Vernacular Englishes in the writing classroom: Probing the culture of literacy. In C. Schroeder, P. Bizzell, & H. Fox (Eds.), *ALT DIS: Alternative discourses and the academy*. Portsmouth, NH: Heinemann.

Foucault, M. (1980). *The history of sexuality* (Vol. 1). Trans. Robert Hurley. New York: Vintage.

Grahn, J. (1978). Murdering the king's English. In J. Grahn (Ed.), *True to life adventure stories*. Oakland, CA: Diana Press.

Inayatulla, S. I. (2013). Beyond the dark closet: Reconsidering literacy narratives as performative artifacts. *Journal of Basic Writing, 32*(2), 5–27.

Lanser, S. S. (1992). *Fictions of authority: Women writers and narrative voice*. Ithaca, NY: Cornell University Press.

Leung, C., Harris, R., & Rampton, B. (1997). The idealised native speaker, reified ethnicities and classroom realities. *TESOL Quarterly, 31*(3), 543–560.

Matsuda, P. K. (2006). The myth of linguistic homogeneity in college composition. *College English, 68*(6), 637–651.

Morrison, T., & McKay, N. (1983). An interview with Toni Morrison. *Contemporary Literature, 24*(4), 413–429. doi:10.2307/1208128

Nero, S. (2016). *Engaging multilingualism in the classroom: Towards a culturally and linguistically sustaining pedagogy*. Talk delivered at York College/CUNY, April 14, 2016.

Philip, M. N. (2002) [1993]. The absence of writing, or how I almost became a spy. In D. Ahmad (Ed.) (2007), *Rotten English* (pp. 459–468). New York: Norton.

Rampton, B. (1990). Displacing the "native speaker": Expertise, affiliation and inheritance. *ELT Journal, 44*, 97–101.

Robinson, H. M. (2019). Post-colonial composition: Appropriation and abrogation in the composition classroom. In V. Milson-Whyte, R. Oenbring, & B. Jaquette (Eds.), *Creole composition: Academic writing and rhetoric in the Anglophone Caribbean* (pp. 320–342). Anderson, SC: Parlor Press.

Young, V. A. (2004). Your average nigga. *College Composition and Communication, 55*(4), 693–715.

10
TRANSLINGUAL ECONOMIES OF LITERACY

Jonathan Hall

A translingual approach to literacy begins with the assumption that a student's entire language repertoire is potentially implicated in any act of reading or writing, and that in the course of interacting with a text, students will necessarily negotiate from multiple identity positions.

As scholars and instructors in rhetoric and composition have come to realize that linguistic diversity is a fundamental aspect of our work (Horner & Trimbur, 2002; Zamel, 2004; Matsuda, 2006; Hall, 2009; among many others), there has been a gradual movement away from thinking about second language writing as a rare phenomenon at the margins of our pedagogy and research, to a new consciousness that sees all student writing, including that of supposed monolinguals, as taking place in a complex translingual space (Horner, Lu, Royster, & Trimbur, 2011) that involves drawing upon multiple languages, dialects, and registers.

This "translingual turn" in composition theory is partly a result of increasing engagement in scholarly alliance with other disciplines such as TESOL, applied linguistics, and second language acquisition, and these fruitful interactions have led us to begin to adjust our theoretical approaches in promising ways. My purpose here is to continue this dialogue by asking how this translingual turn might affect the way in which we apply our research to questions of reading as well as writing. What might a translingual approach have to contribute to current models of multilingual reading? And the reverse—perhaps especially the reverse: what might the literature on second language reading have to contribute to our attempts to articulate a translingual approach to reading in composition studies?

I'll trace certain developments drawn from second language reading research, and then discuss what a translingual approach to reading might look like, and, more broadly, how instructors in U.S. classrooms can nurture our students' translingual transnational literacies. We must seek a more nuanced model of reading, one that would account for transdirectional flows of language, for interactional exchanges of meaning, for what I will call translingual economies of literacy.

In order to anchor these theoretical discussions in actual examples, I will include two case studies. The second of these focuses on the annotation practices of a student at Urban College, while the first one, an experiential introduction to the topic, involves a faculty member, who is a writing instructor and a Spanish language learner. In short, myself.

Case Study #1: Reading Between Languages: A Spanish Language Learner

As I discussed in Chapter 7, over the past few years I've been studying Spanish, combining trips abroad with other approaches, such as participating in a Spanish reading group in New York where we read literary texts aloud and discuss them afterwards. Several years ago, I began to notice that I was reading differently. Specifically, I found that I was beginning to be able to read literary texts, such as a novel by Gabriel García Marquez. The ability to read literature was one of my original motivations for trying to activate my Spanish, which I had last studied what seemed like several lifetimes ago, but on a particular sunny winter day in Buenos Aires, as I browsed in one of that city's many amazing bookstores, something clicked. Previously, when I had tried to read a novel in Spanish, I had felt lost, unable to get more than a very blurry picture of the action, and that only with extensive use of ancillaries such as dictionaries and online translation. But now I wasn't doing any of that, I felt like I had crossed over some kind of a threshold, and I didn't feel lost anymore. I felt like I understood what was going on in the novel, and instead of asking the meaning of a vocabulary word, I was starting to ask the kinds of questions I might have asked in English, about the motivations of characters, about what might happen next, about how it all might end.

It was familiar to me, and yet it was different. I was not translating word-for-word from Spanish to English in my head, but yet—English was, well, *involved* somehow, in a way that I couldn't quite articulate. So I decided to try to figure out what was happening to me by looking at the literature on L2 reading. In this chapter, I share some preliminary observations about that journey with you.

The experience of working my way toward being able to read literature in Spanish has given me a greater appreciation for our multilingual students who are trying to acquire academic literacy in English. My first observation is a general one: simply a more visceral and immediate sense of the difficulty and complexity of the task. It's hard enough to negotiate everyday tasks and social interactions in a second language, but literacy, especially academic literacy, with its insistence on nuanced analysis of complex texts, takes linguistic demands to a whole new level.

Now this process is, to be sure, very different for me than it is for our students. First of all, I'm not in a second language situation, where my environment is primarily in Spanish, except for a few weeks at a time when I'm traveling. These students, most of them, live permanently in the United States, and English is all around them. That's an advantage that they have over me. But an advantage that I have over them is that I'm older and a more sophisticated reader of literary texts. That is, I have English literacy skills which—potentially at least—I may be able to transfer, to some extent, to my Spanish reading and writing, and perhaps even compensate to some degree for some of my purely linguistic shortcomings: my continued limited vocabulary and imperfect command of Spanish grammar, syntax, rhetorical conventions, and cultural references. As we will see, this has been for decades one of the key questions in second language reading research.

My second observation, or perhaps hypothesis, extrapolating from my own experience, is that for our students who come to college with previous literacy in their first language, and with formative experiences and memories in that language: that language will be involved in their reading and writing processes in our courses. I call this phenomenon *a translingual economy of literacy* because it is made up of multiple transactions of meaning, some of which are conscious and obvious to the reader (e.g. meaning monitoring in the L1) and some of which are so tiny and momentary that they occur at a subconscious level that does not overtly intrude into the continuous processing of the text, but which may subtly slow it down or affect its operation. This interaction between a reader's languages during the act of reading is something that we as instructors should simply expect, and not something that we should judge as inappropriate or urge students to overcome. It is not a process that *interferes* with understanding, as an outmoded metaphor would have it; rather, it *is* the process of understanding itself. My own slow gropings toward multilinguality have already helped me to understand, to some degree, our multilingual students' experience of reading, which, I must emphasize, is *not* simply the experience of first reading in one language and then reading in another language. Rather, all of a student's languages are at least potentially active, in a simultaneous fashion, in every instance of reading.

So, from my own mini-auto-ethnography of second language literacy, I derived an intuition about the ways in which multilingual readers may interact with a text. The obvious next question is to investigate whether there may be found explanation of this experience, and/or support for this intuition, in the research literature on second language reading. In the next section I want to share some of my very preliminary observations about that journey.

Is Reading a Problem?

In the field of second language reading research, one question has resonated for years: "Reading in a foreign language: a reading problem or a language problem?" (Alderson, 1984). Of course the first thing that seems out of place here, from a translingual perspective, is conceiving of reading, and specifically of L2 reading, as a "problem" to be solved. When would it be solved? Perhaps when the reader is eventually reading in exactly the same way that a monolingual L1 student would? That will never happen, but what if we re-phrase the question to ask: what are some ways in which readers draw upon their language backgrounds and experience to negotiate meaning by interacting with texts?

One hypothesis from the traditional L2 reading research that jibed with my own experience was that of the "linguistic threshold": "L2 learners must first gain a certain amount of control over L2, or in other words, cross a critical linguistic threshold, before applying their L1 reading skills to L2 reading" (Clark, 1979). Modified versions of this hypothesis later suggested that this "threshold" was not absolute, but might vary by task difficulty, and that very highly fluent L1 readers might be able to compensate, to some degree, for gaps in their L2 proficiency (Bossers, 1991); once again, the language of deficit—"compensate . . . for gaps"—is still present in this formulation. Later researchers refined the question to include background knowledge and socio-cultural experience, and as Elizabeth Bernhardt (2005) summarized, "the question was no longer one of difference and influence, but rather of accountability—how much did first language literacy account for literacy in a second?" (p. 136). This notion of a "linguistic threshold" above which L1 reading proficiency becomes more active in L2 reading raises the question: well, what, exactly, happens in that space identified for "transfer"? How do L1 literacy strategies and proficiencies interact with L2 reading?

Bernhardt (2011) compares second language reading to

> operating in stereo: the first language is the *clear* channel . . . providing phonology. . . . It also provides processing strategies, . . . word recognition strategies, a concept of fluency . . . and so forth. But perhaps most importantly, it is the reader's clear channel of first-language culture and first-language literacy that guides the development of the conceptual model on which understanding is based; it is this model that provides the anticipatory strategies.
>
> *(p. 6)*

As Bernhardt notes, all of this will be obvious to anyone who has ever tried to read in a second language, but remains opaque to many monolingual researchers who persist in believing that reading in a second language is simply a transplantation of reading in a first language. Learning to read in a second language is not like learning to read from scratch: the reading faculty has long been activated, and there will never come a time where the L1 is not, somehow, involved. A translingual reader interacts with a text by choosing among multiple negotiated identities and positions to perform a creative act of reading.

This line of inquiry within applied linguistics and L2 reading has important implications for pedagogy in the language classroom, but also, I want to argue, for the composition classroom, and for research in composition studies as well. We may think of ourselves as writing teachers, but we are just as much reading teachers, and as multilingual students increasingly becomes the mainstream of our classrooms (Hall, 2014) and monolingual English speakers the outlier, whenever we think about reading we need to think about a translingual approach to language, here applied to reading. Evolving out of the original rather primitive distinction between "a reading problem or a language problem," this line of inquiry in L2 reading research opens up a space that I think that composition studies needs to walk into and explore for ourselves, in our own context and with our own students.

Bernhardt's (2011) metaphor of reading in stereo evokes a process that we don't usually think about in our writing pedagogy, an ambiguous area where the student cannot be said definitively to be "reading in English" or "reading in Spanish." Rather each language has a role to play in a single unified act of reading. In a discussion of the language classroom, where a recent trend has been for instructors to re-examine their traditional insistence that all classroom interaction must always be in the target language, Scott and de la Fuente summarize recent research in this area:

> In recent decades, an increasing number of studies have shown that multilingual functioning is a normal process that involves a nearly subconscious interaction between or among a person's different languages. Research on cognition and multilingual functioning has supported the view that two (or more) languages interact collaboratively in understanding and speaking both languages. . . . Indeed, there is some question as to whether bilingual people need, or are even able, to suppress their L1 during L2 retrieval tasks.
>
> *(2008, p. 101)*

This re-conception of the site of reading—and of language use in general—as a shared linguistic space in which languages cooperate and collaborate to produce meaning, to interpret texts, and to initiate contact with others in whatever language is appropriate in a given context—is a real game-changer in the way we in composition need to think about what we are asking our students to do. What it tells us is that even if we give them as a reading assignment a text written in English, expect them to discuss it in the classroom in English, and later to write an interpretive essay about it in English—even in that circumstance, the students' other languages are still involved. The language in which they first learned to read, in which they have read other texts, in which they have experienced relevant life—events which bring depth to their encounter with their assigned texts—this is never going to be irrelevant.

But of course such translingual encounters, in the privacy of a student's own reading practices, take place far from the watchful eye of instructors, and might not please some instructors if they were aware. In the written texts that they turn in, in their oral discussions in the classroom, students customarily do not call attention to their translingual procedures, to the continuing influence—and the continuing operation—of their other languages as they go about their assignments in the English-medium college course, because they understand the implicit economy of the classroom, in which meanings produced or expressed in English are worth more than those in other languages.

Case Study #2: Making Translingual Reading Visible: Anatomy of an Annotation

Given the inherent privacy of the reading experience, and the possible reluctance of students who have been told to do everything in English to show how they actually do it, how can we make our students' reading procedures legible to us—and potentially even to themselves? Pichette, Segalowitz, and Connors suggest that

> Future research should investigate . . . which aspects of reading are affected by transfer. For example, L1 reading maintenance might enhance the transfer of top-down reading strategies concerned with the integration of information across sentences and text, as opposed to enhancing more local processing concerned with single word recognition and grammatical parsing. This effect might be expected because high-level cross-text integration of information is likely to require relatively similar processes across languages, whereas local-level processing is likely to be relatively more language specific.
>
> *(2003, p. 401)*

Consider the case of a student whose L1 is Spanish and L2 is English, at an advanced level, attempting to read a difficult literary text—say a poem written in English by a U.S. poet. Such a student would not translate the English text word by word into Spanish, but as with me and English, it would be equally untrue to say that Spanish would not be involved at all. Nor can we go to the other extreme and say that her meaning-checks would be completely in Spanish—and especially as she reached more advanced levels, she would increasingly ask herself both more frequent and more probing questions in English as well.

It's not surprising that there are few detailed studies of translingual reading, because it mostly takes place in the invisible space of consciousness. We have to look for evidence of this translingual reading process where we can find it, usually when that reading has produced writing. I'd like to share here a glimpse—just a glimpse—that I gained in a summer introduction to literature course into the translingual reading practices of one of my students, who I'll call Cecilia. The student was rather atypical: she was not a student at my campus at all but actually a graduate student studying for a master's degree in Education at another university, and she needed to pick up a literature course to fulfill a certification requirement for her special education teaching program. She had done her undergraduate work not in the U.S. but in her native Mexico.

But this makes her perfect for illustrating my point about multicompetence. Cecilia had some training, some expertise, in the general subject matter of the course-analysis of literature—but the training had been in Spanish, talking and writing in Spanish about Spanish-language texts. Now she was in my classroom, at Urban College, focusing on, in this case, a U.S. poet and a poem written in English. And by chance, she turned in a photocopy of her annotations of a poem by Tess Gallagher—this was not something that I required; she just included it with her paper.

Here are my annotations on Cecilia's annotations (Figure 10.1):

1. Cecilia adds a translingual marginal note next to lines 7–9:

   I feel like hugging you
   para sacar toda la
   energia que llevo dentro de
   mi and

Cecilia is clearly trying to find some kind of an equivalent, in Spanish, for the extravagant English metaphor in the poem, "like a variable star shooting light/off to make itself comfortable." In both cases, the idea is that an excess of energy is building up inside, making necessary a spontaneous act of release. But Cecilia makes no effort to translate the metaphor AS a metaphor, or to translate the words literally. One difference in Cecilia's paraphrase is that she makes it more of a first person experience—"*I* feel . . .", "dentro de *mi*"—whereas Gallagher's speaker makes it sound more like an involuntary spasm, an unexpected and spontaneous gift or release: "a hug comes over me," and comparing herself to a star "shooting light/ off to make itself comfortable, then subsiding."

2. In Line 10, Cecilia also underlines "subsiding" and puts an asterisk next to it, which connects it to another asterisk in the right margin that's clearly trying to define "subsiding" in two languages: "recede, sink (ahogarse) dwindle (morir)." It appears that Cecilia first looked up "subsiding" (or

Translingual Economies of Literacy 149

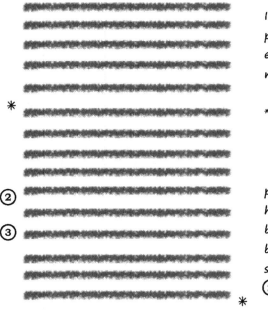

FIGURE 10.1 Cecilia's Annotations on Stanza 2 of Tess Gallagher's "The Hug"

"subside") in an English-to-English dictionary; or possibly more than one and found these three synonyms. But Cecilia's translingual interpretation here is different from all of these: "ahogarse" is "to drown oneself" or "to be suffocated" and "amorir" is "to die," though here perhaps the English equivalent would be a less literal "die down." This is different from Gallagher's metaphor that the star ends up "comfortable" after "shooting light off." Cecilia seems to interpret the metaphor as being not relief or orgasm or the giving of energy to the beloved but death by drowning, something dangerous, a sinking into dark water.

3. Similarly, the translingual comment that follows in the next line does not seem to line up directly with any line. It seems more of a general reflection on the stranger: "he has a place, está bien conformado y bien vestido pero solitario??" ("he's well built and well dressed but lonely??") It's not clear where she is drawing these conclusions from; the man is not really described. Perhaps "he looks homeless because of how he needs." Cecilia did not underline this passage, however.

4. Line 21 *nabs you* leads to, in the left margin, "grab, take, snatch." Straightforward vocabulary look-up-what seems a simple (to a native speaker)

English word "nab" is unfamiliar to Cecilia. It's worth noting that this word does not have a Latinate root, which might have given her a cognate clue to its meaning, but rather a Scandinavian etymology, so she has to look it up. The dictionary is once again English-to-English, and this time, unlike with the glossing of "subsiding," she does not feel a necessity of further exploring the meaning in Spanish; apparently "grab, take, snatch" are familiar enough. In this case Cecilia chooses to stay within English.

Cecilia's annotation in a translingual space, then, is fundamentally different from what an early English language learner would do: although she is apparently consulting references regarding the connotations of some words, she is not just searching for one-to-one correspondences, not just making "vocabulary lists," and not just struggling to understand the surface meaning of the text. In a literature class, this kind of literal glossing is not what is needed and not what this student was doing. Rather, she was trying to understand the poem by calling upon all her language knowledge and all of her transnational experiences. She was trying to feel the poem, to engage in what has been called "affective literacy," which has been described as "seek[ing] out the life principle, messy and complex, threading through reading activities and gestures toward bodily economies of reading and transacting texts" (Amsler, 2011, p. 3). Her nonlinear responses to the poetry are themselves poetic.

How can we elicit that unique translingual understanding, product of the process that Canagarajah (2006) calls "shuttling between languages" from our students? Too often the reading of "L2 students" is judged by how closely their paraphrases and interpretations correspond—or not—to a culturally-bound and language-bound meaning. How can we create spaces of reading, and perhaps technologies of annotation, in which students may come to understand their acts of reading as legitimate engagements with the text, that their insights and the meanings they generate will be valued as actually "participating in the discussion"? That is: how can we help students to create new meanings that would not be available without the translingual process of reading? If they use all the tools and strategies at their disposal in completing assignments in our English-based classrooms, they have the potential to move beyond an extractive model of reading and toward a generative one.

And beyond the classroom, beyond college, as they continue to expand their knowledge of languages and cultures and texts, how can we invite them and empower them to continue to participate, in ways large and small, in the ongoing interaction of texts across supposed linguistic divides? How can we help them to realize that their position between two or more languages, often experienced by them and labeled by the world as a "problem," as a state of exile, is actually a privileged position from which to encounter new meanings created from the friction and collision and intermeshing of languages? These meanings are invisible to the "native English reader," unless we devise techniques and media whereby, in our classrooms and beyond, the translingual meanings derived by our students may be made visible and disseminated. Rather than asserting an arrogance of ownership of "national" literary texts by "native readers," how can we share "our" texts with the world, with other languages, with translingual readers creating and absorbing meanings that have been, until that moment, inaccessible to those of us limited to one language, even the one in which a particular text was originally composed?

Exploring the Translingual Space of Reading

The concept of translinguality—and its several variations such as plurilinguality, code-meshing, translanguaging—represents an attempt to break down the old barriers between languages, indeed to deconstruct the very idea of "a language," to reveal the ways in which every language is a mishmash of heterogeneous linguistic practices and various overlapping language communities, in which drawing a line to declare certain variations as "dialects" or to try to establish a "pure" or standard version of a language are revealed as political acts, as attempts to use power to simplify the very messy boundaries between languages, boundaries which often exist within individual language users.

Translingual economies of reading imply a revaluation of the notion of a "target" language, and indeed of language "proficiency" per se. Our students have insights to contribute, but to get to the point where they feel free to think them, let alone to express them publicly, students need to consciously adopt a linguistic position as they read, which will enable them to make maximal use of all the resources that they bring with them, as well as additional tools with which we can provide them in our particular educational and institutional context. Adrian Wurr (2003) has illustrated the way that many students attempt to segregate languages in their heads, not permitting themselves to access resources, references, and experiences from their L1 that would have both simplified and enhanced their reading experience in L2. Wurr (2003) advocates an approach which would

> facilitate the readers' awareness and use of all the resources available to them in the reading process by integrating theory, methods, materials, and evaluation into a language-rich environment that celebrates and builds on what learners know-their language, culture, interests and common experiences.
>
> *(p. 165)*

Reading in an L2 takes place between languages, in a space that is neither fully L1 nor L2, or is partly both L1 and L2, or which shuttles back and forth rapidly between L1 and L2, and which ultimately questions the distinction between L1 and L2. This is the translingual space of reading, especially in a so-called second language. When we examine translingual practices, we tend to think first about translingual *writing*, to focus on deliberate rhetorical decisions by a writer to include elements from multiple languages in a single text, usually in a provocative attempt to force the reader to deal with those elements-e.g. Gloria Anzaldúa's (2007) strategic incorporation of Spanish into her text, or the student literacy narrative analyzed by Canagarajah (2009), in which Buthainah makes a rhetorical decision to include untranslated Arabic poetry. Such provocateurs actively attempt to create dynamic translingual moments within a text.

But such overt and conscious intrusions, I would argue, represent only a small fraction of translingual transactions, most of which take place during so-called "passive" activities such as reading or listening, which of course are not "passive" at all—they're just harder for an outsider to see. Translingual writing produces something visible—and yet we don't know what processes behind the scenes, perhaps invisible even in the writer's own mind, have contributed to that artifact. Still, writing in general happens much less often than reading does.

Translingual *reading* is a much more common occurrence—indeed a ubiquitous phenomenon which occurs, at minimum, whenever anyone reads a text in her L2—and like all reading, mostly invisible, very difficult for an outside researcher to access or observe. And yet we need answers to questions like: How is the L1 implicated in the reading process? To what uses is it put by L1/L2 readers? How are we to understand this routine—and yet linguistically and culturally complex—process?

Every reader potentially brings her whole communicative repertoire to bear when reading a text. All literacy experiences in the L1 are potentially relevant in the L2 situation, even though a student may try *not* to access them, given the classroom exchange value for meanings expressed in English. L2 literacy experiences, in turn, will affect the way that a student continues to develop as a reader in L1, in a transdirectional translingual flow of strategies and meanings.

So when our students inhabit this translingual space, when they insert themselves into an economy of meaning based on constant back-and-forth exchanges between two linguistic "systems" that are not themselves really separate, any more than national economies are really separate in an globalized world—how will we react to that positioning?

Reading is productive. It produces meanings through interaction with the text, meanings that are not the same as what the author "intended" and not the same as meanings produced by another reader, or even by the same reader at a different time. But the economic value of all meanings is not the same. In U.S. educational institutions, meanings produced and/or expressed in English are much more highly valued than those in other languages. Students could very easily conclude that meanings produced in their other languages are illegitimate, and should be hidden, suppressed, replaced with a translated English version. Those are the ones they know to be in their other languages, notes or commentaries or ideas jotted down in Korean or Spanish or Polish. Even more to be denied-perhaps even to themselves-are the more subtle, more ambiguous, more difficult-to-document-or-make-visible interactions between languages as they read. The notion of a "target language" suggests that use of any other linguistic resource is missing the target.

So if the concept of translinguality necessarily presupposes a deconstruction of the idea of a unified language, then an economy of translinguality, if we want to research it, leads us in the direction of a constant bi-directional or multi-directional exchange between two or more languages: exchanges of words, of meanings, of syntax, of grammatical markers, of rhetorical structures, of community members, and of the markers of community membership.

Transnational Reading and Identification

Translingual reading can take place anywhere, including when the reader is still immersed in their original cultural location, for example in a foreign language class. But if we wish to examine not only translingual but also *transnational literacies*, we will need to consider the differing conceptions of and assumptions about reading that are influenced by the reader's educational background and cultural experiences. The meanings that emerge from translingual transnational literacies go beyond language difference per se; rather, the reader's assigned and claimed and negotiated identities interact with a particular text to create meaning. As Mandell (2015, p. 13) has argued:

> Reading is a matter of identifying with positions generated by a sentence: one considers oneself as able to utter such a sentence, or the one who listens to it, or the one whom it addresses. Multiple points of identification constitute multiple possibilities of interpretation . . . The pleasure of reading comes from the mobility of identifications, from moving from one to another, back, moving onto a third position, and so forth.

In any act of reading, the reader chooses to adopt a particular positionality, an identification for the activity of reading, a positionality that may shift multiple times during the same reading session, and still more when the task turns to performing a version of that reading in writing.

Translingual transnational economies of literacy add transnational background and previous educational experience to the mix. This suggests that, while composition instruction has a lot to learn from research in L2 reading, ultimately the issues raised by the "threshold hypothesis" are broader than whether L1 reading ability affects L2 reading *proficiency*—at some point we have to get beyond L1 and L2, beyond counting languages. Rather, a better question is: how do readers make use of *all* their multicompetent reading resources in all the languages they know, at whatever level?

For example, if I knew no Spanish at all, or only a very little, the task of reading a novel in Spanish would be hopeless. And yet, though I've apparently reached the "threshold" level of proficiency, I'm still never going to read a novel by Gabriel García Marquez like a native Spanish speaker, still less like a Colombian, nor like a literary scholar educated in a Spanish-language university. All of these hypothetical readers bring a wealth of specific knowledge, and various reading schema, to their experience of this text. These differences in linguistic background, in specific cultural and practical experience relevant to understanding the text, and in education and expertise would result in their bringing to bear contexts to which I do not have full access.

But then: those folks are not going to be able to read it like me, either. It would be silly to say that my previous experience as a reader in English would be irrelevant to my project of reading García Marquez's novel. I know a few things about García Marquez, I've encountered his work before, in translation in a class about Faulkner as an undergraduate and in Spanish in a New York City Spanish reading group. I've even done a little bit of translation of one of his stories as an exercise. More broadly, I have a PhD in literature from a U.S. university, with all that implies about the varieties of texts I've read, the various critical approaches and theoretical schools surrounding the study of literature, etc. Obviously, I bring all of that with me as I approach the text of the novel, and I can produce meanings that would not be accessible to my hypothetical native Spanish readers.

Similarly, from one point of view we might articulate as a hopeless task the ambition of an L2 reader in our classrooms to understand a complex literary text originally written in English—and yet this is an assignment which, of course, we give them all the time. These students are never going to read it the same way that a "native reader" of English, inculcated into the culture, might—not that all native readers read the same way. But those native readers are not going to be able to access the meanings that students educated in other languages and other school systems will produce through their translingual transnational processes of reading. The question for us as instructors is how we are going to *read their readings*. That is, will we fall back on our own ethnocentric interpretations—and tell our students that they are wrong? Or will we value the chance to learn from our students, to follow their alternate paths to meaning, their connections of texts to contexts that are familiar to them but not to us or to our U.S.-centered students?

While we are alive, multiple languages course through our bodies like blood, and our brains are the nodes through which those languages constantly speak to each other and speak through us to other speakers, exchange themselves for values that are not equivalent, that differ as language differs and defers, as it simultaneously signifies and fails to signify. Whenever we read, we are reading, we usually think, within a single language, and yet all the languages we know—and perhaps some of the languages we do not think we know—are implicated in every act of meaning, in the ceaseless and infinite exchange that is the translingual economy of reading.

References

Alderson, J. C. (1984). Reading in a foreign language: A reading problem or a language problem? In J. C. Alderson & A. H. Urquhart (Eds.), *Reading in a foreign language* (pp. 1–24). New York: Longman Pub Group.

Amsler, M. (2011). *Affective literacies: Writing and multilingualism in the late middle ages.* Turnhout, Belgium: Brepols.

Anzaldúa, G. (2007). *Borderlands/La Frontera: The New Mestiza* (3rd ed.). San Francisco, CA: Aunt Lute Books.

Bernhardt, E. B. (2005). Progress and procrastination in second language reading. *Annual Review of Applied Linguistics, 25,* 133–150.

Bernhardt, E. B. (2011). *Understanding advanced second-language reading.* New York: Routledge.

Bossers, B. (1991). On thresholds, ceilings and short-circuits: The relation between L1 reading, L2 reading and L2 knowledge. *AILA Review, 8,* 45–60.

Canagarajah, A. S. (2006). Toward a writing pedagogy of shuttling between languages: Learning from multilingual writers. *College English, 68*(6), 589–604.

Canagarajah, A. S. (2009). Multilingual strategies of negotiating English: From conversation to writing. *JAC, 29*(1–2), 17–48.

Clarke, M. (1979). Reading in Spanish and English: Evidence from adult ESL students. *Language Learning, 29,* 121–150.

Hall, J. (2009). WAC/WID in the next America: Re-thinking professional identity in the age of the multilingual majority. *The WAC Journal, 20,* 33–47.

Hall, J. (2014). Multilinguality is the Mainstream. In B. Horner & K. Kopelson (Eds.), *Reworking English in Rhetoric and Composition: Global Interrogations, Local Interventions* (pp. 31–48). Carbondale and Edwardsville, IL: SIU Press.

Horner, B., Lu, M.-Z., Royster, J. J., & Trimbur, J. (2011). Language difference in writing: Toward a translingual approach. *College English, 73*(3), 303–321.

Horner, B., & Trimbur, J. (2002). English only and U.S. college composition. *College Composition and Communication, 53*(4), 594–630.

Mandell, L. C. (2015). *Misogynous economies: The business of literature in eighteenth-century Britain.* Lexington: University Press of Kentucky.

Matsuda, P. K. (2006). The myth of linguistic homogeneity in U.S. college composition. *College English, 68*(6), 637–651.

Pichette, F., Segalowitz, N., & Connors, K. (2003). Impact of maintaining l1 reading skills on l2 reading skill development in adults: Evidence from speakers of Serbo-Croatian Learning French. *The Modern Language Journal, 87*(3), 391–403.

Scott, V. M., & Fuente, M. (2008). What's the problem? L2 learners' use of the L1 during consciousness-raising, form-focused tasks. *The Modern Language Journal, 92*(1), 100–113.

Wurr, A. J. (2003). Reading in a second language: A reading problem or a language problem? *Journal of College Reading and Learning, 33*(2), 157–169.

Zamel, V. (2004). Strangers in academia: The experiences of faculty and ESOL students across the curriculum. In R. Spack & V. Zamel (Eds.), *Crossing the curriculum: Multilingual learners in college classrooms* (pp. 3–17). Mahwah, NJ: Lawrence Erlbaum Associates.

11
TRANSLINGUALITY, GRAMMATICAL LITERACY, AND A PEDAGOGY OF NAMING

Heather Robinson

In his 2006 *College Composition and Communication* essay 'The Place of World Englishes in Composition: Pluralization Continued,' Suresh Canagarajah argues for the incorporation of World Englishes into the teaching of composition, and challenges students to use their "preferred varieties" of English alongside the dominant ones in "rhetorically strategic ways" (2006, pp. 598–599). At the end of the essay, Canagarajah writes,

> The extent to which my radicalism extended previously was to argue for alternative tone, styles, organization, and genre conventions in formal academic writing. I have steered clear of validating nativized varieties at the intrasentential level . . . the moment is ripe to extend my argument of pluralizing English and academic writing into the 'deep structure' of grammar. Still, I must confess that I am myself unsure how to practice what I preach.
>
> *(2006, p. 613)*

In this chapter, I will consider the challenge that Canagarajah identifies and why it remains a challenge—and how instructors might teach grammar with a translingual approach. The goal is a pedagogy that enables a shift in *instructor orientation* from a focus on prescriptive grammar, which prioritizes correctness and linguistic conformity, to a productive, generative *grammatical literacy* that reorients instruction at the sentence level to focus on grammatical patterns and usage in their linguistic context, rather than always comparing them with those of so-called standardized English, which is always closely related to the variety of white, middle class speakers from a particular national region. Of course, the deep structure of grammar, as a linguistic object, cannot be pluralized: a language or variety has its own grammar, and that grammar is internally consistent. What can and must be pluralized, however, are our attitudes towards what grammar is: what we are talking about when we teach grammar, and our embrace of the legitimacy of a wide variety of language use in academic contexts—what the academy and its white gaze will accept, on the sentence-level—from racialized and other linguistically minoritized students. The contention that I put forward here is that analyzing the structure of language, including the languages of racially-minoritized students, can have some positive impact on racist language attitudes in the college classroom.[1]

Therefore, I propose in this chapter a *pedagogy of naming*, which places the recognition of linguistic prejudice and "raciolinguistic ideology" at the center of our discourse about grammar; that is, instructors and students name any discussion of "appropriateness" and "correctness" as an effort to conform to white, middle class linguistic patterns. Rebecca Solnit writes,

> to name something truly is to lay bare what may be brutal or corrupt—or important or possible—and key to the work of changing the world is changing the story, the names, and popularizing new names and inventing or popularizing new terms and phrases.
>
> *(Solnit, 2018, p. 2)*

In the grammar classroom, and more broadly, in the composition classroom, it is particularly important to name what the linguistic purpose of the "grammar" enterprise often is, namely the perpetuation of white ways of using language. It is only by naming the underlying purpose of many school grammars that translinguality can encode and enact a challenge to racial inequality and raciolinguistic ideologies masquerading as a pedagogy that teaches college-level linguistic "appropriateness" (Flores & Rosa, 2015). This means that a translingual approach to grammar instruction cannot merely teach students the grammar and use of standardized Englishes alongside other varieties of English, and/or the other languages with which our students affiliate (Rampton, 1990), but rather must use grammar instruction to take steps towards "dismantling the racialized hierarchy of U.S. society" (Flores & Rosa, 2015, p. 167), particularly as it plays out in terms of linguistic prejudice directed at the varieties and languages of minoritized students, and especially those who are assigned or who claim racialized identities.

The grammar classroom is a critical location in enacting a pedagogy of naming in this way, with the unique opportunity it provides for extended and thoughtful work at the sentence level. However, teaching college-level grammar in a way that creates a space for students to construct a more expansive view of language remains challenging: it is well-known that school grammar courses often teach not a descriptive, comparative grammar, but may rather focus only on the grammar of written "standardized" English, which various authors have shown to be the language of white, middle class citizens, from specific regions of the metropolitan centers of empire, whether the imperial cities such as London and the northern cities of the United States, or cities such as Sydney, Delhi, Toronto, and Kingston (e.g. Flores & Rosa, 2015; Paris & Alim, 2014; Nero, 2005; Coleman, 1997; Smitherman-Donaldson, 1987, etcetera). In such a context, Canagarajah's question might be reconstrued as "is it possible to teach school grammar translingually?", knowing what we do about the "raciolinguistic ideologies" (Flores & Rosa, 2015), which accompany most conversations about "academic writing" and "appropriate language" in a tertiary context. In Robinson (2014), I arrived at a precarious if pragmatic balancing act between accommodating linguistic prejudice, external and internalized, and honoring the linguistic diversity of our students, as per Delpit (1993 [2006]), Delpit and Dowdy (2002), and so on. I this chapter, I want to consider what a translingual approach to grammar teaching might look like, in full recognition of the linguistic ideologies that make such a project challenging.

Raciolinguistic Ideology and the Grammar Classroom

Freestanding grammar courses are scattered across U.S. colleges and institutions, but their role in students' education varies from course to course and institution to institution. They may be framed as linguistics courses, focusing on describing one or many varieties of English, remedial courses, which 'fix' the language skills of the students that take them, teacher training courses, history of English courses, or ELL courses, standing as a preparation for composition courses or upper-division writing courses. For example, the grammar course at Urban College is described in the course catalog in value-neutral terms: "Analysis of English sentence structure, with focus on parts of speech, grammatical voice and mood, and written discourse. Students will examine real-world texts from a variety of genres, as well as their own writing practices" (Urban College course catalog). A sister college within the university, on the other hand, takes a much more prescriptive and corrective approach, including the following as the second of two sentences in the course description: "The course will discuss issues of correctness, grammaticality, common usage, and formal writing, and will help students generate correct, sophisticated, audience-appropriate prose" (Downtown College course catalog).

Whether or not the designers of free-standing courses are explicit in the course description about a focus on correctness, grammar instructors often see the very word 'grammar' as a mandate to focus on the correctness aspect of language teaching. Brown (2009) notes that when instructors think of the definition of the word grammar, "the routine response has been to conceptualize grammar as 'traditional grammar,' as a conflation of prescriptive usage rules and skill-and-drill instructional practices" (p. 218). Such a narrow definition not only limits what is taught in many grammar courses, but it can also limit the linguistic possibilities that students can imagine for themselves, and thus the ways in which they envision themselves participating in the academic and professional world. A course taught along traditional lines, teaching mostly prescriptive, rather than a more descriptively- or rhetorically-oriented type of grammar, is limited in the same way that the New London Group describes "mere literacy" being limited. They write,

> What we might term 'mere literacy' remains centered on language only, and usually on a singular national form of language at that, which is conceived as a stable system based on rules such as mastering sound-letter correspondence. This is based on the assumption that we can discern and describe correct usage.
>
> *(1996, p. 64)*

Similarly, traditional grammar assumes that the same grammatical rules are appropriate for every situation because only one variety of English (or some other national language) is relevant in the educational context, focusing on reproduction of standardized varieties, and correcting any deviations from it. Martin and Rothery (1993) write, to this end, "traditional school grammar became not simply a grammar of etiquette but in addition a grammar of prejudice. It was a grammar that could be used to discriminate against people who spoke non-standard dialects or who wrote as they spoke" (p. 141).

Breaking away from an insistence on decontextualized correctness and on standardized English is no small task in any grammar course, due to the assumptions that college students have, or *should* have access to the forms of standardized English, that students from racially-minoritized backgrounds do not have access to such forms, and that if they work hard enough, they will be able to acquire and deploy them in all academic contexts, and then their language use will become "appropriate." Flores and Rosa (2015) challenge these ideas, arguing that, because of the "raciolinguistic ideologies" that prevail in U.S. and other educational contexts, and due to the United States' cultural regard for the primacy of the white gaze in all educational matters, it does not really matter what a person of color sounds or writes like. That is, if they, from an objective, grammatical perspective, speak and write their local standardized English "perfectly," they will still not be accorded "correctness" and "appropriateness" because they are not white speakers and writers. As Flores and Rosa put it,

> the ideological construction and value of standardized language practices are anchored in what we term raciolinguistic ideologies that conflate certain racialized bodies with linguistic deficiency unrelated to any objective linguistic practices. That is, raciolinguistic ideologies produce racialized speaking subjects who are constructed as linguistically deviant

even when engaging in linguistic practices positioned as normative or innovative when produced by privileged white subjects.

(Flores & Rosa, 2015, p. 150)

This idea dovetails with Leung, Harris, and Rampton's (1997) conception of the "idealised native speaker" of English. They write, "that there is an abstracted notion of an idealised native speaker of English from which ethnic and linguistic minorities are automatically excluded" (p. 546). That is, speakers of English from apparent racially- and ethnically-, and thence (it is assumed) linguistically-minoritized groups are placed, by their teachers and our educational institutions more broadly, into essentializing linguistic categories with disregard for their actual language expertise and affiliation (Rampton, 1990); because of this othering, these students cannot and will not be accorded the status of "native speaker," no matter their objective competence in English, and the similarity of their linguistic performances to those of white speakers. Leung et al. (1997) challenge "the commonsense, fixed, and clearly bounded notions of language and ethnicity" (p. 547) that prevail in our institutions, which are at odds with our students' "actual language use and expertise" (p. 547).

These essentializing linguistic categories are particularly pernicious in the grammar and composition classrooms, with their focus on standardized grammar and the normalizing force of the assumptions that surround the place of grammar in tertiary institutions. Matsuda (2006) describes the unmarked status of standard American English in the composition classroom as having its source in "the myth of linguistic homogeneity: the tacit and widespread acceptance of the dominant image of . . . students as native speakers of a privileged variety of English" (p. 638). This myth, of course, is not restricted to composition, and it leads to suppression of the linguistic diversity of students in any classroom, as well as the labeling as deficient and in need of remediation those students who are not speakers and writers of these varieties. Similarly, other authors have described the "monolingualizing tendency" (Heller, 1995, p. 374) of educational institutions, which are at best disinterested in students' multilinguality, and at worse see multilinguality as disqualifying students from having the status (and associated prestige) of native speakers of English (Leung et al., 1997; Shuck, 2010; Cox, Jordan, Ortmeier-Hooper, & Gray Schwartz, 2010 and essays therein). Finally, Nero (2005) writes, "Despite the obvious linguistic and cultural diversity of the U.S., the monolithic stance of US-born and raised, therefore monolingual English speaker, is still pervasive" (2005, p. 198).

The image of the "privileged variety of English," even at a linguistically diverse institution like Urban College or State University, is thus still associated with an English speaker who is monolingual, monodialectal, and white; even if a speaker is bilingual, they must show no "interference" from their "other" language in their use of English, and nor may they be assigned a linguistic identity based on an assigned racial or ethnic one. As Marnie Holborow puts it, in stark contrast to the superdiversity (Vertovec, 2007) that we see in our cities, in our educational institutions, in their mirroring and idealization of the language practices of global "elites," we see "linguistic superconformity in action" (2013). The reality of this drive to linguistic conformity as a marker of belonging to the global, social elite, means that in courses that focus on the use of English in an academic or professional context, the assumption, from instructors and students alike, is that the focus will be on the attainment of standardized English, with the consequence of erasing other varieties of English from classroom discourse. With this drive to conformity, then, how can the deep structure of grammar possibly be pluralized, when our very understanding of what tertiary grammar is elides anything but standardized English as a target for grammar instruction?

Several authors have resisted the normalizing force of the tertiary insistence on standardized Englishes to the exclusion of all other varieties as admissible in college-level writing. One alternative, outlined by authors such as Paris and Alim (2014), Young (2010), and Canagarajah (2006, 2011) is a pedagogy where linguistic *versatility* is valued, where the barrier between academic, professional, and personal language is porous, where all a person's languages are seen as contributing to that person's academic-linguistic identity, and all those languages are considered to be resources and appropriate in academic environments and academic writing. In a pedagogical environment that prizes versatility, "correctness," or adherence to a particular standardized version of English, is less important than communicative effectiveness. Teaching that linguistic versatility is valid and valuable helps students to value their multiple linguistic identities—more than teaching rigid correctness can. Young (2010) endorses such an approach:

> So when we teach the rhetorical devices of blacks we can add to the writing proficiency of whites and everybody else. Now, that's something, aint it? Code meshing use the way people already speak and write and help them be more rhetorically effective. It do include teaching some punctuation rules, attention to meaning and word choice, and various kinds of sentence structures and some standard English. This mean too that good writin gone look and sound a bit different than some may now expect.
>
> *(pp. 116–117)*

However, such pedagogies can only be effective when "standard language ideology" (Lippi-Green, 2012) is also addressed; otherwise, as Flores and Rosa (2015) put it, "while appropriateness-based models advocate teaching language-minoritized students to enact the linguistic practices of the white speaking subject when appropriate, the white listening subject often continues to hear linguistic markedness and deviancy regardless of how well language-minoritized students model themselves after the white speaking subject." (p. 152). Similarly, Paris and Alim (2014) write,

> For too long, scholarship on "access" and "equity" has centered implicitly or explicitly around the question of how to get working-class students of color to speak and write more like middle-class White ones. Notwithstanding the continuing need to equip all young people with skills in Dominant American English (DAE) and other dominant norms of interaction still demanded in schools, we believe equity and access can best be achieved by centering pedagogies on the heritage and contemporary practices of students and communities of color.
>
> *(p. 87)*

This latter approach—centering pedagogies on the heritage and contemporary practices of students and communities of color—has a lot in common with the translingual pedagogies that we describe and suggest earlier in this book, and so I take this kind of orientation as the baseline for teaching grammar translingually, in opposition to the "appropriateness-based" models of authors such as Elbow (2012) and Fish (2009), which have been shown by Young (2010) and Green (2016) to be a mask for the racist marginalization of minoritized varieties of English, and thus, of their speakers. In the next section, I move on to a discussion of the concrete pedagogical approaches that I think can enact theories of translinguality in the grammar classroom.

Grammatical Literacies and a Pedagogy of Naming

In this section, I lay out what I mean by grammatical literacy, in the context of the pedagogy of naming that I laid out earlier. I will then move to giving three classroom strategies for teaching grammar from a translingual stance. A grammatical literacy approach to pluralizing grammar instruction has its roots in the work of linguists working in the 1960s and 1970s, such as Labov (1972) and Smitherman (1977), whose work in establishing the "logic" (Labov, 1972) of minoritized varieties of English challenged perceptions that varieties such as African-American English were merely "ungrammatical English," by demonstrating that the grammars of these varieties were rule-governed languages, rather than deviant approximations of the white, middle class English of the metropolitan centers. It also draws on the queer pedagogy of Bryson and de Castell (1993), which they describe as "a radical form of educative praxis implemented deliberately to interfere with, to intervene in, the production of 'normalcy' in schooled subjects" (p. 285). Reframing grammar instruction as instruction in grammatical literacy—that is, being literate in the vocabulary and discourse of the structure of language—interferes with the normalizing pressure of standardized English by creating a discourse of description rather than of correction in the ways we talk about minoritized varieties of English. One specific site for intervention is in the ways we talk about how variation manifests itself in student writing; another is to work with developing a vocabulary of parts of speech and clause structure to support learning rules for punctuation that can be applied to all varieties of English.

Patterns of Error → Patterns of Usage

The main contention of this section is that teaching grammar translingually means changing the ways in which we think about grammar instruction, moving from ideas of grammar as instruction in white middle-class English, to speech-writing interface instruction for all varieties of English. It means challenging ideas of what is "appropriate" language in academic writing, and making visible the problems with discourses of appropriateness in the ways that they further marginalize linguistically-minoritized students. In order to do that, college-level grammar instructors might start with reframing their thinking about "patterns of error" towards a framework of "patterns of usage."

It is often the case that grammar, in the teaching of writing, is taught in the framework of "patterns of error," which addresses the observation that what we identify as student "error" is generally not random, but rather, tends to occur consistently throughout a paper. Indeed, one of the purposes of grammar instruction seems to be having students identify their own "patterns of error" in their writing and work to erase them (e.g. Shaughnessy, 1979; Bartholomae, 1980). This erasure, of course, is the process of having students adapt their writing to more closely conform to the patterns and conventions of written standardized English, particularly as they concern punctuation and agreement and tense marking on verbs. As I wrote in Chapter 9, part of enacting a translingual pedagogy is rethinking what we understand as error. Such a reorientation is particularly important at the sentence level, as so-called errors such as variations in subject-verb agreement and verb tense markers, and verb forms themselves, are, from a grammatical perspective, often key characteristics of different varieties of English. For instance, many varieties of English do not vary their agreement patterns within a verbal paradigm, such as using "was" for all pronouns in the past-tense paradigm of "be": I was, you was, it was, we was, they was. In the terms of standardized English, "we was" and "they was" are errors, to be "corrected" into "they were." However, students who are writing "they was" in one of their papers are likely writing it consistently throughout their papers. Thus, an instructor who wants to take a translingual approach to teaching grammar would, rather than asking students to identify this as a "pattern of error," would instead identify it as a pattern of *usage*, if indeed they want to mention it at all. This renaming is a first step in developing a Critical Language Awareness (Alim, 2004), which attempts to "make the invisible visible by examining the ways in which well-meaning educators attempt to silence diverse languages in White public space by inculcating speakers of heterogeneous language varieties into what are, at their core, White ways of speaking and seeing the word/world" (Alim, 2004, quoted in Alim, 2005).

The renaming I propose, in this context, requires a discussion of what a shift from the term "error" to the term "usage" makes visible, linguistic patterns and attitudes both, and laying the groundwork for a comparative linguistic analysis of different varieties of English. While it may be naïve to suggest that students, when identifying a pattern of usage that differs from that of the privileged variety of English that is enforced as the neutral form in their particular educational environment will not "choose" to change a different pattern of usage that conforms to the hegemonic variety, in a particular classroom environment where no benefit accrues from conforming with the standardized variety of English, students may choose patterns of usage other than those associated with standardized English, and make sure they are consistent with the grammatical rules of the particular variety of English that they are using.

However, in order to identify patterns of usage, it is important to develop a common vocabulary for parts of speech, from the word to the phrase to the clause level. Demonstrating a full pedagogy for grammar instruction is beyond the scope of this chapter; however, I will make two suggestions for building grammatical literacy so as to take a step towards pluralizing our attitudes towards the deep structure of grammar.

Parts of Speech

The first aspect of building grammatical literacy concerns naming syntactic categories as we find them, rather than prescribing what the form of the words that fill these various categories should look like. This means defining parts of speech, such as nouns, verbs, sentence subjects and their component parts, phrases (verb phrases and modifying phrases), and clauses in linguistically-informed ways, prioritizing the linguistic vocabulary in its own right, rather than as secondary to identifying and correcting error. Part of the project for teaching grammar translingually is to show that all texts, regardless of what variety the text is written (or spoken) in, are grammatical in that they follow the rules of grammar(s). One type of text that I have found useful for establishing basic principles of English grammar rules—rules that are shared across all varieties of English—is popular songs. These texts are composed using a wide variety of Englishes, and their structure tends to be fairly simple: sentences are not usually longer than two clauses, and they are joined at the clause level by coordinating and subordinating conjunctions, rather than showing the deep nominal subordination that is typical of academic writing (Biber & Gray, 2010, for instance). The subjects of the clauses also tend to be fairly simple, which means that we can focus on the concept of 'Subject,' as a functional unit within a sentence (as opposed to a lexical unit, i.e. corresponding to a particular category of word). In songs, there is often a mismatch between line breaks and clause breaks, which means that students have to be conscious of clause structure, rather than typographic conventions. A song has just enough complexity to provide students with a serious analytic task, but not too much that they get bogged down.[2]

To analyze the structure of the songs, and so develop the kind of grammatical literacy that supports the argument for variation at the sentence level in academic writing, I provide students with a list of categories to look for, with instructions about how to determine which category or categories a word or phrase might belong to. Students also identify independent and dependent clauses; using lists of coordinating conjunctions and subordinating conjunctions as the main way to identify clauses. I show the results of this kind of analysis in the mark-up that follows, an annotated version of the first verse of The Beatles' *Helter Skelter* (Lennon & McCartney, 1968). I use several other songs too, to model the kind of analysis that I'm looking for.

When$_{sub\text{-}conj}$ I$_{SUBJ}$ get$_{VP}$ **to the bottom**	DC
I$_{SUBJ}$ go$_{VP}$ **back to the top of the slide**	IC
Where$_{Coord\text{-}Adv}$ I$_{SUBJ}$ [*stop*$_{mv}$ *and turn*$_{mv}$]$_{VP}$	IC
and$_{Coord\text{-}Conj}$ I$_{SUBJ}$ go$_{VP}$ **for a ride**	IC
Till$_{sub\text{-}conj}$ I$_{SUBJ}$ get$_{VP}$ **to the bottom**	DC
And$_{coord\text{-}conj}$ I$_{SUBJ}$ see$_{VP}$ **you again**	IC
Yeah, yeah, yeah	

Key: IC = Independent clause; DC = Dependent clause, SUBJ = Subject; mv = main verb; VP = verb phrase; sub-conj = Subordinating conjunction, Coord-Adv = coordinating adverb; Coord-Conj = Coordinating conjunction

The previous example shows work at the level of individual words (e.g. mv, sub-conj etc), of phrases that are syntactically important (e.g. VP, SUBJ) and of clauses (IC, DC). We do not discuss sentences; I find that just getting students used to these three levels is a daunting task for them. The students' job is to become fluent in reading for these parts of speech; fluency, or automaticity, is an important element of being able to complete a complex task. As Fuchs, Fuchs, Hosp, and Jenkins write, when a reader is fluent, 'performance is speeded, seemingly effortless, autonomous, and achieved without much consciousness or awareness' (p. 239). To develop grammatical literacy, students must become fluent enough readers of grammatical structure that they can see patterns in the way sentences are constructed, and so identify their grammatical patterns of usage, potentially in direct opposition to the "patterns of error" discourse that can prevail in academic writing instruction. These patterns of usage are what Young (2010), Anzaldúa (1987), and Smitherman (1977), to name just three, demonstrate in their code-meshed texts: writing consistently within varieties and languages, and refusing to call variation from standardized English forms error.

Clause Boundaries, Punctuation, and the Speech-Writing Interface

Parts-of-speech naming can also provide some building blocks for discussions about the speech-writing interface, which, as I describe earlier, is the site of much vexation in the tertiary classroom. Nero (2005) describes "the greater disparity between oral and written language competence of linguistic minorities [and] their often concomitant inability to distinguish between oral and written language" (p. 202); in Coleman's (1997) framing, "our students write with accents." Various conservative authors (e.g. Fish, 2009; Elbow, 2012) have identified a critical need for markers of English vernaculars to be erased from students' academic written English, and describe the difficulties that they see students facing when asked to do this (for critiques of both of these authors' positions, see Young (2010) for Fish (2009) and Elbow (2012) and Green (2016) for Elbow (2012).

Traditional grammar pedagogy often obscures the fact that naming punctuation as our focus can separate out our conceptions of traditional grammar from linguistic grammar, by using linguistic grammar—the structures of language—to inform our placement of diacritics that only appear in writing. Describing this aspect of so-called grammar work as work on punctuation, which speakers of all varieties of English must learn (as opposed to the acquisition that occurs with first languages) can be part of a translingual approach to grammar because it names the target, and separates it out from linguistic "correctness". Learning punctuation is often one of the major areas that students seek instruction in, as it is often not taught in a way that connects punctuation use to grammatical structures. Most people are familiar with heuristics such as "put a comma where you take a breath" and "a sentence conveys a complete thought," and most people know that apostrophes go before an -s ending, but they have not connected punctuation use with syntactic structures in any systematic way. One of the things that makes punctuation very difficult is that it has no reflex at all in spoken language even though clause boundaries and possessive marking, for instance, certainly exist. In this way, punctuation is the only aspect of writing for which speech offers few clues, and which is a system of norms entirely and deliberately manufactured by humans in order to facilitate reading, rather than listening, and as such, we might say that it is particularly resistant to change. As a result, I suggest, punctuation norms tend to be particularly stable, no matter what variety of English a writer is using; for instance, even when Young (2010) codemeshes Dominant American English and other varieties, he uses standardized punctuation, as we see in the passage that follows:[3]

> Code meshing what we all do whenever we communicate—writin, speakin, whateva.

> Code meshing blend dialects, international languages, local idioms, chat-room lingo, and the rhetorical styles of various ethnic and cultural groups in both formal and informal speech acts.
>
> *(Young, 2010, p. 114)*

In this passage, Young indicates to the reader that he is using black English mostly through spelling that differs from that which would be found in a dictionary of standardized English, which suggests a closer connection to a spoken variety of English than is usually seen in written discourses. The punctuation, however, is very traditional, using commas to indicate elements in a list (including an Oxford comma) in two places, and an m-dash to introduce the first list. Clause boundaries are indicated with periods and line breaks. Elsewhere in his essay, Young uses commas between clauses in complex and compound sentences, and a smattering of semicolons and colons between independent clauses. Even as Young's essay reads with an accent, indicated through the consistent use of morphological structures and syntactic patterns associated with black English, his use of punctuation conforms to the conventions of academic writing. This distinction between the variation of word forms (as indicated by spelling), syntactic structures that affiliate a text with a particular variety of English, and the punctuation which facilitates reading, is a crucial one, but they are similar in one important way: all can be described as patterns of usage that build on the consistent application of grammatical rules. So a focus on punctuation can help students see that grammatical rules apply to all varieties of English, that they are systematic and can be learned as well as acquired (in the language acquisition sense), and that "grammar" in its school sense can be separated from the raciolinguistic ideologies that govern much classroom language instruction. While teaching the rules of conventional punctuation is not very translingual per se, being more precise about what we call "grammar" and making the discourse of punctuation one about rules of a code that is native to nobody can change the way we think about correctness in writing. Then we can focus our anti-racist efforts on broadening perspectives on which accents belong in academic contexts, and whose ideas about correctness actually count.

An example of an assignment that uses grammatical literacy, at the level of the clause, to help students work at the speech-writing interface follows. This assignment, brief as the description is, draws upon an understanding of the connection between punctuation and sentence constituents, and can be applied to an analysis of any variety of English.

Just like in the parts of speech assignment, the reasons for use given earlier require a high-level of grammatical literacy; they use technical grammar terms, which must be introduced and agreed-upon in class. This kind of assignment looks quite like one of the "skill-and-drill" assignments so widely derided in current grammar instruction in the composition context, but which Connors

> Replace the missing punctuation in the following passage. I will give credit for correctness, but sometimes there will be more than one correct answer. For the commas that you use, number each, to indicate the reason for its use, based on the list of reasons for comma use are given later.
>
> 1. Between two independent clauses, before a coordinating conjunction.
> 2. Between a dependent and an independent clause, after the dependent clause.
> 3. Between elements of a list.
> 4. After an introductory sentence modifier (Adverbial, Coordinating Adverb, Prepositional phrase, etc.)
> 5. To separate out non-essential material (around a non-restrictive relative clause, or a non-essential sentence modifier that occurs within a sentence).

(2000) suggests were in fact quite effective in increasing students' sentence complexity. I have found this assignment to be productive in terms of establishing a grammatical vocabulary among students which can be used to discuss not only what students are doing in their academic writing, but also to describe their target forms, whatever they may be, while acknowledging that these targets change dramatically from context to context and that they are often informed by raciolinguistic ideologies throughout the secondary and tertiary curriculum.

Conclusion

Because engagements with grammar in educational contexts are so ideological, a "pluralized" approach to grammar instruction must address the political side of what translinguality means, which means a thorough recognition of the raciolinguistic ideologies that afflict language use and teaching. I have suggested two activities that contextualize grammar instruction within the study of language variation, and have offered ways to talk about and use these strategies as part of an anti-racist pedagogy. The strategy of developing grammatical literacy in order to develop students' writing facility in conjunction with their linguistic identity performances was also proposed by Nero (2005) in the ESL-TESOL context, who suggests that instructors should: "cultivate a metalanguage for language—help students develop the language to talk about form, functions, domains of use, identity, etc., and to see that they already know and use language in diverse ways" (p. 203). The latter point is particularly important: as we discuss throughout this book, facility in a variety of language usages is *normal* for many of our students; it is the responsibility of instructors and institutions to *normalize* this plurilingualism in ways that support our students, rather than minoritizing or exoticizing them. Tuck and Yang (2014) produce a strong critique of research that trades on the exposure of the pain and humiliation of marginalized communities, asking "How do we learn from and respect the wisdom and desires in the stories that we (over) hear, while refusing to portray/betray them to the spectacle of the settler colonial gaze?" (p. 223). The same type of question applies to the teaching of students from linguistically-diverse backgrounds: how do we learn from and respect the wisdom of the students who we work with, while refusing to apply settler-colonial, assimilationist frames of knowing to what we ask them to do in a tertiary environment, or treating their linguistic performances as a "spectacle" for our own enjoyment, and, ultimately, dismissal? In this chapter, I have made a tentative attempt to suggest such a way forward, via a pedagogy of naming, and a building of grammatical literacy that can be applied to all varieties of English.

Many instructors teach grammar as an overlay on the work of teaching writing, with sentence-level correctness treated as a so-called "lower order concern," in contrast to the higher-order concerns of engagement with text, and developing and supporting a thesis. An extended focus on language, however, I suggest, can challenge the raciolinguistic ideologies that form the foundation for the entire enterprise of teaching and enforcing academic writing, by exposing the rule-governed nature of the grammatical structures that all writers bring to their texts, and forcing instructors to name the ideologies that they are reinforcing when they teach, for instance, "subject-verb agreement"—that is, conformity to the agreement patterns of white, middle-class English. What instructors do after this naming is a complicated question, but Nero (2005) suggests that "language should be examined and discussed in its totality—its forms, functions, diversity, links to identity and culture, power, as well as language attitudes" (p. 203) in order to make the connection between the linguistic forms that students use, and the forms that we want students to learn in writing, which can include those from heritage languages and code-meshed linguistic performances such as those advocated for by Young (2009, 2010) and Canagarajah (2006, 2011) and their linguistic identities, rather than excluding non-monolingual, non-U.S. born English users from our discourses and constructions of licensed academic identities.

It is important to recognize that much of what I am writing about here is based on competencies that students already have; it's the instructors who need to catch up. As we have suggested throughout in this book, most college students are adept translanguagers, and as W.E.B. DuBois's idea of double consciousness makes very clear, most students who speak and use minoritized languages and varieties of English are well-used to judging their own linguistic productions through the application of a white gaze. In this chapter, I try to challenge this prevailing white gaze by shifting our discourse about grammar from one of "correctness" and "error" to one of patterns of usage, and consideration of the speech-writing interface; I frame this shift in terms of a pedagogy of naming, where a more precise use of language around what we think about as "grammar" can challenge raciolinguistic ideologies by reorienting what we think about when we use the word "grammar" in an academic context.

Notes

1. I am indebted to my colleague Matt Garley for conversations about the topics discussed in this chapter, and for sharing with me his IWAC 2018 presentation (Garley, 2018).
2. This song assignment is based on one that I did in 1993 at the University of Sydney in James R. Martin's Systemic Functional Linguistics class.
3. I thank my colleague Matt Garley for this insight.

References

Alim, H. S. (2004). Hearing what's not said and missing what is: Black language in White public space. In C. B. Paulston & S. Kiesling (Eds.), *Discourse and intercultural communication: The essential readings*. Malden, MA: Blackwell.

Alim, H. S. (2005). Critical language awareness in the United States: Revisiting issues and revising pedagogies in a resegregated society. *Educational Researcher, 34*(7), 24–31.

Anzaldúa, G. (1987). *Borderlands. La Frontera: The New Mestiza*. San Francisco, CA: Spinsters/Aunt Lute.

Bartholomae, D. (1980). The study of error. *College Composition and Communication, 31*(3), 253–269.

Biber, D., & Gray, B. (2010). Challenging stereotypes about academic writing: Complexity, elaboration, explicitness. *Journal of English for Academic Purposes, 9*(1), 2–20.

Brown, D. W. (2009). Coming to terms with what it means to teach and learn grammar. *American Speech, 84*(1), 216–227.

Bryson, M., & De Castell, S. (1993). Queer pedagogy: Praxis makes im/perfect. *Canadian Journal of Education/Revue canadienne de l'éducation, 18*(3), 285–305.

Canagarajah, A. S. (2011). Codemeshing in academic writing: Identifying teachable strategies of translanguaging. *The Modern Language Journal, 95*(3), 401–417.

Canagarajah, A. S. (2006). The place of world Englishes in composition: Pluralization continued. *College Composition and Communication, 57*(4), 586–619.

Coleman, C. F. (1997). Our students write with accents: Oral paradigms for ESD students. *CCC, 48*(4), 486–500.

Connors, R. J. (2000). The erasure of the sentence. *College Composition and Communication*, 96–128.

Cox, M., Jordan, J., Ortmeier-Hooper, C., & Gray Schwartz, G. (2010). *Reinventing identities in second language writing*. Urbana, IL: NCTE.

Delpit, L. (1993) [2006]). *Other people's children: Cultural conflict in the classroom*. New York: New Press.

Delpit, L., & Kilgour-Dowdy, J. (Eds.). (2002). *The skin that we speak: Thoughts on language and culture in the classroom*. New York: New Press.

Downtown College course catalog. Retrieved from https://www.baruch.cuny.edu/courseinfo/detail/ENG3001

Elbow, P. (2012). *Vernacular eloquence: What speech can bring to writing.* Oxford: Oxford University Press.
Fish, S. (2009, September 7). What should colleges teach? Part 3. *The New York Times.*
Flores, N., & Rosa, J. (2015). Undoing appropriateness: Raciolinguistic ideologies and language diversity in education. *Harvard Educational Review, 85*(2), 149–301.
Fuchs, L. S., Fuchs, D., Hosp, M. K., & Jenkins, J. R. (2001). Oral reading fluency as an indicator of reading competence: A theoretical, empirical, and historical analysis. *Scientific Studies of Reading, 5*(3), 239–256.
Garley, M. (2018). *The descriptivist's dilemma: Writing about English grammar in the superdiverse college classroom.* International Writing Across the Curriculum Conference, Auburn, AL, 5 June 2018.
Green, N. A. S. (2016). The re-education of Neisha-Anne S Green: A close look at the damaging effect of "A Standard Approach", the benefits of codemeshing, and the role allies play in this work. *Praxis: A Writing Center Journal.* Retrieved from http://www.praxisuwc.com/green-141
Heller, M. (1995). Language choice, social institutions and symbolic domination. *Language in Society, 24*(3), 373–405.
Holborow, M. (2013). *Applied linguistics and the neoliberal university: American Association of Applied Linguistics Presentation.* Dallas Sheraton, Dallas, TX, 17 March 2013. Invited Colloquium.
Labov, W. (1972). *Language in the inner city: Studies in the Black English vernacular* (Vol. 3). Philadelphia, PA: University of Pennsylvania Press.
Lennon, J., & McCartney, P. (1968). *Helter Skelter.* Northern Songs.
Leung, C., Harris, R., & Rampton, B. (1997). The idealized native speaker, reified ethnicities, and classroom realities. *TESOL Quarterly, 31*(3), 543–560.
Lippi-Green, R. (1997 [2012]). *English with an accent* (2nd ed.). New York: Routledge.
Martin, J. R., & Rothery, J. (1993). Grammar: Making meaning in writing. In B. Cope & M. Kalantzis (Eds.), *The powers of literacy: A genre approach to teaching writing* (pp. 137–153). Pittsburgh, PA: University of Pittsburgh Press.
Matsuda, P. K. (2006). The myth of linguistic homogeneity in U.S. college composition. *College English, 68*(6), 637–651.
Nero, S. J. (2005). Language, identities, and ESL pedagogy. *Language and Education, 19*(3), 194–211.
New London Group. (1996). A pedagogy of multiliteracies: Designing social futures. *Harvard Educational Review, 66*(1), 60–92.
Paris, D., & Alim, H. S. (2014). What are we seeking to sustain through culturally sustaining pedagogy? A loving critique forward. *Harvard Educational Review, 84*(1), 85–100.
Rampton, B. (1990). Displacing the "native speaker": Expertise, affiliation and inheritance. *ELT Journal, 44*(2), 97–101. Web. 20 August 2012.
Robinson, H. M. (2014). Sentence-building pedagogy and the ethics of grammar instruction. *American Speech, 89*(2), 229–242.
Shaughnessy, M. P. (1979). *Errors and expectations: A guide for the teacher of basic writing.* Oxford: Oxford University Press.
Shuck, G. (2010). Language identity, agency, and context: The shifting meanings of "multilingual". In M. Cox, J. Jordan, C. Ortmeier-Hooper, & G. Gray-Schwartz (Eds.), *Reinventing identities in second language writing* (pp. 117–138). Urbana, IL: National Council of Teachers of English.

Smitherman-Donaldson, G. (1977). *Talkin and testifyin: The language of Black America*. Detroit, MI: Wayne State University Press.

Smitherman-Donaldson, G. (1987). Toward a national public policy on language. *College English*, *49*(1), 29–36.

Solnit, R. (2018). *Call them by their true names: American crises*. San Francisco, CA: Haymarket Books.

Tuck, E., & Yang, K. W. (2014). R-words: Refusing research. In D. Paris & M. T. Winn (Eds.), *Humanizing research: Decolonizing qualitative inquiry for youth and communities* (pp. 223–247). Thousand Oaks, CA: Sage.

Urban College course catalog. Retrieved from https://www.york.cuny.edu/produce-and-print/contents/bulletin/listing-of-courses/listing-of-courses-by-department/ENG/ENG270

Vertovec, S. (2007). Super-diversity and its implications. *Ethnic And Racial Studies*, *30*(6), 1024–1054.

Young, V. A. (2009). "Nah, we straight": An argument against code switching. *JAC*, 49–76.

Young, V. A. (2010). Should writers use they own English? *Iowa Journal of Cultural Studies*, *12*(1), 110–117.

12
BUILDING COMMUNITY, BUILDING CONFIDENCE
Transnational Translingual Emerging Scholars

The international graduate student experience is in some ways more difficult to apply the frameworks of translinguality and transnationality to: the administrative designation of "international student" means that any stay on a student visa is time-limited and contingent on successful progress in students' graduate programs, thus limiting these students' transnational possibilities. Translinguality, too, is problematic: highly conventional disciplinary discourse genres and "standards" mean that it is common for faculty to edit students' writing into so-called perfect English, and the Graduate Academic Success Program (GASP) at State University regularly navigates requests that students "get someone to do a native read" of their work. Furthermore, as Chang and Kanno (2010) have shown, requirements to use English while in their U.S. graduate programs differ widely between disciplines, with some disciplines requiring relatively little immersion in English, and some requiring a great deal. And, while the consensus in the literature is that students do better with the "culture shock" of moving internationally if they have contact with U.S. culture beyond their graduate programs, the extent to which students do that also varies widely (see Ravichandran, Kretovics, Kirby, & Ghosh, 2017 and references cited therein). In this chapter, we explore the extent to which students at State University are able to bring disciplinary discourses and "everyday" Englishes together, suggesting that when universities support students in making these connections, students' experience a much greater level of success in overcoming academic "culture shock." The responses from these students also suggest that a focus on communicative effectiveness might be an effective transition to support the development of graduate students' translingual, transnational identities, rather than the current model which often focuses on accent reduction, surface correctness and adherence to disciplinary conventions over providing services and resources that facilitate students' ability to communicate as they apply their disciplinary knowledge and function in their new, "host" environments. In particular, universities that house graduate programs which bring in large numbers of international students would do well to look towards the more "applied disciplines" that we see here—social work and music—to see how students have successfully developed translingual identities as disciplinary practitioners and members of their communities.

In this chapter, we explore the experiences of three graduate students at State University, via interview responses and written work produced within GASP courses. GASP is a program at State University that supports international students with the development of graduate level professional and academic English in their disciplines and in the building of support networks. We examine the degrees to which their disciplinary work and engagement with wider American culture intersect, and suggest that strengthening these intersections creates necessarily translingual spaces which support these students as they seek to negotiate the demands of their academic writing with the experiential learning that is part of their broader education in the U.S. These three students come from a range of PhD programs at State University: one in the social work program, one in music performance, and one in computer engineering. By bringing together the experiences of these three students, we demonstrate how building their ability to trans- between disciplinary discourse and interpersonal interaction can deepen and enhance their engagement in their disciplines, and prove to be personally rewarding. We explore how these students' general English language development and their disciplinary discourse development intersect, and how the support that they receive at State University has facilitated these intersections.

Method

This qualitative study is based on information collected from in-depth interviews with graduate students enrolled courses offered by, or who are otherwise affiliated with GASP. We also read "Intellectual Autobiography" assignments written by students enrolled in one of the academic support courses offered within this program, taught by Nela. Students were interviewed in person in the GASP office; interviews lasted for one hour. There were two interviewers (Jonathan and Nela) present for two of the interviews which we discuss later; the third was conducted just by Nela. The interviews were structured (Wright, Lichtenfels, & Pursell, 1989), though questions were often rephrased to enable students' understanding of what kind of response the interviewers were seeking. Nela's position as Director of GASP and as the students' current or past instructor also gave her access to contextualizing information such as students' written assignments and knowledge of biographical information on

TABLE 12.1 Graduate Student Participant Grid

Pseudonym	City/Country	Years in US	Years at State University	Program
Hanfang	China	≥5	≥2	computer engineering PhD
Xiaoli	Taipei	≥5	5	social work MSW/PhD
Li-kuo	Tianjin, China	≥5	4–5	music

their programs' websites, for instance; she shares her perspectives on students' participation in GASP after we present the interview responses; these reflections also include transcriptions of students' comments made in these courses. Analysis of interview data was inductive: transcripts of the interviews were read to see which themes emerged, and then reread when those themes were identified to group students' responses under these thematic headings. At this point, other materials (student writing samples and biographical information) were brought in to contextualize and develop the themes discussed in this essay, and Nela's reflections provide more context for the students' translingual and transnational identity formations.

Student Participants

Of the nine students who participated in the interviews, we focus on three in this chapter. Three of the students interviewed came from Taiwan, five from mainland China, and one from Honduras. Because the challenges that students from China and Taiwan face when participating in U.S. graduate programs are relatively well-explored, we deepen this exploration by focusing on Chinese and Taiwanese students here. In Table 12.1, we introduce the students who participated in the interviews that form the basis of this chapter; all names are pseudonyms.

The Graduate Academic Success Program

In order to frame these three participants' experiences as international graduate students at State University, we offer a brief introduction to GASP, with which all three students have been involved during their time at the university. GASP has in recent years engaged in a deliberate process of rethinking and redefining the graduate academic success possibilities and outcomes for the graduate students it serves. It has aspired to build a program that provides State University's translingual graduate students with a wide range of support options enabling them to realize their full academic and professional potential and aspirations. The program has sought to carefully articulate values that help guide all aspects of the program and that shape how students experience the university. The mission of the program is as follows:

> As a program, we bring a deep understanding of the academic, cultural, and professional identities of translingual graduate students to everything we do. We believe that English language development goes hand in hand with a focus on graduate academic and professional success. We strive to work with university partners who share our vision to optimize the strengths of the global community of graduate students and scholars at the university.
>
> All translingual graduate students at State University are encouraged to enroll in one of GASP's regular courses, one-on-one academic consultations, and any of our seminars and workshops. Visiting scholars, postdoctoral researchers, and faculty are also encouraged to contact us to arrange academic consultations, program visits, or other short-term educational programs.
>
> *(Mission Statement, 2019)*

GASP's mission statement encapsulates several principles and features of the program that we see coming out in the students' interviews, and in Nela's reflections on their participation. One distinguishing feature of the program is that students are seen as not simply clients who need to be "served" but as partners. Indeed, State University's graduate students themselves have informed this process with their thoughtful suggestions, ideas, and proposals. Many of the newest initiatives that the program has instituted and implemented are a direct result of student engagement with the mission of the program. The program envisions itself as a safe space and "home" for these students, a space that valorizes their plural identities and understands their very presence on campus as an advantage to be leveraged and not a problem to be "solved." GASP recognizes that without these students, the university's claim to global ambitions rings hollow, and, indeed, the students in this chapter who we have been fortunate to engage with have been integral and engaged partners in constructing the continued development of the program. One feature of the program is the detailed reflection assessment (a so-called "needs assessment") to learn more about the kinds of support that students wish us to provide. The program also encourages one-on-one discussions and meetings in which they can candidly describe the type of academic and professional preparedness support they think best prepares them for their academic sojourn at the university.

GASP's program-wide learning goals include supporting students in the following areas:

- To understand the culture, expectations, and conventions of the American university.

- To develop effective reading strategies to understand and make meaning from graduate-level academic texts.
- To be able to deploy graduate-level writing skills to effectively convey ideas for both disciplinary and multidisciplinary audiences.
- To be able to effectively and idiomatically engage in oral communication, discussion, presentation, impromptu speaking, and handling of questions.
- To develop the mindset of self-reflection and goal setting for academic and professional success.
- To be able to navigate diverse academic and professional settings and expectations, adapting English communication strategies (both oral and written) to the needs of the situation.

As we can see from these learning goals, GASP emphasizes not only the development of academic Englishes, but centers the broader communicative goals of the students in its pedagogical structures. Furthermore, as director of the program, Nela leads a commitment to changing the language the GASP instructors use in their teaching practices and programming plans, moving away from a discourse of deficit to a translingual discourse whereby communication transcends individual languages. As we see in the fourth learning goal, the goal of working with students' language use is framed as being that "effective" and "idiomatic" communication. In the three profiles that follow, we emphasize how these individual students navigate the broader communicative demands posed by living, studying, and working in the United States, and how disciplinary discourses and everyday Englishes must be considered to be mutually constitutive in the development of a translingual transnational identity performance.

The students whose voices and messages so distinctly emerge in this chapter came to GASP in two ways. Two of these students (Xiaoli and Hanfang) elected to join the program. Li-kuo was asked to join by his graduate director in order to "strengthen writing skills" but more specifically to prepare for his department's required academic reading and writing assessment.

Xiaoli

Xiaoli is a student in the PhD program in social work at State University, nearing the end of her studies. Additionally, she is living in the United States with her school-aged children, and had ten years' experience as a practicing social worker in Taiwan before moving. More than the rest of the participants in this study, she described a life that is quite integrated into U.S. culture beyond her graduate work. Furthermore, for the last five years she has been the coordinator of the Global Women's Group (GWG) at State University, an organization that supports the spouses of international students in the university's graduate programs; she is also a leader in the social work program. She has for a long period of time examined how different the reading and writing practices were as an undergraduate student as compared to graduate student, and has expressed the importance of reading and writing literacies to graduate student success and professional success especially for translingual students.

Alongside a full discussion of the different English language demands placed upon her by her life as a PhD student and her life as a parent of children in the public school system, Xiaoli spoke in her interview about the necessity of connecting disciplinary discourses with everyday discourse in her work as a social worker. Discussing her field placement with Adult Protective Services, as part of her MSW/PhD studies, she spoke about how different the linguistic demands of engaging with the people with whom she was working were from the kinds of discourses she was used to working with in her formal written work. This excerpt from the interview is long, but we include it in its entirety because we think Xiaoli articulates best the co-construction of academic and everyday discourses on which we are focusing here. Some sentences have been removed for clarity; omissions are indicated with ellipsis points.

> But then I did some home visit. . . . It was interesting because I got a opportunity I mean different experience than other international student because I need to see the poor family and then how the house when the people they were in very bad shape.
> [. . .]
> I asked about these things and then I do the home visit and I realized I need to start like a small talk with a client and you know, because those clients they are aging they are seniors. So some of them they have problems speaking or like some people mumbles and he will be very difficult for me to understand and then sometimes they they're like memory or their mental status is not stable.
> Because we have some question to ask we need to do the assessment right? We need to ask either the client itself or the caregivers. So and so we have our purpose we have question to ask and then I need to understand their answers and then make sure I follow him the dialogue and I got the . . . correct information.
> Yeah, I learn and also so after the visit and I helped to do the documentation. So the documentation will see sometimes I think in the first place is was very difficult for me to understand the person's name when they mention about that. There's their relatives. Who and who so yeah. Or the doctor's name, I need to ask him who is who to make sure. And then the other difficulty would be the medication, what medication they have in a day. So those those I need to see ask him. Can I see them the bottle so I can write it down? Yeah. I feel better because social workers, even they are native speakers, they told me that they have problem with those names and places how to spell this. So if I don't I don't feel I don't have

to feel stress. If I couldn't do that. I can just ask them a question about the right right in front of you if you ask somebody to him,

So my English improved a lot at least my listening and also some cultural and also some small talks so I know how do they do the wedding rings? There's somebody proposed, you know, those that daily life. Nobody talk to you about that in your textbook.

Social work is well-known for the challenges its assessment and reporting documents pose for trainee social workers (e.g. Oglensky & Davidson, 2009), and Xiaoli's narrative here testifies to the additional challenges posed for her by interacting with clients in English. But, importantly, she indicates that it was these kinds of challenging interactions—outside academia—that actually helped her English improve, perhaps more than writing within her discipline would. We see potential in this response for finding a way for academic disciplines to support their international graduate students in their lives in the U.S., in that Xiaoli shows a way in which disciplinary work can intersect with more everyday language use, helping with what Angelova and Riazantseva (1999) might be a goal for international students, especially those who think they might "stay" in the U.S. after their studies are complete: she becoming "bicultural" and "biliterate."

Xiaoli started in GASP over five years ago when she first arrived as a graduate student for a master's program. She has consistently enrolled in a wide range of courses, seminars, and workshops every semester that she has been at the university, except this last year when she was working to finish her research and dissertation in order to graduate in May 2020. Faculty in the program have called her the "great alumna" of the program, and she has in many ways come to embody its aspirational qualities. Xiaoli started as someone who, by her own description, struggled with every day social situations. She felt acutely that her language skills and her limited understanding of the cultural context of the American university made her invisible, and that her academic and professional life, the life she had before she came to the United States, was somehow "hidden", non-existent, and in danger of erasure. She came to GASP because she was determined to speak about the issues that mattered to her in her discipline and to do so in yet another language. Her work on behalf of other international students, especially the community of family members and spouses, was critical to her disciplinary and professional identity as a social worker. She was and is an advocate for those who are on the borders and margins of the university community. She understands that her voice must not be muted because she happens to speak another language. Indeed, she leveraged her mother tongue to reach to other members of the community whose experiences and difficulties might not otherwise become part of the conversations in her disciplinary network. Xiaoli took GASP courses that integrate analytical practices, language development and disciplinary content. The availability of these courses within the program enabled her to experience her professional growth while providing the language development that she needed to perform the types of academic and professional tasks she long aspired to undertake. In her earlier course work in GASP, she completed a series of assignments that in her mind have provided the needed scaffolding, structure, and sensibility that she feels has enabled her to complete her program.

In discussions, Xiaoli has pointed to three elements of GASP that made her want to return again and again to take courses in the program. One was the meritocratic sense that the program works to prepare and support all students for graduate academic success. She thought that although she was initially a Masters' student she might not get into the same courses, or get the same support, time or resources from the program. The second feature that she outlined was that the program leadership, staff, and faculty seem to share the responsibility for student success. She was surprised to see the program change class times to accommodate student schedules, include discipline specific materials in courses, and enact curricular changes inspired by student suggestions, while explicitly asking for student feedback. She felt that it was indeed a communal effort and not a solitary enterprise; this, she said, was "motivating" and showed that the program was quite attuned to students wishes, capacities, and goals. The third feature she pointed to was the clear respect and pride for the heterogeneity of the students in the program. This clear embrace of plurality is something that she deeply appreciates because it coincides with her own interest in supporting diverse communities on campus. Her work with the GWG on campus is an important initiative that she still leads with the support of GASP program staff. The GWG is a group of women whose family members are part of the university community and who come together to engage in discussions about the perils and promises of the plurality they live on campus.

The leadership of the GASP program has been heartened to learn that the shared values and principles that guide its work are evident to the students who are central to this mission. Xiaoli has emerged as a leader among her cohort on campus; she speaks with confidence and clarity in her work, has published articles in peer reviewed journals, and has recently inspired some of GASP's first semester students by presenting her current research at the graduate student symposium. The day she presented her work at a Graduate Student Symposium, a forum for sharing research that GASP offers twice a semester, her peers and faculty congratulated her for exemplary presentation skills, impressive research, and excellent answers to audience questions. Her response to the laudatory comments in many ways can be understood as a call to all of us who claim to do the work of supporting translingual students in their academic journeys. She said "I was simply given the space, time, support, and patience required for me to do what so many other have done before and will do after me. I am growing into my professional and academic identity."

Li-kuo

Li-kuo is a professional cellist enrolled in State University's School of the Arts in the music performance PhD program. Before State University, Li-kuo attended a university in the U.S. Midwest and played in orchestras in the city where that institution was located; at State University, Li-kuo is now teaching as a part-time cello performance instructor alongside pursuing his doctoral degree. Li-kuo describes himself as an accomplished user of disciplinary English, describing some of his acquisition process in his interview responses. He is a long-term English learner, saying that

> English was always in many ways a part of my schooling. I had classes in elementary and secondary school but many of the classes were "old style" classes, in other words lots of grammar, reading, writing examples sentences but not much communicating.

Li-kuo's emphasis on communication in this response is important in the context of his own narrative of how his English use has developed: he sees clearly that it is not enough to be able to produce English; rather, he focused on developing it as a language for communication to help him in his professional endeavors, alongside the musical discourse at which he is very adept.

> The adjustment [to using English in the U.S.] was difficult at times in the beginning I realized that what I learned back home was not enough, I could not understand anything but I the day to day trying forcing myself to think in English, asking speakers to repeat for me and reading music and about music in English was really helpful. I decided that I had to make more efforts, work more, practice, make friends. This was the key, speaking to Americans, forcing myself to speak to English speakers, I had to choice, it pushed me and I liked to push myself. It was like another kind of "music", I had to train my ear, compose new words, like music. Make music in English, that is what I was saying/thinking? I am thinking now to you in both languages, strange, right Professor [addressing Nela]? Remember that I came from . . . [another university in the Midwest] before [State University] this really helped me because I had already been preparing myself for a doctoral program. I knew I had to be better than I was, I had to keep "making the English music", speak, push myself.

Li-kuo's assessment of the limited usefulness of English instruction in China reinforces the findings of several other scholars (e.g. Shang-Butler, 2015). In this excerpt from the interview, Li-kuo talks about the importance that he found in speaking to English speakers, and trying to communicate rather than just "speak." The challenges of communication also are a focus of

Li-kuo's Intellectual Autobiography, as it is through his comfort with communicating in English that he also tracks his professional development as a musician. In his Intellectual Autobiography, he reflects on the linguistic and social demands of teaching and being principal cello in a professional regional orchestra:

> Play cello in a professional orchestra as a principal is a very hard job for me at the beginning. Not only I have to play good but also the relationship between the whole cello section. Principle supposed to have good leadership and very good communication with other strings leadership. Significantly, communicate with conductor is one of the most important part of it.
>
> Teaching students at [Midwestern University] and [Midwestern String Academy] are encouraging me too much to get a doctoral degree because from the results of my students I realize I love teaching. I love to see the big improvement from them. One of the best part of teaching is that I can learn so many things from my students.

In reality, this kind of applied translinguality is what all students who aspire to be part of the professoriate, especially in the U.S.—as these students indicate that they do—are working to develop. We can help students do this kind of applied disciplinary translanguaging with robust support systems that center students' agency.

Li-kuo took two courses in the GASP program. The courses were a two-semester sequence, required by Li-kuo's graduate program. In the first course his program requested that GASP emphasize academic reading and writing strategies that would enable students like Li-kuo to successfully pass a program-wide assessment, so as to be permitted to continue the academic component of their doctoral program. While in the first course in this sequence, Li-kuo stated, "I want to learn to be a successful performer and academic. Can I do both? I need to do both."[1] Li-kuo's observation that somehow he had to "first take the academic writing assessment" and then "enroll in the academic program" confounded him and most of his classmates. While the program's goals were intended to support the students in this rigorous program, in which musical performance and scholarly performance were equally valued, Li-kuo saw this as an impossible request and, at times, one that was not just. He envisioned his two identities as performer and emerging academic as inextricably tied, and was heartened to learn that course content integration and language development were the very definition of this academic skills in the disciplines course, one of the signature courses of the program. In the first semester of the course, Li-Kuo read, wrote, listened to and spoke about his work, his performance and that of his fellow classmates. He read many of the "canonical" music theory essays and peer reviewed journals, and he and his classmates delighted in discussing how these academic texts actually informed their performance and generated new ideas about music.

Li-kuo enjoyed recognizing that "academic language" was another language and he was a musician, whose life, as he said, is "about my love of music, yet another language I speak." He often reminded his classmates that they could complete a writing task in preparation for their assessment because, as musicians, they too "engaged in the stages of writing" or, as he called it, "the stages of composing." He pointed out the incredible similarities between their process of composing music and the process of composing writing for the GASP writing course. He enjoyed completing the Intellectual Autobiography, which is a signature assignment for GASP. Every GASP student does this assignment; offers a narrative of students' academic and professional identity. The assignment is both written and video recorded. Li-kuo explained to the class his process for completing the assignment. He first completed his "video performance;" he watched it, listened to himself, "read" himself and then came back to the writing component. He said he started from his "already established" identity, that of a talented musician who has performed around the world, taught in his native China, taught in the United States, and was recruited to this university for his incredible talent, an identity that, as he would say, "is not emerging" but is "more like arriving."

Exploring and leveraging his strengths in his identity as a "music artist," as he would say, enabled him to "build up" his identity as an emerging academic writer in a language that is not his own. He saw the Intellectual Autobiography as an "authentic" assignment and not one invented to practice language skills; rather it is an assignment connected to real tasks that students must perform, such as the development of an artist statement or, in Li-kuo's case, the biography that would later be put on a website in the department in which he would teach as a part time lecturer. The work of the Intellectual Autobiography was a spiral assignment, one assignment creating different types of assignments for specific and relevant academic and professional reasons, but each one providing an opportunity to revisit language, structure, and ideas that would, eventually, lead to more effective, clearer and, in some cases, persuasive writing. That kind of writing would also enable students to develop a voice and, as Li-kuo would suggest, a distinct style. The point where Li-kuo was able to describe this assignment as "mine" was a break through moment in many ways for Li-kou and for his classmates.

Throughout the semester, it became clear that he was much less worried about the end-of-semester assessment and more interested in readings on the history of western music, on western musical and artistic movements, and how they differed from artistic traditions of his native China. Li-kuo welcomed the focus on ideas, on the music instead of "the fact that my English is not perfect"; he saw the class, as he called it, "real" and not "remedial," and during a one on one meeting, he expressed his interest in the course for the following semester when he could "put to practice" many of the writing experiences he discovered and uncovered in the class. At the end of the semester, Li-kuo took the assessment along with his classmates. The students requested, and GASP suggested to the music program, that the students should take the assessment in the last week of classes (rather than during the exam period) so that it could be understood as simply another authentic professional task and not as a high stakes "English Exam." The music program was amenable to the suggestion, and Li-kuo as his classmates welcomed this change of venue and format. He expressed a remarkable calm and ease in the days leading up to the assessment, and, on the day of the assessment, he pointed out that they would pass because they had learned that they were not only musicians but writers and thinkers.

The following semester Li-kuo did indeed take the writing course without the reticence that he expressed when he first was asked to join the program. Li-kuo and his cohort started their academic course work in addition to their performance work. The courses they took in the program built on the practices and discoveries of academic writing identities, disciplinary expressions and professional preparedness from the previous semester. In the second semester of the course, Li-kuo expressed his delight with another signature element of the program's courses: several one-on-one meetings with the instructor combined with class meetings to build on the sense of a "community of writers" that was established in the first semester. Li-kuo invited some of the faculty to hear him perform at the end of the semester, and he poignantly added the following to his invitation: "please do come and watch me perform in a different but equally important way, it is my way, I may not always perform well with the pen, or computer but those lessons continue to shape my work."

Hanfang

Hanfang, a student in the computer engineering PhD program at State University, came to the U.S. as an undergraduate junior at a large Midwestern university, then continued there as a graduate student in a STEM field. When her advisor changed jobs and locations, Hanfang moved with him:

> I continued for my graduate study in same school. So in my senior year I'm like interested in software engineering but I realized computer architecture hardware design super important as I push myself to like join a hardware secure lab completely new area for me. Yeah. So then in my second year of the PhD . . . my advisor of me they would I mean he's going to move to [State University] and for me like would I should like go with him and I say sure of course because I love the location of [State University].

At times, Hanfang's challenges with academic English seemed almost insurmountable. At these times, Hanfang reminded herself about the stakes and found strategies to survive, to gradually improve in-class comprehension, and ultimately to thrive. One strategy that she describes in detail is that of purposeful listening, pushing her auditory comprehension of spoken English in a classroom context, which can often be a challenging one:

> Yeah, so I think because it has this is my opportunity to stay here. So I forced myself to stay. So I was I would listen to the professor. I probably in the first class, I got only half or maybe 30% of the content and I understand and I was counting down the time to defend myself because last the class of but I know I have to sit there and get through it. So I think I understand when I got like almost 90% 100%. It was the last class of the semester.

Hanfang was fortunate in having a professor for that course who was herself experienced in translingual transitions, and so could give her practical advice:

> Yeah and during that time. I asked my professor. She's from Korea and she speaks good English accent. I asked how did you improve your English and she told me that you probably you don't have time for English, but she would suggest me. She suggested me to watch TV show. So and then I asked my roommate so I started the first TV show I watch is *Prison Break* and it funny I watch the TV show and then I took notes. I wrote down those four camera. I didn't know that. However, I didn't I wasn't sure if I can use those idioms that are all about life in prison. I remember the first semester most of the time I stayed silent.

As this excerpt from the interview with Hanfang shows, while her comprehension of English improved because of her instructor's advice, she still "stayed silent" most of the time. These everyday discourses did not offer Hanfang the kind of support that she needed with her academic Englishes; even now, when Hanfang is an accomplished writer of academic Englishes, she expresses the following about "general writing," and also describes her advisor's heavy-handed editing of her written work:

> And also I hate general writing. . . . [My advisor] said 'I had no idea about how to write how to do the writing.' Yeah and I say, why is that I never think this so negative comments. Before like and I then I start to look at it. There were pages like he has commented on every sentence I wrote and eventually I said, well, that's a really good one and I can't I understood why my advice what I wrote before just because there's a big difference big Improvement. For that academic writing and I along with I think the professor never also told us about like some academic writing say you cannot use the that word "get" in your paper, but you

should use "provide" in that paper. These kind of things like have to really learn how to do the kind of professional academic writing for the idea for papers. I think that's that's kind of challenging for me because if you think about engineering and you know, really it's not that hard you don't have to really be definitely {literary}. I read a lot and read a lot like technical report and papers and that's who we rely on time.

Indeed, unlike Li-kuo and Xiaoli, translinguality of the kind we have seen in the earlier sections is a long way away for Hanfang. Disciplinary communicative expectations seem to have meant that she has had very little opportunity to make connections between English and her other languages in her disciplinary work, and the Englishes that disciplinary work have not required her to develop everyday communicative competencies. Hanfang is clear that what she wants to focus on is "academic writing," and specifically writing in her particular discipline. She is impatient with what she calls "general writing" and although she is now very accomplished in academic writing in English and is working on her dissertation, she recounts still struggling with more everyday genres. Her experience reflects that narrated in Chang and Kanno (2010), where two of the students, in "technical disciplines," had very limited demands placed on their "discursive" English competence by their disciplinary discourses. Hanfang's experience of being able to limit her use of an exposure to everyday Englishes stand in direct contrast to the experiences of Li-kuo and Xiaoli, who have to move regularly between their disciplinary discourses and everyday genres in order to do their professional and academic work,

For Hanfang, as for Yi-fen in Chapter 6, English has become her professional language in her discipline:

> I tried to like create a resume in Chinese version. I had a really hard time. I had no idea about how to create a resume in Chinese, but I know how to create a resume in English. And now I after I took that us to deal with the present and the future and I feel that also now, I'm bad at don't like Chinese academic words writing really now.
>
> Because my major is engineering I need to know what's going on in the real world so that I can keep myself in the state of art stage and never lose the track. I don't know. I pray I think I hope because I'm not a person like have to stay in one place. I always loved moving. Yeah, and so you may want be one of these people where there's a project here and next year there's a project somewhere else. Look, they're working you ask or come back to China or another that different countries to work. I don't know what it's like now. I don't have a clear plan about that. You just feel like I think I just want to pick a place where I feel comfortable right now.

Hanfang was "exempt" from course work in her graduate program at State University. However, her program, which is very rigorous and exacting, and her responsibilities as a teaching assistant, seemed to compel her to explore courses with GASP. In a skills inventory meeting—what is often called "needs assessment"—faculty in GASP met with Hanfang so that she could tell us what kinds of course offerings and support might best be suited to her language and academic skills, responsibilities and tasks. In this meeting, Hanfang shared her academic experience prior to her arrival at State University, and articulated what kinds of support she was seeking at GASP.

After the skills inventory advising meeting, it quickly became clear that Hanfang was a very experienced teaching assistant who in fact had already taken an extensive International Teaching Assistant Program at her previous university and was about to teach her first class at State University later in the week. During the advising session, she selected GASP's Studio course for her formal instructional engagement with the program. It was, according to her, an "inspired choice"; she was intrigued by the design and goals of this course. The course is designed as a "Studio" informed by principles of Studio teaching (Tassoni & Lewiecki-Wilson, 2005; Sutton & Chandler, 2018 and essays therein). In Studio, students work on academic and discipline academic or professional projects, and there is a continued focus on cooperative and collaborative learning and on fostering student independence. It also features the best of small group work along with one-on-one academic consultations. Hanfang requested a focus on oral and research based presentational communication skills although she did work on some writing tasks. She saw these Studio sessions as an opportunity to showcase her dual role as emerging scholar and teacher. She asked if she could in fact work on "relevant and discipline specific projects" and was genuinely surprised when she noted that in a discussion of the syllabus and course work, the emphasis was placed on discipline specific projects selected by the students.

Hanfang also chose to develop role-plays as well as effective ways to address student content related questions during her office hours with her students. Hanfang relied on her Studio classmates' thoughtful suggestions to her "role plays" and eventually took on a leadership role in the Studio course due to her positionality as the only doctoral student Teaching Assistant with experience studying, living, in the Midwestern USA, in a course filled otherwise by first semester doctoral students, who were recent arrivals to the United States, and students in Masters' programs. She also selected to work on refining a conference presentation at a global conference in which she would have the opportunity to present her current global research, present her work for a possible award, and subsequent funding.

The work she did in the course was, she said,

> fulfilling, I feel that I am an emerging scholar and not simply my mentor's assistant, I understand the possible value of my work and I feel that

> I am really a faculty member and not an extra pair of hands needed for grading.

This was a theme that she returned to many times, and which echoes the feeling that other ITAs have also shared: that they have been recruited to do the work of their discipline but that they are as she would say "not good enough to be seen, heard, or contribute." Hanfang told the class one day that "being an ITA at times was as frustrating as being a woman researcher in computer science." She explained that in many cases she found herself struggling to make her voice heard not because of her "English language skills" but because of her gender and "ITA" status. She saw herself as in many ways being "the other" because of her gender, her race, and this elusive status that enabled her to be both an insider (she is a faculty member) but an outsider (the international graduate student); she often stated, "I want to remove the dreaded 'I' in ITA" then perhaps my status might change and I can simply be a "TA," because she felt that she did the same work of her fellow American born TAs but she was in a constant struggle to "legitimize myself in a place that claimed to have wanted me to come to State University . . . do they want me or the 'idea' of me, just an international statistic?"

Hanfang came to see Studio as a "safe space where I can breathe and be a computer scientist with ideas," the educator who has just helped students make sense of a confusing concept. Indeed it was in a studio individual session in which she presented her conference presentation. She had "scaffolded" the presentation herself, provided an outline, drafted the presentation, audio recorded herself and later video recorded herself. She asked the instructor and later her studio classmates to "be hard on me, critique me, I have to be prepared to defend my ideas, I can handle it, I really can." It is important to note that at the start of the semester these sessions in which students offered constructive critiques about their work unsettled Hanfang and she freely admitted that perhaps she was not ready for the "challenges of a conference." Towards the end of the semester she attended the conference, and her presentation was so well received that she was able to network with people whose work she had read in global journals. Her innovative idea, it turns out, had impactful and commercial possibilities. One of the colleagues told her, "you found your voice," and, as she proudly shared with her classmates and instructor, "I never lost it, I learned how to be heard in contexts like these."

Conclusion: Support Program Design and Participation

Sharma (2019) writes that international graduate students need "Effective support programs [that] use inclusive, accessible, and engagement-driven practices in order to foster students' intellectual and social agency, especially by advocating for the students' success and wellbeing" (vi). As we have seen, these three students' access to GASP has made a big difference in their "intellectual and social agency," particularly, we suggest, as the program has provided space and support for connecting and developing students' professional and linguistic identities. As Nela recounts in her reflections on and contexualization of the students' interview responses, the students see their involvement with GASP as having been very important for their "success and wellbeing," supporting them as they make connections beyond their academic programs, as well as they undertake the academic tasks required of them.

One of the contributions of this chapter is that it provides a portrait of what kinds of support structures that graduate students themselves identify as being important in their translingual transnational development. They identify, specifically, the ability to create a program of courses and support services that meet their own assessment of their needs, venues to perform emerging professional identities in front of a supportive audience, and a group of faculty who are willing—and equipped—to help them navigate the cultural and linguistic demands of the research university, and the students' emerging professional and academic lives. As Hanfang said to Nela, effective support for international students helps them not to find their voice, but rather, to "learn how to be heard in contexts like these."

Note

1. These quotations included in Nela's descriptions of and reflections on the students' participation in GASP come from Nela's notes, in which she included transcriptions of various interactions with Li-kuo, Hanfang, and Xiaoli, as well as other students.

References

Angelova, M., & Riazantseva, A. (1999). "If you don't tell me, how can I know?" A case study of four international students learning to write the US way. *Written Communication, 16*(4), 491–525.

Chang, Y. J., & Kanno, Y. (2010). NNES doctoral students in English-speaking academe: The nexus between language and discipline. *Applied Linguistics, 31*(5), 671–692.

Mission Statement. (2019). *Graduate academic success program.* State University.

Oglensky, B. D., & Davidson, E. J. (2009). Teaching and learning through clinical report-writing genres. *International Journal of Learning, 16*(9).

Ravichandran, S., Kretovics, M., Kirby, K., & Ghosh, A. (2017). Strategies to address English language writing challenges faced by international graduate students in the US. *Journal of International Students, 7*(3), 3–7.

Shang-Butler, H. (2015). *Great expectations: A qualitative study of how Chinese graduate students navigate academic writing expectations in US higher education.* Unpublished doctoral dissertation. University of Rochester.

Sharma, S. (2019). Focusing on graduate international students. *Journal of International Students, 9*(3), i–xi.

Sutton, M., & Chandler, S. (Eds.). (2018). *The writing studio sampler: Stories about change*. Fort Collins, CO: The WAC Clearinghouse/Boulder, CO: University Press of Colorado.

Tassoni, J. P., & Lewiecki-Wilson, C. (2005). Not just anywhere, anywhen: Mapping change through studio work. *Journal of Basic Writing, 24*(1), 68–92.

Wright, P. M., Lichtenfels, P. A., & Pursell, E. D. (1989). The structured interview: Additional studies and a meta-analysis. *Journal of Occupational Psychology, 62*(3), 191–199.

13
CULTIVATING A CULTURE OF LANGUAGE RIGHTS

Nela Navarro

Sites of Negotiation

Toni Morrison, in her 2015 article in *The Nation*, wrote "There is no time for despair, no place for self-pity, no need for silence, no room for fear. We speak, we write, we do language. That is how civilizations heal" (Morrison, 2015). In this chapter, I explore the centrality of language rights in the work of addressing violence done to historically marginalized groups in the context of the language and writing classroom. As Morrison writes, acknowledging and fostering the right to language, and individuals' and communities' sovereignty over their languages, not only helps them to face the world; it is also central to the healing that is needed to build a more equal, more just future. I take the intertwined nature of healing, courage, and justice that Morrison offers as my starting point for this chapter.

Translingual approaches to the existing composition classroom require a significant rethinking of writing spaces and teaching practices. Such approaches invite a "thinking beyond" the existing prescriptive spaces and practices and "towards" spaces as sites for negotiation and practices that nurture the complex process of meaning making. These spaces challenge institutions that claim to uphold and embody plurality, tolerance, respect, and inclusion of "others" who they admit into the hallowed halls of their universities. After all, many institutions of higher learning, particularly in the United States, actively pursue these "multilingual" students so that their very presence can lend legitimacy to their claims of creating truly global universities that prepare students for the promises and perils of twenty-first century living.

University administrators from a range of offices recruit, invite, and welcome language minority students into these spaces, students both domestic and "international," who enhance the university's image and standing. This process of recruitment with the aim of diversifying the campus has perhaps unintended consequences. In many cases, administrators using the language of addressing students' "needs" rather than the language of being attuned to the capacity and aspirations of students (Hakuta, 2011) creates distinct and separate programming that highlights the students' sense of marginality and exclusion rather than cultivates a sense of community and inclusion. The seemingly small but rich space of a writing classroom can be seen as a promising site for enactment, cultivation, and protection of language rights. What might a human rights or, to be more specific, a language rights based lens offer to a discussion of translingual spaces and practices in a college classroom?

Language Rights as Human Rights: Definitions and Declarations

Exploration and discussion of language rights and linguistic rights have traditionally emerged in the context of discussions of language as an integral part of maintaining the nation-state. Indeed, earlier scholarship on linguistic rights has focused principally on "dominant or official" languages being imposed on a people, or the role that linguistic rights might play in stabilizing national discord resulting from historical, cultural, and linguistic differences. A transnational perspective allows us to consider language rights at levels other than that of national governments, including how this framework impacts institutional assumptions and pedagogical practices involved in higher education language and literacy instruction.

Language as a human right was introduced as part of the original United Nations' Universal Declaration of Human Rights in 1948 in Article Two: "Everyone is entitled to all the rights and freedoms set forth in this Declaration, without distinction of any kind, such as race, color, sex, language, religion, political or other opinion, national or social origin, property, birth or other status" (UDHR, 1948). It was not until the late 1980s and 1990s that linguistic rights were recognized in an official capacity in many transnational discussions, treaties, and international law.

Although language as a human right was understood to be outlined in article two of the Universal Declaration of Human Rights, which included language as one of the key categories for equal rights, many advocates of linguistic rights felt that this was not enough to promote linguistic rights. What's more, there were also those who felt that "separating" language from the basic categories for human rights endangered the very right to language that advocates of a new declaration of linguistic rights wanted.

As part of this exploration of language rights, human rights, and linguistic rights, it is important to work with a common definition, such as the one outlined in the United Nations Special Rapporteur on Minority Rights (de Varennes, 2011): "Language rights" and "linguistic rights" are human rights that have an impact on the language preferences or use of state authorities, individuals and other entities. Language rights are usually considered broader than linguistic rights. In international law, these rights are usually examined in the context of cultural and educational rights. Language rights are therefore understood to be a part of basic human rights.

> The rights of minorities are often thought of as constituting a distinct category of rights, different from traditional human rights. Such a view fails to recognize that the use of descriptive expressions such as "minority rights" or "language rights" may be useful, but also imprecise. Most of what are widely recognized as minority rights are in fact the direct application of basic human rights standards such as freedom of expression and non-discrimination. This means that language rights are not collective rights, nor do they constitute "third generation" or vague, unenforceable rights: by and large, the language rights of minorities are an integral part of well established, basic human rights widely recognized in international law, just as are the rights of women and children.
>
> *(de Varennes, 2012)*

It is critical to understand that language rights are not simply a part of a "newer generation of rights" (de Varennes, 2012) or simply lesser human rights; rather, what we refer to as language rights derive very specifically from the general human rights standards protected by international law.

Despite concerns by human rights advocates such as de Varennes that there was no need to speak of linguistic rights as a separate category, advocates for linguistic rights drafted the Universal Declaration of Linguistic Rights. The document was adopted on the last day of a global conference on linguistic rights held in Barcelona in June of 1996. This document has been signed by many global non-governmental organizations and enjoys wide support by global advocates of linguistic rights and, particularly, by those concerned with linguistic genocide and the plight of endangered languages.

This declaration was also presented to UNESCO, but to date it has not gotten approval from this body or any of the United Nations related bodies. The declaration has been critiqued as being naïve, for embracing the idea that "all languages are equal" and, in so doing, for negating the protections and rights they seek to uphold for the very languages that need this protection the most.

Critics also point out that the declaration's definition of a "language community" as "any human society established historically in a particular territorial space" is quite limited. It seems to suggest that those who are not part of this category have no option other than to assimilate, since, for example, having the right to education in the "language of the territory" does not necessarily mean having the right to an education in your own language. Supporters of the declaration point out that it is this very document that enshrines the need to protect against linguistic genocide and to protect and sustain endangered languages.

The critiques and lack of adoption by the United Nations bodies has not deterred proponents of the Declaration of Linguistic Rights. The Girona Manifesto was developed in 2011 by the International Pen Club as a commemorative document to celebrate the 15th year anniversary of the original declaration in Barcelona, Spain. This new manifesto abbreviated the original declaration as a way to garner more support and facilitate the planning and implementation for entities that have adopted or intend to adopt the manifesto. It also developed a focus on linguistic rights as a way to defend and promote freedom of expression. The manifesto has been translated into numerous languages and informs the work of many educators, particularly those who are concerned with advancing linguistic rights in educational contexts. The following principles articulate in clear language the critical role that language plays in the human experience.

Girona Manifesto on Linguistic Rights

1. Linguistic diversity is a world heritage that must be valued and protected.
2. Respect for all languages and cultures is fundamental to the process of constructing and maintaining dialogue and peace in the world.
3. All individuals learn to speak in the heart of a community that gives them life, language, culture, and identity.
4. Different languages and different ways of speaking are not only a means of communication; they are also the milieu in which humans grow and cultures are built.
5. Every linguistic community has the right for its language to be used as an official language in its territory.
6. School instruction must contribute to the prestige of the language spoken by the linguistic community of the territory.
7. It is desirable for citizens to have a general knowledge of various languages because it favors empathy and intellectual openness, and contributes to a deeper knowledge of one's own tongue.
8. The translation of texts, especially the great works of various cultures, represents a very important element in the necessary process of greater understanding and respect among human beings.
9. The media is a privileged loudspeaker for making linguistic diversity work and for competently and rigorously increasing its prestige.
10. The right to use and protect one's own language must be recognized by the United Nations as one of the fundamental human rights.

(International Pen Club, 2011)

The Girona Manifesto and the Pen International Club who led the charge to draft this document also included the concept and term "translation" as it understood translation to be inseparable from linguistic rights, a position that many who drafted the Universal Declaration of Linguistic Rights hoped would be included in the 2011 document. The Pen International Club sees translators as "central to the promotion of the right of all linguistic communities to be treated as equal" (International Pen Club, 2011).

Language Rights and Minority Rights

Language rights in the context of accords and treaties were usually connected to discussions about minority rights. This association in many ways complicates the discussion of the language rights of minority groups because there is no internationally agreed upon definition as to what constitutes a minority. The larger community of human rights scholars and practitioners and state agents, however, seem to agree for the most part that definitions of minorities must include both objective factors (statistics, data, facts, etc.) and subjective factors (the group's understanding and definition of themselves as a minority group).

This inclusion of the subjective factor, intending to give the minority group agency in determining and defining their status, is critical. This focus on the subjective also shifts the task of determining who is a minority away from the nation-state. For this reason, a common definition used to define a minority group presented by the United Nations Sub-Commission on Prevention of Discrimination and Protection of Minorities is the following:

> A group numerically inferior to the rest of the population of a State, in a non-dominant position, whose members—being nationals of the State—possess ethnic, religious or linguistic characteristics different from those of the rest of the population and show, if only implicitly, a sense of solidarity, directed towards preserving their culture, traditions, religion or language.
>
> *(OHCHR, 2019)*

Although this definition of minority rights is imperfect, the inclusion of "non-dominant" in the definition is significant, since it clearly illustrates the crucial relationship between language rights and minority rights. Given the centrality of language to human experience and the key role it plays in the expression of identity, rights issues related to language are especially critical for linguistic minorities who aspire to maintain and nurture their cultural and linguistic identity, often in the face of exclusion and discrimination. The United Nations Human Rights Office of the High Commissioner's 2013 report on the language rights reminds us that language rights are clearly present in a wide range of provisions that are outlined in international human rights law.

> Linguistic rights can be described as a series of obligations on state authorities to either use certain languages in a number of contexts, or not

interfere with the linguistic choices and expressions of private parties. These might extend to an obligation to recognize or support the use of languages by minorities or indigenous peoples. Human rights involving language are a combination of legal requirements based on international human rights treaties and standards on how to address language or minority issues, as well as linguistic diversity within a state. Language rights are to be found in various provisions enshrined in international human rights law, such as the prohibition of discrimination, the right to freedom of expression, the right to a private life, the right to education and the right of linguistic minorities to use their own language with others in their group. They are also elaborated on in a variety of guiding documents and international standards.

(Izsák-Ndiaye, 2015)

Although there are differences in the wide range of international human rights laws, accords and standards, it seems that they agree on fundamental duties that states and institutions must meet in order to comply with their responsibilities regarding language. These international documents highlight four focal areas:

1. Dignity: Article 1 of the Universal Declaration of Human Rights declares that all human beings are born free and equal in dignity and rights. This is a fundamental principle and rule of international law, and especially important in issues surrounding the protection and promotion of minority identity.
2. Liberty: In private activities, language preferences are protected by basic human rights such as freedom of expression, the right to a private life, the right of minorities to use their own language or the prohibition of discrimination. Any private endeavor can be protected, whether commercial, artistic, religious or political.
3. Equality and non-discrimination: The prohibition of discrimination prevents states from unreasonably disadvantaging or excluding individuals through language preferences in the provision of any of their activities, services, support or privileges.
4. Identity: Linguistic forms of identity, whether for individuals, communities or the state itself, are fundamental for many. These too can be protected by the right to freedom of expression, the right to a private life, the right of minorities to use their own language or the prohibition of discrimination.

> Linguistic rights issues: (i) should be considered in any activity that involves state authorities and language preferences; (ii) are closely associated with issues of national, collective and individual identity; (iii) have an impact on the participation and inclusion of minorities;

(iv) if not properly addressed in a balanced, reasonable way, can lead to sentiments of alienation or marginalization and potentially instability or conflict; and (v) arise in extremely diverse circumstances and conditions. There is no 'one-size-fits-all' approach to implementing language rights in all the world's hugely diverse national contexts.

(Izsák-Ndiaye, 2015)

These four points though presented in the context of nation-state and institutional responsibilities could inform the practices of educators who are working with language minority students. Each principle can encourage us to rethink how our language minority students are viewed, treated, represented, and talked about in our classrooms and programs.

Each category (dignity, liberty, equality, and identity) invites us to rethink the ways in which we create expectations, give assignments, and assess and support language minority students. Thinking about these issues is not simply an act of philanthropy or kindness designed to "bridge the gap"; rather, it is an integral part of an educator's responsibility to uphold the rights of our students, one that may lead to careful considerations of the curricular designs we create, the classroom conditions we cultivate, and the ways in which we offer students space to enact their rights. Each category may be considered in terms of the following suggested questions:

- **Dignity:** How might a translingual writing class highlight the importance of respecting and promoting minority identities?
- **Liberty:** How might a translingual writing class cultivate opportunities to uphold language preferences and freedom of expression in the chosen language?
- **Equality and non-discrimination:** How might a translingual writing class promote equal access to classroom experiences and support services?
- **Identity:** How might a translingual writing class promote the plurality of identities of language minority students without essentializing the language identity link.

(May, 2013)

A Language Rights Lens for the Writing Classroom

Employing a language rights lens to the work of a translingual college composition class enables us to affirm the importance of language rights and to think deliberately and carefully about how policies, practices, and products in our classrooms open up opportunities to uphold rights and to examine ways to prevent possible rights violations. It is critical to consider the implications of a language rights-based approach for our students in the college classroom. Conceptualizing classroom practices in terms of a language rights frame allows educators to ask: What might this approach yield in the classroom? How can students' rights be better protected? How can their experience be better understood?

- A rights-based approach has the potential to enhance and improve access to the educational experience of the college writing classroom.
- A rights-based approach can generate discussions of empowerment and equality for minoritized groups within the language minority (LGBTQ, religious minority, women, etc) in the classroom.
- A rights-based approach can promote more effective use of university wide resources that support students.
- A rights-based approach can promote conflict reduction, misunderstandings in class, and the broader university community.
- A rights-based approach could promote diverse approaches to plurality and diversity in the classroom and in the broader university community.

While there is clearly a wide range of possibilities that a linguistic human rights framework can offer, it is important to acknowledge the limitations of this very framework. Critiques of this framework include concerns about the potential inequality that can result as a consequence of highlighting the status of a specific minoritized language or language minority group. Another concern is the underlying assumptions about the uniformity of the "collective" language minority group. Perhaps the most significant concern raised about the limitations of this framework is that this frame often envisions language as a singular construct. This last critique has been raised by scholars who are deeply interested in the differences between language communities and speech communities, who frame their work around social community theory, and who discuss and debate how these language minority communities are defined (Morgan, 2004; Saville-Troike, 2008).

Language Rights

An understanding of language rights as a human right is critical for the work of the university writing class. It disrupts the hegemony of singular structures, privileged arguments, idealized writing projects, and a standardized lexicon of "composition." Learning spaces are constituted and the key role that language plays in these writing classrooms is highlighted.

These discussions also demand that we see language as not simply a "tool" the students use to express, but as *the expression* of who they are. We must also be reminded that they have a right to their languages. Furthermore, these rights are asserted in the declaration of human rights and in legal frameworks around the world. They are rights that are considered by many as inextricably tied to basic human and civil rights.

The students in our classrooms are not (and should not be) waiting for their "minority rights" to be enacted in those spaces. Educators and students alike are sometimes unaware of the fact that language minority students have language rights, and that those language rights are the same as those enjoyed by students in the "dominant language" group. The nature of the writing classroom, in which language use, critical thinking, and independent thinking are core components of the work students undertake, provides an optimal opportunity for them to enact and express their identities.

Students annotate reading texts in the margins, take notes and sometimes do so in their languages, not usually because they cannot do this in the dominant language, but because the idea has emerged in their language, and they choose to annotate, note-take, and draft in that language. This enables them to do what we "expect" them to do in the college composition class, that is to engage with the ideas of the texts and develop their own ideas and claims. Students may connect and synthesize to other readings and other thinkers who are writing in another language, not because they did not understand the reading in the dominant language, but because they do not see themselves, their experiences or ideas, represented in the texts of the dominant language. They also may want to connect to other texts because they want to "bring in," introduce, and engage with ideas that they know well, in the same way that we, as educators have selected texts that are familiar to use and that represent our ideas, values, and experiences.

Our language minority students can and do express their identity and ideas using structures that are different. They may be ones that we might often not recognize because we have prioritized one way of writing, in the dominant language, over another, the language of the minoritized. For example, students may have crafted a careful claim and presented it as a "singular" thesis, but we request that they introduce the thesis in the first paragraph even as this structural practice is very specific to one kind of thesis development practice, in one particular language, Academic American English. In Spanish and Chinese, the languages of many language minority students in our American classrooms, for example, one does not "start with an argument" as in American Academic English; rather, one arrives at the argument, at the end of the writing project.

In other words, many of the struggles that our language minority students face are not because they struggle with ideas or with language use but because we have neglected to explicitly remind them that these are particular conventions for a very particular and limited audience/reader, in this case, an American Academic English reader.

We have in a sense placed limitations on their linguistic liberty/freedom to access or leverage the resources that their language might afford them as they work through their writing projects.

Cultivating and Protecting a Culture of Language Rights

Exploring translingual writing spaces with a linguistic human rights-based lens shifts the paradigm of how educators and administrators talk about supporting language minority students and how they design programs and practices that support these students. It invites us to question traditional approaches that favor separate spaces for students who are "speakers of *other* languages," and to question the underlying assumptions of classrooms and activities that aim to "mainstream" and assimilate students in the standards and conventions of the dominant language.

These "separate but equal" approaches are hardly equitable and, depending on programmatic implementation strategies, are outright discriminatory. These deficit model approaches to working with and for language minority students as part of a "transition students to the mainstream" project risks diminishing the students' sense of their authentic selves. It can even lead to "covering," that is, to minimizing an identity that is perceived as minoritized and disfavored (Yoshino, 2006). Students may envision especially covering as a necessary to academic life and to academic survival. They may engage in covering even if there are risks to their identity, and well-being. They may especially choose to do so in the college composition class, where their "voice" and status as a minority language student is so clearly visible and "exposed." Language minority students may also recognize that, in the context of these classes, their very status as minority language students has "placed" them into these classrooms in the first place.

Speaking of academic writing as if it is only "done in English" reinforces the monolingual paradigm and its implicit assumptions that has been in place for so long in first year writing classrooms (Canagarajah, 2013; Horner & Tetreault, 2017). This approach, for example, places the responsibility on language minority students' ability to reach the "native" reader and not on the usually monolingual reader's ability to read in different ways, across divides, and engaging with new ideas. A recognition of the rights of minority students involves, in part, taking seriously ideas that often emerge precisely as a result of the language minority student writer's ability to navigate and negotiate across linguistic borders and divides.

Cultivating the rights of language minority students by explicitly acknowledging their translingual status rather than "addressing the needs of their language minority status" affirms the student's right to their identity. Pointing out to students that they are not learning how to "write for the first time" but rather that they are writing for a different audience changes the classroom dynamic from one in which English hegemony is expected and promoted to one in which it is understood that college composition classrooms are exactly the places where languages collide, converge, and create ideas that can be expressed in writing projects.

References

Canagarajah, S. (2013). *Literacy as translingual practice: Between communities and classrooms.* New York and London: Routledge.

de Varennes, F. (2012). *Language, rights and power: The role of language in the inclusion and exclusion of indigenous peoples.* UN Expert Mechanism on the Rights of Indigenous Peoples, OHCHR, Geneva, Switzerland. Retrieved from www.ohchr.org/Documents/Issues/IPeoples/EMRIP/StudyLanguages/FernandDeVarennes.doc

Guerra, J. C. (2016). *Language, culture, identity and citizenship in college classrooms and communities.* New York: Routledge/NCTE.

Hakuta, K. (2011). Educating language minority students and affirming their equal rights: Research and practical perspectives. *Educational Researcher, 40*(4), 163–174.

International Pen Club. (2011). *Girona manifesto.* Retrieved from https://pen-international.org/who-we-are/manifestos/the-girona-manifesto-on-linguistic-rights/read-the-girona-manifesto.

Izsák-Ndiaye, R. (2015). *Comprehensive study of the Special Rapporteur on minority issues on the human rights situation of Roma worldwide, with a particular focus on the phenomenon of anti-Gypsyism.* UN Doc. A/HRC/29/24.

May, S. (2013). *Language and minority rights: Ethnicity, nationalism and the politics of language.* London and New York: Routledge.

Morgan, M. (2005). Speech community. In *A companion to linguistic anthropology* (pp. 3–22). Hoboken: John Wiley & Sons.

Morrison, T. (2015, April 6). No place for self-pity, no room for fear. *The Nation.* Retrieved from www.thenation.com/article/no-place-self-pity-no-room-fear/

OHCHR. (2019). *Minorities under international law.* United Nations Human Rights Office of the High Commissioner. Retrieved from www.ohchr.org/EN/Issues/Minorities/Pages/internationallaw.aspx

Saville-Troike, M. (2008). *The ethnography of communication: An introduction* (Vol. 14). Hoboken: John Wiley & Sons.

Universal Declaration on Human Rights (UDHR). (1948). *United Nations.* Retrieved from www.ohchr.org/EN/UDHR/Documents/UDHR_Translations/eng.pdf

Yoshino, K. (2006). *Covering: The hidden assault on our civil rights.* New York: Penguin.

14
CONCLUSION
Negotiated Identities

Ask the students. That has been our guiding principle throughout this project, and listening to student voices has been key to our research. But this attentiveness to the articulated experiences of students' translingual identities and transnational realities does not take place in a vacuum, because students, like everybody, are social beings and writing is a social and contextual activity.

In this concluding chapter, we will bring together the various influences on negotiated student identities that we have been investigating throughout the book: everyday translinguality, the influence of monolingualism, institutional structures and assumptions, imposed national identities, transnational translingual literacies, and the varied experiences of our students in and out of the classroom, all connected in Figure 14.1.

Everyday Translinguality

One of our central concerns here has been an attempt to make visible the routine, everyday translinguality that many of our students experience and perform. If an instructor in the U.S. writing classroom comes from a monolingual background, these translingual studies may first manifest as an amazing discovery that there are billions of people out there who know more than one language. And more than that: they frequently use more than one of them in a single day. And yet more: that these languages mix together in their heads, to the point where even the concept of "a language" or separate languages begins to get called into question. As we know from research into bilingual speakers' language processing, multilingual speakers have all of their languages running simultaneously, ready to be used (e.g. Bialystok, Craik, & Luk, 2012). Translingual speakers and writers can thus make instantaneous adjustments as they enter

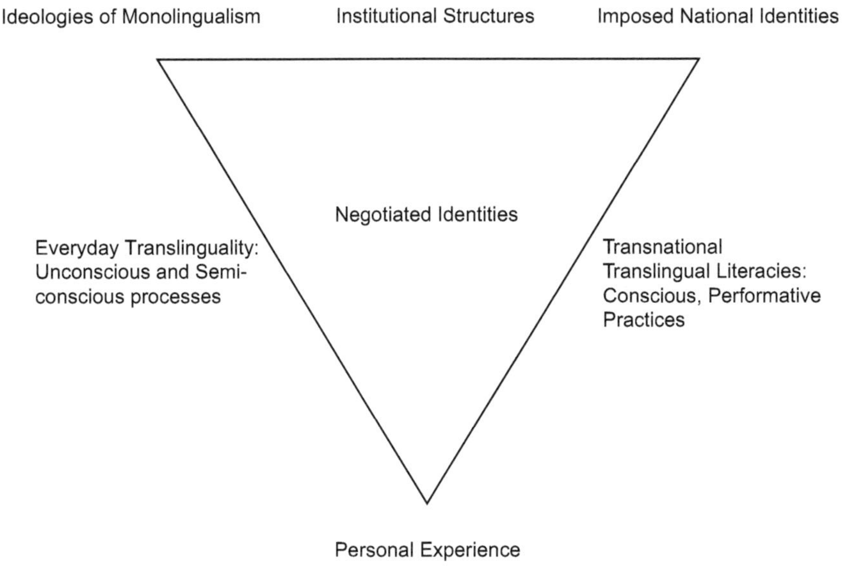

```
Ideologies of Monolingualism      Institutional Structures      Imposed National Identities


                                   Negotiated Identities
Everyday Translinguality:                                         Transnational
Unconscious and Semi-                                             Translingual Literacies:
conscious processes                                               Conscious, Performative
                                                                  Practices




                                   Personal Experience
```

FIGURE 14.1 Negotiated Translingual Transnational Identities

a conversational situation, and rapidly assess which words and other language features will be most appropriate to communicate in that particular context. In studies of "translanguaging" this process is sometimes presented as "selecting features" from one's full linguistic repertoire, depending on the context (Otheguy, García, & Reid, 2015). Canagarajah (2009), from a slightly different angle, argues that what are initially survival skills, when conducting commercial or personal relationships in a language contact zone, eventually become almost instinctual. Canagarajah (2009) posits that these same linguistic negotiating skills may become assets when students sit down to write—but only if they feel free to do so, liberated from monolingualist dogma about "first language interference," and empowered to make use of their full linguistic repertoire as they read (especially), compose, and revise.

To those who grew up in a translingual milieu, or to those who make these adjustments through necessity when thrown into an immigration or sojourner or expatriate or other type of transnational situation, this naive amazement at such linguistic dexterity might be laughable.

Or at least it would be laughable if it weren't symptomatic of a slow recovery from a pervasive indoctrination in monolingualist ideology.

Monolingualism

Monolingualism is an ideology. We can distinguish it from simply speaking only one language, which can be designated as monolinguality, a neutral fact in itself—although we might suggest that no one literally has knowledge of just one language. But if this is so, those of us in the U.S. (and elsewhere) often seem to be living in a state of denial. Monolingualist ideology aligns with other ethnocentric belief systems, and it often serves as a proxy for discrimination or assertion of in-group dominance. Monolingual stances have in recent years been used as a political weapon to incite fear and discord, often operating as a stand-in for racist, anti-immigrant behaviors and actions (e.g. Madani, 2017; Wang, 2018; Dayal, 2019; Lam, 2019; Solé, 2019). Monolingualism is not identical with racism, but it is rooted in similar systems of identity, and so when nationalist or populist politics is on the ascendant, what begins as a passive, unexamined assumption inhering in the culture becomes weaponized into fears that a majority language is somehow in danger. The cynical appeal, sometimes explicit and other times implied, is to the idea of "one nation, one language" at the macro level, with a corollary of "one person, one language" at the micro level. From this perspective individual translinguality becomes perceived as a threat to a common identity. Languages from elsewhere, and the individuals who speak them, become symbols of a frightening, encroaching, globalized world.

This fear of linguistic fragmentation represents, however, only a minority strain in U.S. culture. For the United States not only has never had an official national language, but it has never actually been a monolingual place. How could it be, as a "nation of immigrants," who would hardly forget their other languages, or voluntarily stop using them once they have arrived in the United States? And this is not to speak of the languages of Native Americans; these languages, as well as the people who speak them, have historically been marginalized, and systematically repressed and in some cases suffered linguistic genocide (Reyhner, 1993). In a time where fears of "other" languages and language fragility is one feature of broader anti-cosmopolitan sentiments, the recognition of translingual realities may be seen as an initial step in interrogating the underlying ideologies that support systemic exclusions.

Institutional Structures and Assumptions

Our context for the studies presented here has been U.S. academic institutions, and one of our central concerns has been to analyze the institutional structures that both derive from and continue to re-enforce monolingualist assumptions. All three of this book's writers have made careers within this system, and so cannot escape being implicated in its practices, and this is one reason we have each devoted a chapter to examining our own positionality with regard to language privilege and ideologies.

Lippi-Green (2012) argues that universities—along with the rest of the education system, with news and entertainment media, the corporate sector, and the judicial sector—are "dominant bloc" institutions, engaged in a process of "language subordination," which re-enforces "mainstream" language and cultural values while ensuring that "language is mystified, authority is claimed, misinformation is generated, non-mainstream language is trivialized, conformers are held up as positive examples, explicit promises are made, threats are made, non-conformers are vilified and marginalized" (p. 68). Of course, we in academia do not want to recognize ourselves in these kinds of neo-colonial roles; we wish to see ourselves not only as politically correct but as actively progressive, as engaged in resistance to all forms of discrimination and injustice, as empowering the oppressed and as speaking truth to power. But have we really found ways to stand outside the power structures of the institutions in which we work and the society in which those institutions are situated?

As instructors in the U.S. writing classroom, we cannot escape these uncomfortable questions about how even the most well-intentioned pedagogy may end up re-enforcing exclusionary values and assumptions. Our classroom practices inevitably force us to negotiate, on the one hand, institutional demands that we "produce" students who are capable of imitating and composing texts that not only make use of standardized English, but of more specific academic registers. As instructors—and especially as adjunct instructors—we are rewarded according to the degree that we produce "conformers," in Lippi-Green's (2012) terms. We can—and often do—think of this process as empowering students to take on middle-class roles by taking on middle-class language; this is an especially tempting rationalization at Urban College, where many of our students are first in their family to go to college, and do in fact explicitly think of higher education as a means to achieve socio-economic mobility, and, indeed, the university of which Urban College is a part is often lauded for its success in this area. Many of our students will not complain about the "language subordination process" (Lippi-Green, 2012): this is what, through years in the U.S. educational system, many raciolinguistically-minoritized (Flores & Rosa, 2015) have been taught to be the only "appropriate" language for educational and professional purposes. So if our students will not call us out on participating in language subordination, and our institutions continue to promote it as a positive good and reward us for doing it well, why should we take up transing pedagogy? Throughout this book we have offered considerations of how to center translinguality and transnationality in the ways in which we work with students, taking steps to support their agency in their own language use and language identities. The strategies that we consider in this book are neither easy nor comfortable. They require a reorientation away from the hegemonic—that is to say, white, middle class, masculinist, straight—epistemologies that pervade higher education. But if we want to take the project of translinguality and transnationality seriously, and integrate our understanding of how language shapes identity into our classroom practice, this is work that we must do.

Institutional demands for language standardization are inimical to a translingual approach, which regards students' language processes as more agentive, as making active choices as to how their written and spoken work will appear to particular audiences, and as using all their available linguistic knowledge to help them understand written or spoken texts. This is an issue in all writing classrooms, but it becomes more acute whenever we are focusing on a population of mixed races, classes, and immigration statuses, as at Urban College, and on "international" students, both undergraduate and graduate, at State University. We have argued that such students are better thought of as transnational, because otherwise we have no hope of escaping from the transactional connotations of an international exchange. If we have trouble empowering U.S. citizens and residents to be agents of their own language practices, the complexities increase exponentially when we consider students whose status is legally defined as temporary, just passing through, not really here, not part of our mainstream population. The Graduate Academic Success Program that we have explored in some detail in Chapter 13 had its institutional origins in just such a desire to create a space outside the regular flow of academic coursework, in this case for international graduate students.

Imposed National Identities

We have focused in several chapters on "Chinese students," though we have tried to caution against over-generalizing or stereotyping on the basis of that superficial label. China is a big country, with many differing regions, and the students who come to State University bring with them a variety of language backgrounds—they all speak "Mandarin" or "Putonghua," but that is often only one element in a complex linguistic profile.

China is a translingual place, that is, what we call Mandarin is the result of conscious and strenuous effort at first creating a standardized language by beginning with elements of a Northern dialect and then incorporating elements from others (Moser, 2016). The old linguistic saying that a language is a dialect with an army and a navy very astutely describes the Chinese situation, where multiple mutually-unintelligible language varieties are described as "dialects" nonetheless.

Monolingualism as a means of creating or re-enforcing national identity then, is not confined to the United States, nor to other English-speaking countries where it also thrives. The Chinese government has been promoting a conscious and explicit language policy for decades (e.g. Moser, 2016), seeking to meet the communication needs of a modern technological society, and to a large extent they have succeeded: with Putonghua the standard and standardized language of the entire educational system, almost everyone can make use of it to at least some extent. But our focus on our transnational students from China has revealed that many of them still are in contact—understanding and using—with some of those languages. Monolingualist ideology has not fully succeeded in rooting out alternate means of communication, especially spoken communication.

At the same time that the Chinese government has promoted Putonghua, they have also insisted on English instruction in all Chinese schools, usually beginning in the third grade or so. Our students tell us that the pedagogical approaches to English, at least in their experience, did not produce levels of proficiency sufficient to support their study abroad in the United States. English is taught as a required foreign language, focusing primarily, in an approach certainly not limited to China, on grammar, vocabulary, and high-stakes testing. Therefore, a common experience that transnational graduate and undergraduate students encounter when they arrive at State University is the sudden realization—at once stimulating and frightening—that they will be actually using English for both academic and social purposes. We have detailed in previous chapters the varying degrees to which students have been able to connect to American life, ranging from near isolation to remaining in the comfort of a Mandarin-speaking enclave, to, in at least one case, a full immersion in American life, both on the personal and professional level. Administrators planning programming, as well as classroom faculty, must be very careful in making generalizations and assumptions about "Chinese graduate students," and still more careful about "international" graduate students more broadly, because their common visa status often conceals a much deeper diversity in their language background, in their previous academic experiences, in their degree of initiation into their disciplinary identities, and in their future plans and ambitions.

Transnational Translingual Literacies

The first half of this book emphasized "Everyday Translinguality," focusing on making visible some of the unconscious and half-conscious processes that translingual students routinely employ to carry out common tasks, both academic and non-academic. We demonstrate that translinguality is a real and common event, not the invention of over-zealous theorists in rhetoric and composition. A colleague of ours, an applied linguist less than a decade out from graduate school, reflected recently that he had already found it necessary to re-orient his research approach, which in his dissertation had been framed as "language contact," in light of recent developments in the areas of translanguaging and translingualism: how can one study language contact if, under new theoretical approaches, languages, as traditionally conceived, do not really exist? Translingualism, translanguaging, and other trans- approaches have sometimes been framed as an discipline-internal dispute among proponents of alternate approaches to the teaching of writing, usually a rhetoric and composition approach vs. a second language writing approach, a contention that one of us has vigorously contested elsewhere (Hall, 2018). We see translinguality as an already-existing phenomenon in the world that various disciplines are only now catching up to. It requires, in most cases, a paradigm shift, and often a transdisciplinary approach, and both of these adjustments are always uncomfortable for those who have been in the field for a long time—or even, as in the case of our colleague, for a relatively short time. And we envision translingual*ism* as a necessary counterweight to the pervasive monolingualism that we have already outlined.

The second part of the book explores "Transnational Translingual Literacies," a phrase that encompasses several important meanings. First of all, it signifies that, in contrast to the ubiquitous, almost automatic and unnoticed translingual processes that define Everyday Translinguality, we turned instead to more thoughtful, deliberate, and conscious negotiations that students engage in with regard to their language identities and their transnational realities. As one of the elements of transing pedagogy is increasing student metacognition, we should consider encouraging students to embrace and analyze their own language backgrounds and practices, and to examine the ways that they will—and will not—immerse themselves in the processes of standardization and cooperation that are the usual hallmarks of the American education system. It is our responsibility to create spaces that will enable them to become aware that there are, in fact, choices to be made in terms of language, in terms of national and cultural identity, in terms of future aspirations, regardless of what they may have thought they were going for when they enrolled in college.

Translingual pedagogy, or transing pedagogy in general, then, recognizes that students have the right to their choices and opportunities to explore their own language repertoire in a safe, welcoming, and nurturing environment. The opening chapter in this section introduces three of our key terms: *translanguaging*, *negotiation*, and *performance*. This idea of language *identity as performance* suggests the shift in our focus away from linguistic chronicling of the background language processes of everyday translinguality and toward a student's more active and pedagogically-stimulated engagement with the conventions of academic writing, now presented not as inevitable and unchangeable but rather as created in every act of writing as a negotiation between readers' expectations and writer's intentions. The writing assignment is now configured as an invitation and incitement to self-examination and experimentation, borrowing techniques—and the suspension of immediate technical judgment—from creative writing pedagogy and practice. Students may mix and match registers (including academic disciplines and non-academic expertise), dialects, language "codes," meshing potentially heterogeneous elements together to show how they cohere in the writer's own language identity. The student also needs to think about how hard they want to make the reader work to understand elements taken from aspects of the student's language identity that are not shared by the instructor—and we see in the examples chosen that sometimes students hit that mark and allow the reader to understand, and sometimes they leave the reader not fully following their presentation, but always we see students negotiating rhetorically, not just grammatically, realizing that they have not only to present their content but to invent their reader as well.

Personal Experience

All the students in our various studies occupy, to a greater or lesser degree, complex spaces in terms of their translingual and transnational identities. For the students at Urban College, the great American taboo subject of social class is one border they need to cross, as this is not an institution for the already-elite but rather part of a system with historic roots in trying to promote upward mobility. Their varied language identities are often fairly hidden while in the classroom, though they are ubiquitous in the hallways, and one key aspect of transing pedagogy is trying to find ways to connect those two spaces, to avoid having students freeze up into a standardized template once they step through the door to meet their instructor. In fact, transing pedagogy is often a matter of re-configuring the classroom as not a place apart from students' real lives but rather as part of a network that connects inside and outside, academic and non-academic, standardized English with other Englishes, English with multiple languages, dialects and varieties, shared transnational cultures with local communities, home with school identities.

As we showed in Chapter 2, students at Urban College are often immigrants themselves or the children of immigrants, and so they often maintain strong transnational ties to places, cultures, and people outside the U.S. Caribbean cultures and languages, including Spanish and Haitian Creole, as well as various varieties of English from Jamaica, Trinidad, Guyana, and elsewhere, are strong influences, but every continent is represented, with the Indian subcontinent, especially Bangladesh, as another strong location on the Urban College transnational network. So Urban College students are legitimately transnational in their own right, but they are in a quite different position from the transnational students in the State University studies, not only because of the institutional differences but even more because of the differences in their visa status: most of the Urban College students are either U.S. citizens or permanent residents, though the institution welcomes international and undocumented students as well.

But all of the students in the State University studies are here in a contingent manner, by definition of their student role and their legal status. Officially they are here to study, train, and then go home. But as we saw in our interviews with transnational graduate students, many of them have plans that do not necessarily involve returning to China. Some of them are hoping to find a way to stay in the U.S. through permanent employment, sometimes in an academic capacity, while others envision a continuing transnational existence, travelling the world in search of the next engineering project or the next orchestral gig. They usually maintain strong relationships to family and friends in China through their digital devices, while some have already developed networks of expatriate friendships in the U.S., sometimes with people they had known during their earlier education in China. It is a challenging thing they are doing, studying at an advanced disciplinary level in a new language, and it's up to the U.S. institutions to find ways to support that daring act of self-assertion and self-creation.

Negotiated Identities

Finally, to return to the diagram with which we began this concluding chapter, the concept of identity, including but not limited to translingual and transnational identities, has been central to our concerns throughout. In Chapter 4 we described transing identities as being performed, dynamic, and complex. We may also add that they are negotiated. In U.S. society one cannot simply choose one's racial identity; if you try to do so, the society at large will push back. This illustrates that there is an inescapable social component to identity—or one might call it a rhetorical component. That is, one may claim an identity, but that claim both creates and requires a response, a partner, a reader.

So in the writing classroom, the construction of the "instructor identity" is crucial. If instructors present themselves as the representative of the "standardized language," there is the risk that students will adopt and write for this representative of the "accepted standard language." If on the contrary the writing instructor models flexible responses and negotiable genre and structure, then students may experiment with their language identities and their identities as writers.

The writing classroom, then, is an opportunity for a rhetorical and linguistic negotiation, and thus for assertion, experimentation, and testing of identity on the parts of both student and instructor. The way to empower students is not to disempower instructors but rather to promise a complex response, an authentic one that includes the instructor's personal engagement, not just a bureaucratic or institutional assessment. Yes, instructors unavoidably represent the institution, and must give grades, but the instructor may also be an active and honest reader of student writing, and most especially a negotiator of identity, suggesting that there is flexibility—though not infinite flexibility—in the response of the reader, helping students to imagine readers who correspond to their intentions in the text.

It is a tricky proposition for an instructor to employ transing pedagogy, to trans an assignment, to invite negotiation of identity. We should consider, for example, Alison Jaggar's (1989) thesis that those in subordinated positions see more. By embracing a translingual and transnational stance in our teaching, we are saying that we want to know what raciolinguistically minoritized students see—but we have to make the ways in which they express what they see count, so that they don't have to be filtered and shaped for a white gaze and a white ear. Furthermore, we encourage—or rather implore—instructors to consider that performance is what students are doing in their classroom, and therefore we cannot require students to display an "authentic" linguistic identity in their writing assignments, because such requirements often reinforce essentializing and reifying identity categories. Building on Deleuzean ideas of focusing on becoming rather than being, Ellsworth (2005) calls for a pedagogy that "address[es] a student that is not coincident with herself, but only with her change . . . a learning self that is in motion" (p. 7). Any identity that is negotiated in any particular course or assignment is just an identity for the nonce, a step along the way to the next re-invention of identity in a future rhetorical and linguistic context.

So students' assertion of identity comes from a dynamic interaction with social categories and forces. Their rhetorical repertoire includes their everyday translingual practices, which have to contend with pervasive ideologies of monolingualism to which no one, in this culture, is immune. Their writing also unavoidably takes place in the context of institutional structures and assumptions that limit what even the best-intentioned instructor may be able to do in the context of inflexible course requirements and one's own institutional identity—i.e. tenured faculty may have more room to experiment than contingent faculty. Academic institutions participate in national—or nationalistic—constructions of identity, and these inevitably disproportionately affect those students who do not readily fit the profile of the student for which the curriculum was originally designed—often long ago, and not adjusted for changing times. Our students, not just at Urban College and at State University but everywhere, necessarily operate in the intersection of personal and academic experience, and they need to be invited to participate in the conscious, performative practices that can lead to re-negotiated identities.

We have called for future research—and, especially, for activism—in and out of the classroom, on language equity in our pedagogy and our administrative practices. What is needed, we suggest, is a global language rights perspective on student languages in the translingual classroom. Future work on students' language rights will need to take account of translingual and transnational developments, under various terminologies, in fields ranging from applied linguistics to second language writing to second language acquisition to rhetoric and composition. We hope that the framework laid out in this chapter, and our approaches to transing identities, pedagogies, and administrative procedures that we have explored in this project as a whole, can help in a small way to point toward that necessary re-evaluation of the place of language rights in our classrooms, in our support programs, on our campuses, and in societies as a whole.

This final chapter has revisited the role of translinguality and transnationality in the formation of language identity, and the consequences for pedagogy in U.S. writing and language classrooms. But many questions have only begun to be opened up: What does translinguality mean for English native speakers, who may well speak several varieties of English, and use "a broad and diverse repertoire of language resources" (Horner, Lu, Royster, & Trimbur, 2011,

p. 308)? What does it mean for our pedagogy if we move a consideration of students' transnational experiences from the margins to the center of our work in the classroom? How does translanguaging construct an audience? What do we get if we teach students a more nuanced perspective on native-speaker/non-native speaker status? What do we gain—pedagogically, experientially, and in research—from making translinguality and transnationality visible?

As researchers, attention to transnational translingual literacies requires an encompassing approach to students' language backgrounds, translingual influences and practices, transnational networks of connection, and disciplinary commitments, as well as an invitation to them to explore, if they wish, their personal experiences negotiating and claiming identities. We end where we began, with a simple approach, "Ask the Students." To which we may add: Then listen to what they say.

References

Bialystok, E., Craik, F. I. M., & Luk, G. (2012). Bilingualism: Consequences for mind and brain. *Trends in Cognitive Science*, *16*(4), 240–250. doi:10.1016/j.tics.2012.03.001

Canagarajah, A. S. (2009). Multilingual strategies of negotiating English: From conversation to writing. *JAC*, *29*(1–2), 17–48.

Dayal, M. (2019, July 12). "I hope Trump deports you": Customer threatens Puerto Rican woman for speaking Spanish. *Yahoo Lifestyle*. Retrieved September 29, 2019 from www.yahoo.com/lifestyle/i-hope-trump-deports-you-customer-threatens-puerto-rican-woman-for-speaking-spanish-183528034.html

Ellsworth, E. (2005). *Places of learning: Media, architecture, pedagogy*. New York and London: Routledge.

Flores, N., & Rosa, J. (2015). Undoing appropriateness: Raciolinguistic ideologies and language diversity in education. *Harvard Educational Review*, *85*(2), 149–301.

Hall, J. (2018). The translingual challenge: Boundary work in Rhetoric & Composition, second language writing, and WAC/WID. *Across the Disciplines: A Journal of Language, Learning, and Academic Writing*, *15*(3), 20.

Horner, B., Lu, M.-Z., Royster, J. J., & Trimbur, J. (2011). Language difference in writing: Toward a translingual approach. *College English*, *73*(3), 303–321.

Jaggar, A. M. (1989). Love and knowledge: Emotion in feminist epistemology. *Inquiry*, *32*(2), 151–176.

Lam, K. (2019, January 27). Duke professor sparks online outrage after telling Chinese students to only speak English. *USA Today*. Retrieved September 29, 2019 from www.yahoo.com/news/duke-professor-sparks-online-outrage-003742833.html

Lippi-Green, R. (1997 [2012]). *English with an accent: Language, ideology, and discrimination in the United States* (2nd ed.). New York and London: Routledge.

Madani, D. (2017, October 16). High schoolers protest after teacher tells student to speak "American". *HuffPost*. Retrieved September 29, 2019 from www.huffpost.com/entry/new-jersey-speak-american-student-protest_n_59e5510be4b0a2324d1d2061?ncid=edlinkushpmg00000313

Moser, D. (2016). *A billion voices: China's search for a common language*. Hawthorn, Victoria: Penguin.

Otheguy, R., García, O., & Reid, W. (2015). Clarifying translanguaging and deconstructing named languages: A perspective from linguistics. *Applied Linguistics Review*, 6(3), 281–307. https://doi.org/10.1515/applirev-2015-0014

Reyhner, J. (1993). American Indian language policy and school success. *The Journal of Educational Issues of Language Minority Student*, 12(Special issue III), 35–59.

Solé, E. (2019, July 11). Elderly women kicked out of Burger King for telling manager, "Speak your Mexican at home . . . this is America". *Yahoo Lifestyle*. Retrieved September 29, 2019 from www.yahoo.com/lifestyle/elderly-women-kicked-out-of-burger-king-for-telling-manager-speak-your-mexican-at-homethis-is-america-180334383.html

Wang, A. B. (2018, May 17). 'My next call is to ICE!': A man flipped out because workers spoke Spanish at a Manhattan deli. *Washington Post*. Retrieved from www.washingtonpost.com/news/business/wp/2018/05/16/my-next-call-is-to-ice-watch-a-man-wig-out-because-workers-spoke-spanish-at-a-manhattan-deli/

APPENDICES

APPENDIX A

First Day Thinking

1. What languages do you speak?
2. Where did you learn them?
3. What Englishes do you speak?
4. How did you learn them?
5. What geographical regions are they associated with?
6. What communities do your languages connect you to?
7. Do they differ in prestige? How?
8. Do you change the way you speak depending on the context in which you are speaking?
9. How do you change your speech?
10. Why do you change it?

APPENDIX B

AutoBio and Literacy Narrative Assignment: Guidelines Document

Dear Student,

Please write a two-page introduction/autobiography & literacy narrative. Please also add a page with photos. The photo pages should be separate from the two-page autobiography & literacy narrative. The photo/photo should show you doing something you enjoy. You can also include photo/photos of you or with people you care about or in a place that is important to you. Please remember as we discussed in class, you are telling me a story/communicating something about you to me.

Include the Following: (3 pages)
Bio: Page 1

> What is your name? Where are you from?
> What is your major? Why did you choose this major?
> Is English your native language? What other languages do you speak? What languages have you studied? What was your experience studying languages?
> What are your strengths as a student? What are things you would like to improve?
> What is difficult for you when you write or speak in English? What is easier?
> Do you like to write? Explain your answer.
> How did you do in your last writing class? (EAD 154,155 (if retake).
> What did you improve? What do you need to work on? (use the language of the EAD grading rubric)

What goals do you have for our class?
What do you like to do in your free time?
Please tell me anything you would like me to know about you.

Literacy Narrative Part: Page 2

When was the first time as a very young boy or girl that you realized that words/language/writing is very important?

Photo/Photos: Page 3

NOTE: Please do not forget to include your photo/photos on a separate page! FORMATTING:

Thank you!
Prof Navarro

APPENDIX C

Language Narrative Assignment [Chapter 2]: Introduction to Writing, Rhetoric, and Language Course

For this assignment, I'd like you to consider the question "What languages do you speak?" And I'd like you to write about where you speak your languages, and how they fit together. How does this composite of languages affect your identity? How does it connect you to your different communities? And what do you value most about them?

[NOTE: Students were offered two variations on this part of the assignment—one asked "What Englishes do you speak?" and the third asked them to describe their "relationship with English." All three options included the following second paragraph:]

You may use your answers to your "Education & Language Background Survey" as a starting point, but don't simply copy your answers there—choose the most important or the most interesting ones and expand them in more depth. Develop those answers by reflecting on what each of your languages means to you, using

- specific incidents from your experience that illuminate your attitudes and/or your learning process
- at least three quotations/references to three different readings from Part 1 of the course

APPENDIX D

Questions for Transnational Graduate Student Interviews

I. Language background/Early education/Translingual experience (prior to U.S.)

   A. What languages/local dialects did you hear growing up? In your family, at school, in the streets, etc. Which did you use among your friends? Which do you identify as a "native speaker" of?
   B. What was/is your relation to Putonghua/Mandarin? (Is there another name that you use for the "standard" dialect? E.g. Hanyu).
   C. When did English enter the picture in your education? What roles did it play at primary and secondary levels? Was it a required course? Do you think that the way it was taught prepared you well for the reading and writing tasks you would need to perform later on at Rutgers?
   D. Did you take private English lessons in addition to what you were taught in school?
   E. Besides formal education, what other experiences did you have with English before coming to the U.S.? E.g. English language media, travel, English-speaking visitors.

II. Disciplinary language/English medium instruction (college & grad levels)

   A. In your undergraduate courses, were courses taught in English, Putonghua, or a combination? Specify as much as possible: i.e. were readings in English? Instructor lectures? Class discussions? Instructions and questions (e.g. "What is the homework?") Study groups or informal discussions with classmates?
   B. What were you asked to read as an undergraduate in your field and in what language?

- C. What writing assignments were you given as an undergraduate in your field and in what language?
- D. What has the adjustment been like for you to a U.S. institution and English medium reading and writing?
- E. If you've been teaching, how is that going, with regard to English? What's the hardest thing about teaching U.S. students?
- F. If you had to give a lecture about a technical topic in your field to a Putonghua-speaking audience in China, would that be difficult for you?
- G. What's the hardest thing about reading in your field?
- H. READ ALONG: Let's read a little. Take us through your process regarding a reading in your field.

III. Transnational experience/"International student" status

- A. Why graduate school in the U.S.?
- B. When did you first start thinking about grad school in the U.S.? Was there a particular person's advice or an incident that helped lead you in that direction?
- C. What was the process like a. on the Chinese end (bureaucracy, exams, etc.), b. on the U.S. end (applying to grad programs (how many?), visa issues, and c) regarding language (TOEFL or Versant exams, etc.)?
- D. Do you feel like you're living in two places? If so, when do you get that feeling?
- E. Outside the classroom, how much do you associate with a) other Chinese students b) other international students, and c) U.S. students? How often do you use your non-English language(s)?
- F. What are your future plans/ambitions? Do you see yourself in academia/business? Here/China/Somewhere Else? Why? Future use of English and other languages.

APPENDIX E

Initial Assignment

In this initial writing and oral presentation assignment, you will prepare a scholarly and professional "introduction" of yourself to the Graduate ELL and ITA Program.

Rationale: The ability to provide a formal written and oral introduction to your future colleagues is an essential part of graduate school, often on the first day of a course. It is your opportunity to share what has motivated you to pursue graduate study in your chosen field, reflect on academic and career goals, and discuss potential areas of research interest. Your "introduction" will also form the foundation of the larger portfolio of work you will produce for this course.

Requirements: This assignment is comprised of a written and an oral part.

Part 1: Intellectual autobiography (in-class writing and for homework, 500 words minimum, due Monday, February 4.

Address the following *suggested* questions in a personal narrative (see sample in class). You can follow any order you prefer. Remember, this is a narrative of some significant experiences in your intellectual life and not just a list of answers. It should tell a story.

- Who are you? How do you identify yourself? Where are you from? Where did you go to school? What was your education (both formal and informal) like?
- Have you had any professional work experiences? If so, which ones have most influenced who you are today, and why?
- What special achievements or accomplishments would you like to highlight?
- Why did you choose to pursue graduate study? What challenges do you see ahead of you?

- What are your academic and career goals at the present time? Do you have any research interests, and if so, what?

Part 2: Oral Introduction (in-class video-recorded presentation, 3 minutes minimum, due Monday, February 4.

Select three–four key ideas, topics, or experiences to highlight in an in-class oral presentation. These elements should be selected to answer the question: What do you want your colleagues to learn about you? Your oral introduction should include:

- An introduction that gets our attention and sets up the main idea of your speech.
- A body that discusses the three–four key ideas, topics, or experiences you wish to highlight, with details.
- A brief closing section that rephrases the main idea of the speech and leaves us with something to think about.

Grading: While each part of your initial assignment will be evaluated separately, you will receive a combined assignment grade for both parts. Your intellectual autobiography will be evaluated for accurate completion of the requirements mentioned previously, thoroughness of your response, organizational structure, and language clarity. Your oral introduction will be evaluated for accurate completion of the requirements, engaging presentation, vocal clarity/body language and overall presentational skills.

Key Considerations

- Focus on what's important and don't get buried in background or extraneous information. Focus on core themes, topics, and experiences.
- Always be truthful. This is about your life, experiences, and getting to know your colleagues better.
- Assume an interdisciplinary audience. Stick to common, everyday words and define technical terms. Maintain a conversational tone in writing and speaking.
- Feel free to have fun with this! This is the place to try out new ideas and identities—in this safe, interdisciplinary environment. Creativity is encouraged.
- **Optional**: watch your video and write a brief reflection on your performance and how you conveyed ideas.

APPENDIX F

End of Semester Writing Reflection

Prof Navarro

**END OF SEMESTER WRITING REFLECTION
PROF NAVARRO**

Dear students,

You will remember that I said you would write an **Individual Writing Reflection**. This is a **two to three page [not including the cover page]** reflection in which you will do the following:

Assignment Guidelines

- Write about what you have learned about your academic writing process particularly academic writing and what you have learned about yourself as a writer.
- Describe specifically **using the language of the writing rubric** what you have done to improve and what needs to be improved. **Be very specific,** do not write in general ways. Please answer these questions: What aspects of your writing still need some work? What did you learn about yourself as a writer? What did you learn about your own writing process? Which essay did you enjoy writing and why? Which essay gave you the most trouble and why?
- What surprised you the most about your work in our class? What is the value of learning how to write well?
- At the conclusion please give some useful advice to a new EAD I. What do you think they should do to become a better reader and writer in EAD I?

Format

- One–two pages 12-point font, one inch margin, New York Times or Arial and add page numbers.
- Include a separate Cover Page as you do for your essays.
- Staple or Paper Clip this Reflection.
- Give the **Reflection a unique name/title**.
- Choose an image/photo or illustration that best represents the writing process for you and add this image to the cover page.

Due Date: Friday, December 15, 2017

Must be submitted via [CMS] assignments NO EXCEPTIONS!! NOTE: I will PRINT AND include this in your portfolio.

INDEX

academic English 111
academic language 183
accent hierarchies 39–43
activism 211
acts of identity 46–47
affiliations 10, 24, 49, 50, 51, 52, 55, 56, 71; acts of identity 46–47
African-American Vernacular English (AAVE) 54–55, 122, 130, 131–132, 139
agency 74–75, 84, 101
Ahearn, L. M. 24, 74
Ahmad, D. 6
Alexander, J. 106
Alim, H. S. 161, 162
Angelova, M. 179
annotations 147–148, 149–151
Anzaldúa, G. 165
applied linguistics 2, 4, 14, 98; linguistic identity studies 44; "trans-" 8
Argentina 89, 91
Ashcroft, B. 121
aspirations 10–11, 31
assessment 99
assigned identity 46–47, 48
assignments 110; creative writing 126–128; "Intellectual AutoBiography" 174

Baillif, M. 125
"Banglish" 31
Bartholomae, D. "Inventing the University" 103

Benesch, S. 44
Bernhardt, E. 145, 146
bilingualism 30, 62–64
biographies, international students 76–81; see also Intellectual Autobiography
Blackledge, A. 44
blogs 108–109
Blommaert, J. 7, 12, 44, 51; on identity 48
brainstorming 107, 108
Brathwaite, K., *History of the Voice* 53
Britzman, D. 97, 108
"Broken English" 28, 28–29
broken English 122
Bryson, M. 162
Butler, J., on gender identity 45

Canagarajah, S. 14–15, 31, 51, 113, 120, 124, 125, 136, 150, 152, 156, 158, 161, 203
Caribbean English 31, 56, 123
Cervantes, M., *Don Quijote de la Mancha* 66, 67
Chang, Y. J. 73, 85, 173
Chiang, Y.-S. 44
China 33, 34, 69, 72, 74; and imposed national identities 206–207; Shanghai International Studies University 68; see also graduate students; international students
classrooms 15, 97, 100, 103, 106, 192; language rights 197–198; virtual writing 108–109
clause boundaries 166, 167

code-meshing 2, 102, 120, 121, 128, 129, 133–134, 135, 136, 139, 165, 166–167, 169, 208
code-switching 30, 120–121, 128, 129, 130
collecting quotations 109
Colombia 60, 63, 64, 65
complexity, of identity 49–50
composition studies 7, 98, 99, 126, 156; linguistic identity studies 44; "patterns of error" 163; "trans-" 8; translingual approaches 104; translingual turn 14, 142
connective thinking 76
Connors, R. J. 147, 167–168
contradictions of transing pedagogy 102–103
cosmopolitanism 15
courses, grammar 158–159
Cox, M. 44, 109–110
creative writing 126–128, 133; first-person narration 137–140
Crenshaw, K. 50
Creole 55, 56
Critical Language Awareness 163–164
critical pedagogy 2
cultivating and protecting language rights 200
culture 66, 75, 84
culture shock 173
Currah, P. 9, 51, 100
Cushman, E. 101, 104

de Castell, S. 162
de Varennes, F. 193
desire 104
dialects 151
dignity, as human right 196, 197
discursos 68
diversity 22, 23, 28; of graduate students' spoken languages 35–36; of international students' spoken languages 32–34; of students' spoken languages 28–29, 30–31
"dominant bloc" institutions 204–205
Dominican Republic 91
double consciousness 169
Dovchin, S. 22
drafting 107, 108
DuBois, W.E.B. 169
Duranti, A. 74
dynamic, identity as 48–49

"Ebonics" 30, 41, 122
editing 112

Elbow, P. 98, 162
Ellsworth, E. 211
embodied engagement 111–112
embodiment 105
English 87, 91, 93, 94; academic 111; "broken" 122; Caribbean 123; "idealized native speaker" 160; Indian 113; and monolingualism 87–89, 90; non-native speakers 96; "proper" 93; Standardized 123
English as a Second Language (ESL) 6, 7, 8, 27, 46, 93
English for Academic Purposes (EAP) 32, 33, 34, 72, 73, 75, 112
English Language Learner (ELL) 6, 73, 92
equality, as human right 196, 197
errors *see* patterns of error
español 60, 63, 64, 68
essays 67, 72, 75, 98
everyday translingualism 22, 23, 28, 202, 203, 207

faculty 13
first-person narration 52–53, 137
Fish, S. 162
Flores, N. 111, 159
formal assignments 14, 107, 110, 119, 120, 125–127, 154, 167–168, 174, 183
Fuchs, L. S. 165

Galarte, F. 103, 104
Gallagher, T. 148, 149
Garcia, O. 51
Garrison, E. 103
gender identity: Butler on 45; intersectionality 50
Generation 1.5 44
genres 109–110
Ghana 11, 54
Gilyard, K. 44
Girona Manifesto 194–195
Glick Schiller, N. 11, 41
Graduate Academic Success Program (GASP) 73, 83, 173, 174, 175, 189, 206; computer engineering program 184–188; Intellectual Autobiography 183, 184; learning goals 176–177; mission statement 176; music performance program 181–184; needs assessment 187; social work program 177–180
graduate students 14, 25, 75, 173; culture shock 173; insiders 25; interview responses 81–85; linguistic identity

35–36; outsiders 25, 26; recruitment 192; support programs 188–189; *see also* Graduate Academic Success Program (GASP); international students
grammar 15, 75, 156, 157, 169; clause boundaries 166, 167; naming parts of speech 164–165, 165; "patterns of error" 163; patterns of usage 164; pedagogy of naming 157, 158, 162–163, 169–170; prescriptive 156, 159; punctuation 166, 167; speech-writing interface 166; translingual approach to 157
Green, N.A.S. 162
Griffiths, G. 121
Guatemala 91, 92, 93
Guyana 11; Creole 55

Haiti 11, 52
Hall, J. 49
Harklau, L. 44, 50
Harris, R. 44, 50, 71, 122, 160
Hartse, J. H. 111
higher education 103, 105; *see also* graduate students; international students; universities
Holborow, M. 160–161
Honduras 93
Horner, B. 7, 54
Hosp, M. K. 165
Hughes, L., "Mother to Son" 54–55
human rights 196–197; language 192, 193; *see also* language rights
Hurston, Z. N. 120, 128

identity 12, 24, 26, 44, 45, 70, 71, 72, 73, 74, 75, 101, 125, 142, 211; acts of 46–47; assigned 46–47; Blommaert on 48; complexity of 49–50; as dynamic 48–49; formation 48, 49; gender 45; as human right 196, 197; imposed 13; narratives 48–49; negotiated 1, 45, 56, 104, 146, 153, 202, 210, 211; performances 45–47, 119, 208; self-disclosure 125–126, 127; translingual 51; transnational 23; West on 47; *see also* linguistic identity; translingual identity; transnational identity
immigrants 46, 73, 91, 209; and accent hierarchies 39–43; othering 126
imposed national identities 206–207
Inayatulla, S. 119

inclusion 15
Indian English 113
insiders 25, 56
institutional structures and assumptions 204–206
instructors 15, 23, 24, 73, 107; embodied engagement 111–112; faculty 13; insider/outsider positionality 25; insiders 25–26; linguistic performance 41; negotiation model 124–126; outsiders 25–26; rights-based approach to classroom practices 197–198; teaching performance 127–128; transglobal citizen researcher/teacher 26; transing pedagogy 98–100
Intellectual Autobiography, Graduate Academic Success Program (GASP) 183, 184
international graduate students *see* graduate students
international students 13–14, 25, 72, 73, 75, 173; agency 74–75; aspirations 10–11; biographies 76–81; challenges faced by 71; Chinese, language affiliations 81–85; culture shock 173; diversity of 23; English for Academic Purposes (EAP) 32, 33; everyday translingualism 22, 23; Graduate Academic Success Program (GASP) 175–177; imposed national identities 206–207; insiders 25; language expertise 73–74; linguistic identity 32–34; narratives 24; negotiated identities 210–212; outsiders 25, 26; recruitment 192; support programs 188–189; transnational identity 23; *see also* Graduate Academic Success Program (GASP)
International Teaching Assistant Program 187–188
intersectionality 50, 56
interviews 24, 25, 71, 72, 174, 175; participants 175; responses from Chinese graduate students 81–85

Jaggar, A. 210
Jargon 28–29
Jaworsky, B. N. 10
Jenkins, J. R. 165
Jordan, C. 44

Kanno, Y. 44, 73, 85, 173
Kazan, T. 111

Kramsch, C. 113
Kubota, R. 111

Labov, W. 162
language 10, 24, 66, 67, 70, 97, 112, 151; academic 183; code-meshing 120, 128, 129, 133–134, 135, 139, 165, 166–167, 169; translingual assumptions 4–5; World Englishes 15; *see also* grammar
language acquisition 7, 75, 167, 211; Spanish 88–89, 90, 92
language affiliations 50, 71, 72, 73; of Chinese international students 81–85; international students 76–81; *see also* affiliations
language contact 207
language crossing 102–103, 107–108
language difference 4–5, 22
language expertise 73, 74, 85
language inheritance 50, 55, 72, 74
language rights 15, 191, 192, 193, 199; in the classroom 197–198; cultivating and protecting 200; Girona Manifesto 194–195; and minority rights 195–197; Universal Declaration of Linguistic Rights 193–194
Lanser, S. 129, 130, 136, 139
Le Page, R. B. 10, 46
learning 100, 103; *see also* second language literacy
Lee, J. W. 98, 103, 104–105, 105–107
Leung, C. 44, 49, 50, 71, 73, 122, 160
Levitt, P. 10
liberty, as human right 196, 197
liminal space 59, 64, 69, 70, 97, 100
lingua franca English (LFE) 113
linguistic affiliations 122
linguistic human rights 15
linguistic identity 1, 2, 11, 13, 21, 24, 29, 30, 31, 44, 47, 63, 87, 139; African-American Vernacular English (AAVE) 130–132; and agency 74–75; as dynamic 48–49; of graduate students 35–36; of international students 32–34; narratives 48–49; performances 45–47, 50, 72; transing 51
linguistic performance 41; of Chinese international students 81–85; *see also* performances
linguistic threshold 145
linguistic versatility 161
linguistically-minoritized students 27; *see also* minorities

Lippi-Green, R. 204, 205
literacy: grammatical 156, 162–163, 164–165, 165, 166, 167, 168; translingual approach to 142, 143; transnational 153

Mandarin 69, 74
Mandell, L. C. 153
marginalized groups, language rights 191, 192
Marquez, G. 154
mastery 135
Matsuda, P. K. 122, 160
Medina, C. 100, 111
metrolingualism 23
miller, s.j. 103
Milson-White, V. 56, 101, 102
minorities 55, 73, 101; cultivating and protecting language rights 200; identity 49; and language rights 195–197; rights-based approach to classroom practices 197–198; *see also* human rights; international students; language rights
monolingualism 29–30, 87, 91, 95, 104, 203–204, 206; learning Spanish 88, 89, 90, 92; in the United States 95
Moore, L. J. 9, 51, 100
Morrison, T. 112, 129–130, 139, 191
multicompetence theory 4, 148, 153–154
multilingualism 132–136
Muñoz, V. 103

naming parts of speech 164–165, 165
narratives 22, 26, 29, 30, 31, 32, 48–49, 50, 55–56, 71, 72, 74, 75, 126, 136; first-person narration 137–140; graduate students 35–36; international students 24, 32–34, 76–81; students 26–27, 28, 29, 30–31; *see also* Graduate Academic Success Program (GASP); interviews
national identity 12
native language 72
needs assessment 187
negotiated identities 1, 45, 56, 104, 146, 153, 202, 210, 211
negotiation model 124–126
Nelson, M. 53, 98
Nero, S. 6, 21, 44, 46, 121, 160, 166, 168
network building 99, 100, 103, 105, 107, 109, 174
New Literacies 2

New London Group 159
non-discrimination, as human right 196, 197
non-native speakers 73
non-resident aliens *see* international students
norms 101
note-taking *see* annotations

one-on-one student conferencing 111
Ortmeier-Hooper, C. 44, 45
othering 39, 61, 68, 126, 139
outsiders 25, 26, 44, 56

Pakistani: culture 135–136; language 55
Paris, D. 161, 162
parts of speech, naming 164–165, 165
Patois 28, 30, 40–41
patterns of error 163
patterns of usage 164, 165
pedagogy 13, 14, 15, 51, 66, 75, 91, 142; assignments 110, 119; creative writing assignments as translingual spaces 126–128; grammatical literacy 162–163; linguistic versatility 161; of naming 157, 158, 162–163, 169–170; negotiation model 124–126; queer 104, 105, 106, 108, 162; transing 97; translanguaging 104–105; translingual 119; translingual writing 120; translingualism 5; writing 99; *see also* grammar; transing pedagogy
Pen International Club, Girona Manifesto 194–195
Pennycook, A. 113
performances 50, 72, 101, 107, 208; African-American English 131; identity 45–47; of mastery 136; narratives 56; reading translingual and transnational identities 52–55; teaching 127–128; translanguaging 128–130; translingual 51; videoblogs 53–54, 55; *see also* narratives
Perriton, L. 105
Perry M. 100, 111
Peru 90
Pichette, F. 147
Pierce, B. N. 44
Polkinghorne, D. E. 48
Polskie 59, 61
positionalities 153
possibilities of transing pedagogy 105–107

post-colonial theory 4, 121
post-structuralism 4
prescriptive grammar 156, 159
prestige English 13
pre-writing 107
proficiency, threshold level 153–154
proof-reading 112
protecting language rights 200
punctuation 166, 167
Punjabi 132, 133
Putonghua 82, 206, 207

queer studies 105–106; "trans-" 9; transgender studies 8; transing 9–10
quotations, collecting 109

racial privilege 39–40
raciolinguistic ideologies 159–160, 161, 162, 168
Rampton, B. 12, 44, 50, 71, 73, 102, 104, 107, 122, 131, 160
reading 143; threshold level of proficiency 153–154; translingual space of 151–153; transnational 153–155; *see also* literacy; second language reading; translingual economies of literacy
reflections *see* narratives
"reified ethnicities" 73
research methodology 24
research universities, policies 23
researcher positionalities 24–26
revision 110–111
Reynolds, M. 105
Rhodes, J. 106
Riazantseva, A. 179
rights-based approach to classroom practices 197–198; *see also* human rights; language rights
Roberge, M. M. 44
Robinson, H. 158
Rosa, J. 111, 159

scaffolding 188
Schmida, M. 44
Schwartz, G. 44
Scott, V. M. 146
second language literacy, Spanish 143–144
second language reading 14, 145, 146, 147; annotations 147–148, 149–151
second language writing (SLW) 3, 8, 14
Segalowitz, N. 147

Index

self-disclosure 125–126, 127
Shang-Butler, H. 73
Shanghai International Studies University 68
Shanghaiese/Shanghainese 33, 68, 81–82
Sharma, S. 72, 188
slang 28–29, 30, 122
Smitherman, G. 162, 165
social work program, GASP 177–180
Solnit, Rebecca 157
Spanglish 138
Spanish 64, 65, 69, 80, 89, 90, 93, 94, 95; learning 88–89, 90, 92, 143–144; *mija* 64; translinguality 30; *see also español*
speech-writing interface 166
standardized English 5, 7, 29, 31, 40, 122, 123, 130–132, 156, 161, 205
Stryker, S. 8, 9, 51, 100
students: agency 74–75; aspirations 31; demographics 28; diversity 29; everyday translingualism 28; formal assignments 14; Generation 1.5 44; linguistic affiliations 27, 28–29; linguistic identity 21–22, 27, 28, 29, 30, 31, 44; linguistically-minoritized 21, 27; narratives 29, 30, 31; raciolinguistically-minoritized 205; reading translingual and transnational identities 52–55; translanguaging 122–124; translinguality 3; videoblogs 53–54; *see also* classrooms; graduate students; instructors; international students
superdiversity 12, 23
syntax 137

Tabouret-Keller, A. 10, 46
Taiwan 84
TESOL 2, 14, 93
thesis 67
They Say, I Say 107
"threshold" level of proficiency 154
Tiffin, H. 121
traditional grammar 159
"trans-" 7–8, 10, 12, 44, 54, 56, 70, 97, 100, 101, 105; as prefix 9
transgender studies 8, 53; transing 9, 10
transing 9, 10, 51, 55, 87, 100–102
transing pedagogy 97, 98, 100, 113, 205, 208, 209, 210; antecedents 103–105; assignments 110; collecting quotations 109; contradictions of 102–103; and desire 104; editing 112; embodied engagement 111–112; as methodology 98–100, 106; political focus 101; possibilities of 105–107; recognized genres 109–110; revision 110–111; virtual writing 108–109
translanguaging 14, 104, 104–105, 105, 119, 120–122, 123, 203, 208; code-meshing 120–121; creative writing assignments as translingual spaces 126–128; negotiation model 124–126; as performance 128–130; syntax 137
translation 34, 66, 67, 75, 134, 194–195
translingual economies of literacy 144, 151, 153–154, 155
translingual identity 13, 14, 74; of Chinese international students 81–85; international students 76–81; *see also* identity
translingual practices 2
translingual turn 142
translingualism 4, 5, 7, 8, 101, 102, 208; everyday 22, 23, 33; as subject matter 5
translinguality 3, 4, 5, 6, 7, 12, 22, 23, 30, 35–36, 50, 56, 61, 88, 91, 97, 101, 104, 151, 153, 186, 207–208, 211–212; everyday 15, 22, 202, 203, 207; graduate students 173; performances 51; reading 52–55
transliteration 134
transnational identity 11, 12, 14, 21, 23, 74
transnational reading 153–155
transnational translingual literacies 207–209
transnationalism 8, 10, 50
transnationality 6, 11, 56, 97, 101; connections 3; graduate students 173; reading 52–55
transpedagogies 103
trilingualism 31, 132–136
Tuck, E. 169

United Nations 60, 194; Special Rapporteur on Minority Rights 192–193; Sub-Commission on Prevention of Discrimination and Protection of Minorities 195; Universal Declaration of Human Rights 192, 196
United States 11, 13, 23, 33, 34, 50, 52, 55, 69, 71, 75, 84, 85, 90, 91, 159, 191; accent hierarchies 39–43; African-American Vernacular English (AAVE) 54–55; institutional

structures and assumptions 204–206; monolingualism 95, 203–204; and transnational identities 6
Universal Declaration of Linguistic Rights 193–194
universities 24, 71, 89; English for Academic Purposes (EAP) 32, 33; International Teaching Assistant Program 187–188; monolingualist assumptions 204–206; policies 23; Shanghai International Studies University 68
urban space, metrolingualism 23
Urdu 132–136, 133, 135, 136

vernacular transcription 121
videoblogs 41, 53, 54, 55
virtual writing 108–109

Waite, S. 98–99, 104, 105–107
Weinrich, M. 9
West, C. 10; on identity 47
women, intersectionality 50
World Englishes 15, 28, 52, 53, 128, 130, 156; normative 101
writing 56, 98, 99, 112, 152; academic 113, 186; brainstorming 107, 108; editing 112; genres 109–110; "patterns of error" 163; pre- 107; revision 110–111; teaching 97; trans- approach to composition teaching 101; translingual 120; virtual 108–109; *see also* affiliations; biographies; composition studies; creative writing; English for Academic Purposes (EAP); essays; literacy; narratives; network building; pedagogy; translanguaging
Wurr, A. 151

Yang, K. W. 169
Young, V. A. 44, 120, 161, 162, 165, 166, 167

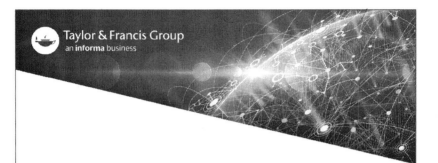